Why Austerity Persists

Why Austerity Persists

Jon Shefner
Cory Blad

polity

First published in 2020 by Polity Press

Polity Press
65 Bridge Street
Cambridge CB2 1UR, UK

Polity Press
101 Station Landing
Suite 300
Medford, MA 02155, USA

ISBN-13: 978-1-5095-0986-7
ISBN-13: 978-1-5095-0987-4 (pb)

A catalogue record for this book is available from the British Library.

Library of Congress Cataloging-in-Publication Data
Names: Shefner, Jon, 1958- author. | Blad, Cory, author.
Title: Why austerity persists / Jon Shefner, Cory Blad.
Description: Medford, MA : Polity Press, [2019] | Includes bibliographical
    references and index.
Identifiers: LCCN 2019016713 (print) | LCCN 2019980321 (ebook) | ISBN
    9781509509867 (hardback) | ISBN 9781509509874 (pbk.) | ISBN
    9781509509904 (ebook)
Subjects: LCSH: Economic policy. | Economic development--Government
    policy--Case studies. | Government spending policy. | Social policy.
Classification: LCC HD87 .S5424 2019 (print) | LCC HD87 (ebook) | DDC
    336--dc23
LC record available at https://lccn.loc.gov/2019016713
LC ebook record available at https://lccn.loc.gov/2019980321

Typeset in 10.5 on 12pt Plantin
by Fakenham Prepress Solutions, Fakenham, Norfolk, NR21 8NL
Printed and bound in the UK by CPI Group (UK) Ltd, Croydon

For further information on Polity, visit our website: politybooks.com

Contents

Abbreviations

AFDC	Aid to Families with Dependent Children
ALEC	American Legislative Exchange Council
ANC	African National Congress
BEE	black economic empowerment
CONAIE	Confederacíon de Nacionalidades Indigenas de Ecuador/ Confederation of Indigenous Nationalities of Ecuador
EC	European Commission
ECA	Employment Contracts Act
ECB	European Central Bank
EEC	European Economic Community
EMU	Economic and Monetary Union
ESAP	Economic Structural Adjustment Programme
EU	European Union
FDI	foreign direct investment
FEE	Foundation for Economic Education
FIRE	finance, insurance, real estate
FUT	United Workers' Front
GEAR	Growth, Employment, and Redistribution strategy
HIPC	Heavily Indebted Poor Countries
IFIs	international financial institutions
IMF	International Monetary Fund
ISI	import substitution industrialization
MDRI	Multilateral Debt Relief Initiative
MTFS	Medium-Term Fiscal Strategy
NAFTA	North American Free Trade Agreement
OPEC	Organization of the Petroleum Exporting Countries
PAH	Plataforma de Afectados por la Hipoteca/Platform for the Mortgage-Affected

PRI	Partido Revolucionario Institucional/Party of the Institutionalized Revolution
PRSPs	Poverty Reduction Strategy Papers
RDP	Reconstruction and Development Program
SAREB	La Sociedad de Gestión de Activos Procedentes de la Reestructuración Bancaria/Bank Restructuring Asset Management Society
SNP	Scottish National Party
TANF	Temporary Assistance for Needy Families
UKIP	UK Independence Party
VAT	value-added tax
ZANU–PF	Zimbabwe African National Union–Patriotic Front
ZAPU	Zimbabwe African People's Union
ZCTU	Zimbabwe Congress of Trade Unions

Acknowledgements

Jon Shefner would like to acknowledge his collaborators in his work on austerity over the years. These include his coauthor on this project, Cory Blad, and also George Pasdirtz, Aaron Rowland, Steven Panageotou, and Julie Stewart. He's learned from all of these friends and coworkers, but from none more than John Walton, whose pioneering work on austerity protests serves as a constant inspiration. Jon additionally thanks Fred Block, Paul Gellert, Frances Fox Piven, and Gay Seidman for comments, inspiration, and encouragement. Jonathan Skerrett at Polity has been a generous and helpful editor. The book has benefited significantly from the work of Polity's reviewers. Emily Landry and Charles Walton provided substantial help in the research and editing process, Emily especially providing excellent and painstaking assistance as the work was completed. Jon also thanks Karen for everything, always. Finally, Jon wants to note that working with Cory Blad again has been a great joy.

Cory Blad would like to thank several people who have contributed to this effort in one way or another. Ricardo Dello Buono, Emanuele Ferragina, and Samuel Oloruntoba each contributed to his thinking on austerity and contemporary political economic trends. Conversations with Vicki Dabrowski and Elena Díaz González provided new insights and have encouraged him to broaden his understanding of conditional possibilities. As always, Julia, Zoë, and Sanna continue to provide inspiration and demonstrate infinite patience.

1

Many Paths to Austerity

On February 2, 1989, during his inaugural address, Venezuela's President Carlos Andrés Pérez emphasized the need for a debtors' cartel and called for a new international policy aimed at reducing Third World debt. Since the Mexican government's announcement of its inability to pay its debt in 1982, and subsequently accession to austerity measures, debt had become the central issue of the developing world. The President's contentious inaugural rhetoric soon proved empty, however, when he agreed to International Monetary Fund (IMF) requests that austerity policies be imposed as conditions of debt relief. Venezuelans interpreted the agreement as a betrayal; during Pérez's previous term as President (1974–9), he had served as a strong voice for social democratic foreign and domestic policies.

The IMF conditions followed a design by then familiar across the Global South. The government implemented austerity measures, including increases in gasoline prices and transportation fares, lifting price controls over goods and services, freezing public hiring, imposing a national sales tax, as well as raising domestic interest rates and devaluing the currency. These measures, combined with shortages of various food commodities, hurt many Venezuelans; they responded with peaceful marches in the capital city Caracas, with protest immediately following in other cities.

Within days, the demonstrations escalated to full-scale rioting and looting. President Pérez called out the army, suspended constitutional guarantees, and imposed a curfew as riots spread to at least 16 cities and towns. Weeks of rioting resulted in at least 300 reported dead, along with over 2,000 wounded and over 2,000 jailed. Participation in the riots was widespread, with students, workers, and slum dwellers taking part in the looting of shops and sniper attacks on government forces.

The riots forced the government to reinstitute price controls over basic foodstuffs and services and allow pay increases in private and public sector jobs. The President used the protests as temporary leverage in negotiations with the IMF, World Bank, US Treasury, and commercial banks to obtain further loans.[1] But despite the dramatic protests and his initial backpedaling, Pérez continued to follow IMF prescriptions over the course of his increasingly discredited presidency. The government allowed no further wage increases and slashed social protection programs and spending while increasing interest rates and privatizing some state-owned enterprises. New trade policies included lowering tariffs in order to open the market to competition from imported goods. Global elites benefited from the changes, as interest rate increases diminished credit access to local businesses, while new foreign investment laws removed restrictions on remittance abroad of dividends, established parity of treatment of foreign and local investors, and enlarged the list of activities designated as priority areas for foreign investors. In short, the IMF-driven policies paved the way for the neoliberalization of the Venezuelan economy.

Greece's experiences with austerity began in the wake of the Great Recession of 2008. Europe's great powers offered stimulus packages for their own national economies, while imposing austerity on some of the weaker members of the European Union (EU). Greece was an easy target, as its debt was thought to be a product of its overgenerous welfare state.[2] By 2011, the Greek government had already instituted austerity measures as a condition of Eurozone bailout, but new punishing measures were on the horizon. The parliament voted to impose more austerity as conditions for its further relief. The new plan called for cuts of "14.32bn euros ($20.50bn; £12.82bn) of public spending, while raising 14.09bn euros in taxes over five years" (BBC 2011). Specific measures targeted state workers, cutting public sector workers' wages by between 20 and 30%, and shrinking civil service employment by drastic attrition, with replacement of retirees ranging only between 10 and 20%. Additional cuts targeted health and education spending, social security income and pensions, public investment, and subsidies to local governments (BBC 2011).

Over the course of the next four years, the Troika (the European Commission, the European Central Bank [ECB], and the IMF) continued to demand austerity despite persistent street protest and the outcry of elected officials. Austerity, Troika members believed, would ensure that bailout monies would be repaid, while avoiding the contagion of economic failure spreading to the rest of the Eurozone. Social protection and government services were regularly slashed. In 2013, 15,000 additional layoffs were imposed on the public sector. In 2014, the government "cut another 4,000 public-sector jobs, reduced benefits for the unemployed, cut pensions, and implemented a reform of the labor code that drastically curbed the right to strike" (Panageotou & Shefner 2015: 317). Social costs were substantial, with unemployment surging, especially for youth. Those "at risk of poverty or social exclusion increased from 27.6 percent to 34.6 percent in 2012" (Panageotou & Shefner 2015: 318). Suicides, homicides, and armed robbery all increased, while access to healthcare diminished. Social movements took to the streets repeatedly in protest at the ongoing hardships caused by austerity.

The political struggles evolved as an emerging left-wing party, SYRIZA, became increasingly prominent in the opposition, leading the waves of protest against austerity. That continued until its candidate, Alexis Tsipras, became President in January 2015, having been elected with promises to roll back the austerity agreements and grow the economy without leaving the Eurozone (Elliott 2015). Tsipras soon found his promises impossible to keep. By July, the President and his party found themselves in the uncomfortable position of pushing the same kinds of austerity measures that they had critiqued. In exchange for ongoing bailout, the Greek parliament again voted in favor of another round of punishing austerity (Daley & Kanter 2015). SYRIZA paid the price and lost power in July 2019.

Venezuela's and Greece's experience are similar in many ways, despite the 20-year gap. Austerity was imposed on less powerful nations by coalitions that were dominated by more powerful nations supported by global/regional financial actors; specific measures were similar in their targeting of state social protection expenses; state debt was seen as the problem that austerity would fix; and the hegemony of austerity as a policy was demonstrated in part by its imposition by government leaders whose actions belied their previous critique.

These two brief scenes of austerity lay the ground for the goals of this book: to recognize the long and global history of austerity; to clarify the different economic ills to which austerity has been applied as the purported cure; and to point out similarities and differences in the way austerity has been implemented since the early 1980s. These goals require some elaboration.

From 1973 to the current day, austerity has increasingly become the go-to policy to resolve the "problem" of national debt. This has been a truly global phenomenon, emerging in the 1970s in what was then called the Third World in response to debt crises incurred by government borrowing. Over time, as we will show, austerity responded not only to public debt, but also to private debt that was guaranteed by national governments. Austerity was often rhetorically framed as "shock treatments," with the expectation that such policy imposition would be short-lived, but history demonstrates the extended life of such measures in many nations. Over time, the use of austerity has moved well beyond resolving public debt: it has also been imposed in response to slower economic changes, as a strategy to protect creditors' investment, and as an instrument for governments to take on private debt, all as part of a wider neoliberal shift that has diminished government efforts to address citizen needs through various social welfare measures. That is, austerity has been viewed as the medicine to cure a number of economic ills, while the components of austerity policy have remained largely similar.

We make four central contributions in this book. First, we want to point out that austerity is a truly global set of policies that have been brought to bear in response to different economic ills across the past 40 years. That global history has been ignored by recent research following the 2008 financial crisis. In the wake of austerity in the Global North, academics and journalists published a great deal of critical research, admirably demonstrating how austerity policies failed to stimulate equitable economic growth in developed nations. However, this recent scholarship suffers from spatial and historical blinders in its discussion of austerity, as it fails to recognize its extensive history in the Global South. Development scholars remember the dramatic impacts of austerity across Latin America, Africa, and Asia. The pain of those years was recognized by many who labeled the 1980s "the Lost Decade" owing to the reversal of previous state-funded social gains. Austerity continued to be the policy of choice in the Global South into the 1990s and 2000s. Indeed, its global scope increased as more Asian nations were forced to follow the same policies even while many ex-Soviet nations found austerity defining their reintroduction to capitalism. The fact that recent researchers who wrote critically of austerity in the Global North ignored its precedent in the Global South and elsewhere demands this historical correction. This book addresses austerity in both the Global South and the Global North, in powerful nations and those less so, in democratic nations and authoritarian ones, pushed by external actors and internal ones. Our goal is to demonstrate the continuities and differences in application of those policies across time and place.[3]

The failure to recognize the global scope of austerity by even critical scholars has implications beyond the scholarly omission: this position provides cover to the policymakers of the Global North, who willfully ignored the largely detrimental history of austerity in the developing world as they applied the policy to the Eurozone. The critique of austerity in the Global South was wide and deep (Pastor 1987; George 1988; Walton & Seddon 1994; Portes 1997; Dello Buono & Bell Lara 2007, to cite just a few). Reminding readers that this critique preceded the more recent research (Crouch 2011; Lynn 2011; Blyth 2013; Karger 2014) leads us to our next point.

Our second contribution is to demonstrate that the actors most important to the imposition of austerity have varied over time. Examining the "architects of austerity" (Major 2014) demonstrates that austerity policies are linked to changing loci of power in the global economy. Powerful states, international and national banks, and international financial institutions have played significant roles in the imposition of austerity, as have a variety of ideologues employed by academic institutions, government, and business. Importantly, and related to austerity's hegemonic status, the relative importance of these players changes across time and place. The IMF and the United States were central players in the developing world, but play a reduced role in austerity in the Eurozone, where the ECB, German and French bankers, and credit rating agencies became more important. Indeed, in several of the cases we examine, austerity was willingly introduced by domestic policymakers. Austerity has remained an important tool of control by global economic elites; examining who has wielded it over time helps us understand shifting powers within the neoliberal global economy.

Third, we argue that austerity has been used as a tool to make the poor and the working and middle classes pay for those changes in the global political economy that might otherwise have forced economic elites to diminish their profits. Harvey (2005: 12) makes the point that neoliberalism was a response to a global "crisis of capital accumulation" which occurred simultaneously with rising political and economic threats to elites. Neoliberalism, for Harvey (2005: 19), is best understood as a "political project to re-establish the conditions for capital accumulation and to restore the power of the economic elites."[4] Austerity has provided an important and consistently used tool for those elites. Examining austerity across time and place provides important documentation of how the majority of national populations are hurt as elites restructure economies in ways that benefit them. Neoliberal economic restructuring in itself has hurt many; in addition, the risks taken on by the powerful in the restructuring process have led to errors such as those that led to the Great Recession. Within the nations where it has been imposed, it is the poor and the working and middle classes who bear the costs, suffering from both risky behaviors and more planned components of the global transition. Cross-nationally, austerity adds to the policy toolbox that maintains inequality between Global North and South nations, as many of the latter continue to be dependent on the former for investment, supplying low-skilled jobs on commodity chains, and remain the locale of much natural resource extraction.

Capitalism is not everywhere and always the same. The classic work of Cardoso and Faletto (1979) masterfully unpacks dependency and development in Latin America as they examine historical variations in capitalist control. Importantly, forms of control shift over time, and are sensitive to specific places and histories. Cardoso and Faletto remind us that capitalism always varies owing to changing priorities of external and internal social forces. The former, in our argument, have been responsible for imposing austerity. The latter are more diverse in their relationships to austerity; they, too, may impose and implement it, but they also sometimes resist and occasionally overturn it.

Finally, our goal is to show that both the long history of its imposition and its global reach suggest that austerity has taken on the status of a hegemonic policy. Regardless of the economic ill diagnosed as the root of diverse problems – debt crisis in the Global South, financial crisis in the Eurozone, diminished state spending flexibility in the United States – austerity has become the medicine of choice. The different problems have found different champions, as we note above, but their common settling on austerity confirms it as a hegemonic policy. Arrighi (2010) points to the importance of financialization as a key strategy during hegemonic transitions. Although austerity policies have not played that same historical role, the consistency of their implementation suggests they have provided stability in power holding and accumulation during neoliberalism. The fact that austerity has now been applied to weak and strong states, to states with divergent political structures, and in globally common but also locally varied ways, further demonstrates its hegemonic status.

Yet hegemony, in the Gramscian sense, cannot persist without some manifestation that the hegemonic ideology, or in this case policy, indeed addresses some material needs. The postwar industrial expansion in the United States, for example, facilitated hegemony because it addressed the material needs of certain working-class populations for a time. In contrast, austerity has benefited very few. Despite repeated failures, however, austerity policies continue to be the policy of choice for economic elites. Examining the global actors who became increasingly important in establishing neoliberalism's hegemonic status helps us understand these choices (Plehwe et al. 2007; Mirowski & Plehwe 2009; Jones 2012; Mirowski 2013; Major 2014). These range from intellectual pioneers such as those found in the Mont Pelerin Society, established in Switzerland in 1947, to foundations set up by rich business families in pursuit of their economic interests and philosophies, to economics departments across the globe, and finally to think tanks that brought theorists, politicians, businesspeople, and others together as a coherent ideological force – what Mirowski (2013) calls the "neoliberal thought collective." While we do not seek to repeat the work done by others, we also examine which players and institutions were especially influential in forging the austerity consensus in different cases, and what that tells us about changing global economic power.

Together these four contributions help us answer the central questions in this book: How can we understand such persistence in the face of such problematic outcomes? How has the hegemony of austerity been maintained in the face of such dramatic evidence of its failure, and a resulting absence of popular support? First, we need to explain our definition of austerity.

What Is Austerity?

Austerity as a term has been widely used, and in varied ways. It has been used to define specific policies, but also to describe a wider governing ethos, as well as to articulate an ideology. For policy-makers in the Global North and South, austerity has been touted as a crisis management tool; in the Global South it has the added distinction of being considered a pathway to economic development. Finally, for many across the globe, austerity has become a way of life.

The varied definitions tell us how commonplace austerity has become, and how our understandings of its role in neoliberalism has evolved. Early academic critics found the implementation of austerity measures a "condition of structural adjustment and debt restructuring" (Walton & Seddon 1994: 99). Specific policies included cutting public expenditures, reducing basic subsidies on survival goods, currency devaluation, and price increases. A decade later, authors of the 2004 SAPRIN report evaluated the multinational experience of austerity in the Global South, and differentiated it from "stabilization" programs, which "imposed strict fiscal and monetary discipline on indebted countries as a condition for receiving short-term balance of payments credits." What became known as second- or third-wave neoliberalism relied on the imposition of austerity policies to move nations toward "structural adjustment policies" which "were designed to open markets and reduce the state's role in the economy." These latter measures included trade liberalization, investment deregulation, and privatization of state enterprises, among a variety of other reforms (SAPRIN 2004: 2). Many critics of the impact austerity has had on the Global South focused on its political project, finding the point of such policies to be not only extractive, but also to force a singular economic vision on recalcitrant nations. The labeling of the "Washington Consensus" (Williamson 1990) made it clear that the power to force a unified perspective was imposed by powerful actors in a historically unequal relationship.

As the 2008 crisis generated more work on austerity in the Global North, researchers revised their definitions as their foci changed. Blyth, for example, offers this:

> Austerity is a form of *voluntary deflation* in which *the economy adjusts* through the reduction of wages, prices, and public spending to restore competitiveness, which is (supposedly) best achieved by cutting the state's budget, debts, and deficits. Doing so, its advocates believe, will inspire "business confidence" since the government will neither be "crowding out" the market for investment by sucking up all the available capital through the issuance of debt, nor adding to the nation's already "too big" debt. (Blyth 2013: 2, emphasis added)

Schui offers this understanding of the meaning and components of austerity, even more dramatically omitting mention of specific actors and their political intentions:

> Austerity policies are proposed to restore balance in government finances and regain economic dynamism and competitiveness. The former objective is pursued mainly by cutting back on government expenditure that funds individual and collective forms of consumption for example pensions, health care and education. ... The second objective, stimulating growth, is mainly sought by lowering the cost

of labour, that is, reducing wages and hence individual competition. Renewed economic dynamism is also expected to result from the reduction of government expenditure and debt: a smaller state is believed to leave more space for private initiative and inspire confidence among private investors and consumers. (Schui 2014: 2)

As comprehensive and clear as they are, Blyth's and Schui's definitions fail to make clear that, during the past 40 years of austerity, it has been states that have cut their own budgets and have done so under extreme pressure by global economic actors. Blyth's book more than makes up for this omission, but for the purposes of our argument, states' actions are crucial to understand, as the unattributed action of global actors not only cuts the state budget, but also employs states to do the dirty work of austerity. To us, the power relations between indebted states and those global powers advocating austerity are central to the historical unfolding of the phenomenon.

In contrast, Harvey (2005) defines neoliberalism as an economic *and* political project, the latter focused on rebuilding elite class prerogatives, which had eroded in post-World War II welfare states. Giddens also understands the political and disciplinary role played by the imposition of austerity policies, although he holds a less critical perspective: "The point of austerity, in the context of the EU countries today, was not just to bring the books into closer balance but to help enforce change and reform, partly through its very shock value" (Giddens 2013: 60).

Austerity, in our view, is an economic tool that always betrays political intentions. Austerity facilitates the wider neoliberal project by weakening welfare states and policies, and diminishes the protections won by labor. The policymakers who implement austerity aim to open protected parts of national economies, so limiting the double-movement capacity of states to alleviate the savagery of unrestrained capitalism. Polanyi (2001) long ago recognized that states, in addition to social movements, seek to control what many have called the free market, and its harsh impacts on humans and the environment. State regulation policies, as well as the construction of welfare programs, result from the recognition of the need to blunt these impacts. With the turn to austerity, government officials prioritize the workings of a seemingly free market, giving in to neoliberal arguments that human welfare will be best served when almost all human needs are resolved through market mechanisms.

In this book, we define austerity as a subset of a larger palette of neoliberal measures, and focus on a consistently applied bundle of policies that are brought to bear in response to different diagnoses of economic ills. Austerity is among the first steps in the neoliberal process of economic and political restructuring to the benefit of elites.[5] The signal policies of austerity are those that limit the state's economic ability to provide for the social protection of its citizens, and as such are always both political and economic in scope and intention. The class project so well described by Harvey (2005) uses the state as a tool in new ways, not shrinking it, as neoliberal advocates have claimed, but instead marshaling its powers to diminish welfare provision and creating a favorable environment for deeper structural changes. Instead of shrinking the state, austerity policies demonstrate the state is a contested terrain; they occur during periods in which the political and economic interests of national and global upper-class constituencies are prioritized. Paradoxically, when states impose austerity, their own legitimacy can be challenged if citizens recognize that these policies reinforce a preference for the needs of the economically powerful. When they baldly exert power in the defense of elites, states' own ability to mobilize citizens in their own defense diminishes. In protests and political campaigns, dissenting citizens recognize the global origin of austerity policies, but it is the states that suffer from declining legitimacy when such policies are challenged. The paradox of how the state weakens itself and its citizens is central to this book, as is who forces the imposition of austerity, how that has changed across time and place, and what the purposes of that action are.

Because we identify austerity as a tool embedded in a larger political and economic project, our focus is on how specific policies are used, and how they affect nations and citizens. The policies we define as austerity include: reducing social welfare spending in such areas as healthcare, education, and housing; cutting consumer subsidies; public sector wage cuts and layoffs; legal restrictions on deficit spending; tax increases; currency devaluations; and raising interest rates. These measures yield both immediate and enduring impacts on citizens' living standards, and create a context in which states are forced to become the enemies of their own citizens.[6] We include privatization of state enterprises within this definition of austerity policies although others do not, because creating such enterprises can be rooted not only in economic development strategies, but also in welfare state provision and legitimation efforts. States often build both economic and political power through their employment practices, which are then disrupted with privatization. Additionally, privatization often occurs simultaneously with other austerity measures. Global policymakers have forced these policies to be implemented in largely consistent ways across Global South and Global North nations, with the exception of currency devaluation, as the Economic and Monetary Union precludes devaluation as a component of austerity because it would harm all members of the EU.

We argue that austerity has been used to address different social and economic causes throughout its recent history. The ways austerity has been understood in academic and journalistic responses to the 2008 European crisis differs from the way austerity policies were written about during decades of application in the Global South. Both experiences provide further contrast to moments when austerity has been an expression of social solidarity during wartime, or when it has been the policy of choice in a context where its imposition becomes seemingly inevitable. Our definition highlights the policies and how they are similarly imposed, while acknowledging that different dominant actors have imposed austerity across time and space, using various crisis diagnoses.

By acknowledging different national experiences within a global framework, we argue that austerity has been a hegemonic policy. This means neither that the imposition of austerity policies has a singular chronology, nor that it has been imposed by the same actors either globally or nationally, nor that it has responded to the same pressures. Instead, we emphasize exactly the opposite: how such actors and causes have varied, and why the use of such policy has differed by time and place. For example, the use of austerity in Latin America during the 1980s responded not just to national debt, but also to efforts at state-centered development. Asia escaped such pressures until the 1990s, however, even though many nations pursued similar development goals and strategies, because those governments friendly to the United States played a role in the Cold War that was different than in Latin America. For another example, governments took on public debt in Latin America, while those in the EU absorbed private debt. And, as we will see, the IMF was a principal actor early, less so later on, and, in at least one of our cases, largely absent.

In other words, governments came to austerity through different paths, pushed by different actors, and in response to different global and national pressures. But they arrive at the same destination just the same. The paths to austerity have been flexible, and some elements of the policies themselves have differed, but the common arrival demonstrates that the policy has been hegemonic.

Gramsci wrote that hegemony requires some balance between

coercion and legitimacy, the latter supplied by some shared material progress, or at least the shared interpretation that the hegemonic system provides material benefits. That is, some social groups, in addition to capitalists, had to interpret their material and cultural standing as improving for capitalism to be truly hegemonic. Here we differ from the Gramscian interpretation. We will show that austerity has caused broad hardships, and has generated both official and social movement opposition in ways that defy this traditional component of hegemony. Like others, we emphasize the role played by neoliberal ideologues in and out of government who played the role of Gramsci's organic intellectuals of neoliberalism and austerity (Plehwe et al. 2007; Mirowski & Plehwe 2009; Jones 2012; Mirowski 2013; Major 2014). We suggest that it is in part these actors, and the interests to whom they cater, who have replaced the Gramscian requirement of popular sectors benefiting by a hegemonic system. There are, of course, other factors. The proliferation of new communication media and the explosion of consumer culture have reinforced capitalism, as has the erasure of seemingly possible alternatives with the fall of communism. These cultural changes are arguments beyond the scope of this book, but these global trends, too, have contributed to the creation of a hegemony without popular sectors benefiting, unlike Gramsci's original conception. Instead we see a hegemony with even more restricted beneficiaries than did Gramsci.

We do, however, address the elements of a hegemony without beneficiaries, or one with only restricted beneficiaries, in this book. These elements are central to austerity and neoliberalization. We argue that in addition to ideologues pushing away alternatives, structural changes in how profits are made have reinforced why and how austerity has become the central economic strategy. The increased prominence of financialization globally requires a new prioritization of investors and increasing the security of their profits. Austerity measures, focusing on debt repayment, have accomplished that greater security for investment capital. The role of debt itself, always an instrument of profit extraction, has become even more highly prioritized as a money-making strategy, much in ways that Arrighi (2010) wrote of previous hegemonic regimes. Austerity measures have also reinforced labor discipline among the global workforce; with the shrinking of wage controls and other protections, the ability to contest neoliberalism through legal platforms diminishes. Privatization through austerity has expanded markets for investment, as both state-owned enterprises and remaining sources of welfare provision transition into businesses more intent on profit than employment or addressing needs. Finally, austerity with restricted beneficiaries helps us understand how poor and rich nations alike are subjected to the process, the former more immediately and fiercely at first, as they provide a laboratory for the more powerful rich nations.

Our argument of hegemony without popular beneficiaries, but with restricted ones, informs our sample. To demonstrate how widely austerity has been imposed, we examine rich countries and poor, those from the Global South and North, those with socialist governments and firmly capitalist ones. We look across time and place to find nations where austerity has violently responded to socialist policies, and where it has slowly but steadily become the seemingly inevitable choice. We examine nations where the spur has been public debt and those where it has been private debt. Finally, we examine how the powerful actors have changed by time and space as further confirmation of the hegemony of austerity.

One more comment on definitions: when we use the term "free market," we are echoing how that term is used by its neoliberal advocates, not endorsing that such an institution can or should exist. The term is an important part of the ideological toolbox used to explain and rationalize austerity and other neoliberal policies. Following Polanyi and others, we don't believe a free market exists, nor could it. All market relations are dependent upon state regulations. Even neoliberal policies that purport to lift regulations in favor of an unrestrained market are indeed regulations in their own right. A market truly free from government regulations is illusory. The question of state regulations is always: Who benefits from them?

Comparative Austerity: Commonalities and Distinctions

Examining austerity in a global comparative context is a complicated endeavor because these policies have been used to address different economic problems. Austerity has consistently been used to facilitate market liberalization, but experiences vary from country to country. While austerity is relatively ubiquitous, it is neither evenly imposed nor equally voluntaristic. Not only does the form of austerity shift from, for example, transformative "shock therapy" to self-imposed spending reductions, it also varies in terms of severity. The question then becomes: How best to create a comparative framework to understand the commonalities and distinctions between national state austerity imposition and experience?

Austerity experiences in the Global South are distinct from those in the Global North. While this is an overly broad characterization, we root it in a history of empire, colonization, and dependency. First, the conceptual distinction between the Global South and North is rooted in the historical expansion of colonialism and in many senses defines the contemporary relationship between the generally more affluent North and poorer South. The purpose of colonial acquisition and conquest – resource exploitation and accumulation of wealth – remains a defining feature of the relationship between wealthy and poor nations.

Second, the subsequent legacy of colonialism is differential power. The political autonomy of Global South governments, particularly within the context of political economic decision-making, is traditionally subsumed under external political and ideological authority structures. This legacy of external political economic control over former colonial national states hindered the development of autonomous political economic authority in the Global South.

This history creates distinctions between Global North and South countries, which can influence the scope and experience of austerity policies. Yet the purpose of austerity policies – to condition political economic governance along market-oriented, liberal capitalist lines – is consistent across all countries that have pursued neoliberalism, regardless of relative affluence and colonial history. We follow a descriptive framework that is designed to highlight common aspects of austerity imposition, while remaining sensitive to historical, economic, and political differentiation between country cases. The framework allows us to make largely consistent comparisons based on variables that define either conditions influencing austerity imposition, or the experience of majority populations in the countries we examine. Our goal is to provide a means of analyzing the commonalities and differences regarding the effects of austerity policies in select countries. Using this framework helps us comprehensively describe austerity imposition and effects nationally, while explaining why austerity is so widespread globally. In doing so, we demonstrate how austerity policy can overwhelm other political and economic conditions and histories.

The three dimensions of difference – regime type, degree of austerity imposition, and relative economic status – allow us to examine the specifics of national cases while remaining sensitive to global power dynamics rooted in historical colonial and development contexts. Each dimension must be thought of as existing along a continuum, as we briefly outline below.

Regime Type

Our focus on regime form revives the importance of politics in a discussion too often relegated to only economics. Advocates of neoliberalism and austerity trumpet the efficacy of the market in economic decision-making, demonizing the regulatory or welfare functions of the state as intervening in what they think is a purer, more rational kind of transaction. By addressing austerity across states that vary in levels of democratic function, we make it clear that in the imposition of austerity, as in other economic policies, states can never be neutral arbiters. There are always different constituencies supporting and opposing different economic policies owing to their considerations of how such policy will aid or harm them. Austerity is never a "rational choice"; it is always a political one driven by different political conditions and constituencies.

Examining regime form also allows us to take on the argument that austerity is about shrinking the state. State employment often does indeed shrink through austerity, whether through privatization of parastatal enterprises or by jettisoning social services. But the function of the state is as important as its size. What our case examination of the politics of austerity shows is that shifting state priorities are as important as shrinking size.

Finally, our comparison across different kinds of political settings can reveal the power of austerity's architects even over local political institutions. We first examine Chile and how a violent and costly coup ushered in austerity. But austerity need not be reinforced by authoritarian politics. As we will see, policies that reinforce inequality are fully consistent with democratic processes.

Examining regime type reminds us that, while rooted in economic theory, austerity is a largely political process. These policies are not democratically requested; rather they are imposed by state actors who are then responsible for implementing, maintaining, and defending policies that negatively impact large sections of their nations' populations. We pay particular attention to the role political processes and institutions play in austerity imposition: attempting to legitimate austerity in the face of worsening material adversities, and responding to anti-austerity mobilization. Political conditions have informed our case selection: we examine cases in authoritarian-leaning countries as well as those in more democratic countries.

Degree of External Imposition

This variable further illustrates the political nature of austerity policies. These are not independently designed policies, but rather politically imposed restrictions designed to solely promote economic growth. By examining the actors and institutions responsible for enabling austerity policies, we understand the differences in the experiences of the Global South and North in addition to the historical shift in the role of powerful actors and their goals.

The dominant role of external institutions imposing austerity, aided by internal national elites, is a common element of austerity in the Global South. In the Global North, internal elites intent on maintaining their national power or their position in an economic union helped promote austerity, which changed the nature of external pressure. Recognizing and identifying the external–internal dynamic and how it contributed to policy implementation highlights essential aspects of domestic and international power. The implementation of austerity as a means to reduce social service provision, lessen governmental regulation, and facilitate capital mobility is an aspect of the political economic transformations supporting the market-dominant orientation demanded by neoliberalism. In this sense, Global North proponents use austerity as a means of conditioning advanced capitalist states.

The role of international financial institutions such as the IMF and the World Bank in the Global South worked in a different fashion, imposing austerity policies and conditions as conditions linked to new loan acquisition or debt servicing agreements. Many countries in the Global South did not voluntarily implement austerity in support of neoliberal political economic restructuring – it was a requirement linked directly to existing debt and new capital acquisition. We argue that this distinction is important not only in terms of how societies experience austerity, but also in relation to movement mobilization and other reactions to conditions resulting from austerity imposition. For example, in postindustrial economies such as the United States and the United Kingdom, the perceived "need" for austerity emerged over time. As deindustrialization, trade liberalization, and production deregulation took hold, it became more and more difficult for state institutions to meet a growing need for social funding and service provision (O'Connor 1973; Jessop 1996). The "need for austerity" emerged as a result of this seeming failure of state institutions in the United States and United Kingdom to meet demand, coupled with a decline in capacity to sustain services.

Finally, any comparison of austerity must remain sensitive to the historical shift of austerity proponents from international financial institutions (IFIs) such as the IMF and World Bank to private capital interests such as national financial and credit ranking institutions, as well as regional actors such as the EU. Linked to the internal–external dynamic, there has been a clear privileging of private capital in the expansion of global financialization. While still tied to debt and loan conditionality, the role of private capital investment has complicated contemporary austerity promotion. Traditional IFI-imposed austerity was part of a larger ideological effort to transform developing economies into liberal market systems. The rise of private capital in this process seems increasingly focused on austerity as a means of ensuring debt repayment and/or maintaining conditions of positive capital investment. The participation of actors like the EU also highlights the hierarchy of power within a regional union.

Breadth and Depth of the Impacts of Austerity

The relative affluence or poverty of a country plays a distinct role both in how austerity is imposed and in what its effects might be. As previously stated, austerity is neither applied nor experienced evenly. Those in more precarious material conditions may suffer far more than those in more comfortable situations during periods of austerity. This difference has implications for anti-austerity mobilization and the effects of austerity on respective national populations.

Factors including unemployment rates, real wages, household income, inequality, and food security allow for a more detailed comparison of how the implementation of austerity policies impacts people in various countries. Examining differential impacts using these measures allows for international and national comparisons that will further highlight the divide between economic conditions in the Global North and South. In particular, the role of the state in creating consumerist middle classes (Alavi 1972; Tomba 2004) and in attempting to mitigate the worst conditions of abject poverty (Grindle 2004; Hall 2006) is commonly impacted by austerity imposition. Affluent countries with a developed social service infrastructure are better able to distribute austerity restrictions and mitigate material hardships than are dependent states. Indeed, the impact of austerity can restrict the ability of states to promote economic diversification and long-term development by privileging private capital with short-term profit motivations. As foreign investment in commodity-dependent countries tends to focus on those commodities, austerity can restrict such countries in ways not experienced in the more diverse, finance-dominated economies of the Global North.

In short, the telling of the story of austerity since the 2008 financial crisis has been incomplete and too focused on the developed world. This has resulted in an incomplete understanding not only of how neoliberalism has operated as a political economy, but also of how austerity has been used by different actors. We seek to provide a more complete understanding of the application and impact of austerity policy as a signal marker of neoliberalism. Recognizing variety and similarity within austerity policies is crucial in understanding neoliberalism's flexibility, persistence, and penetration.

Structure of the Book

Chapter 2 focuses on experiences of austerity that preceded the 2008 crisis, focusing on Latin America as the laboratory for austerity policies. During the first decades after World War II, Latin America was a site of substantial growth, much of it due to policymakers following a program of development through import substitution industrialization. The debt crisis followed, precipitated by many nations undertaking debt that, for a variety of reasons, they were unable to repay. IFIs, primarily but not only the IMF, joined the United States by imposing a set of conditions in reply to requests for debt renegotiation. With austerity came substantial social costs; the pain of those years was demonstrated by the often-used term the "Lost Decade of the 1980s," during which social and economic development advances were reversed.

All debt payments are extractive, of course, given the function of interest payments. During the 1980s and 1990s in the Global South, however, growing debt was pushed higher by rising interest rates, which facilitated a massive transfer of wealth from Southern nations to Northern banks. The experiences of Chile, Ecuador, and Mexico provide examples of austerity trajectories in differing political environments. In Latin America, as the global economy penetrated international trade, labor markets, and credit availability, austerity became the vanguard of other neoliberal policies that were touted as strategies for economic development. The cases addressed in this chapter varied from dictatorship, to emerging democracy, to one-party populism, and from an economic power like Mexico, to a nation with a thriving middle class like Chile, to a very poor nation like Ecuador. This comparison further demonstrates that neither variety of political system nor economic strength could successfully resist the early imposition of austerity.

Chapter 3 examines other cases of austerity prior to the pre-2008 crisis, again in the Global South. African nations, struggling for development gains, experienced similar relationships with international actors pushing austerity, but in different postcolonial political settings. South Africa and Zimbabwe provide different histories of austerity in Africa in nations with diverging democratic histories. Emerging from apartheid, the South African government found its economic policymaking flexibility soon limited by global economic actors. The economic progress expected from political freedom proved illusory as debt payments were prioritized and austerity was imposed. Zimbabwe, emerging from colonialism into a democratic and then increasingly authoritarian government, was pressured by both the World Bank and the IMF to increase food costs and reduce spending on education and healthcare across the 1990s. In both cases, the spread of neoliberalism meant that the pressures from global powers found willing allies even within governments founded on reversing racial and class exploitation.

Chapter 4 continues our examination of the Global South. In Asia, nations that had made significant development gains faced new extraction via austerity policies. Indonesia, an Asian giant that enjoyed substantial growth, was impacted by crisis and forced into years of austerity policies. The way to the 1997 crisis in Thailand was paved by previous neoliberalization of the nation's economy, and followed by austerity. New Zealand, although geographically in the Global South, shares many characteristics of advanced capitalist nations. It provides an interesting comparison owing to its limited economic diversity, which is balanced by careful attention to infrastructure and investment. Its inclusion offers an important case study of how a welfare state can be brought under sustained austerity.

Prior to austerity, Asian nations' growth found champions in the West, despite the similarity of some of their state-centric development policies to those that elicited criticism in Latin America. The end of the Cold War freed neoliberal ideologues to demonize all state economic interventionism and respond with austerity. In Asia, the increasing openness of the global economy helped the crisis emerge, and here again, the answer was austerity. All the cases in chapters 2–4 demonstrate the multitude of ills that the United States and IFIs diagnosed as requiring austerity, and the predominance of IFIs in the new austerity regimes.

Chapter 5 expands our analysis by examining policies that created the context for austerity in the United States, as creeping and cumulative scarcity came to define the environment to which governments had to respond. Policies familiar to those in the United States, such as tax reforms, decrease public resources that could be used to resolve economic need, and simultaneously limit governments' policy options. Deindustrialization in the industrial North, and then across the United States, further diminished economic wellbeing and cut jobs, while reducing tax bases that government relied on to address social needs. The policy responses we document, in the presence of ideological cover that argued for decreased economic regulation, confronted federal, local, and state government with a contradiction. As social needs increased, driven by rising inequality, the strategies with which governments could address such needs were limited by previous policymaking. With fewer policy tools ready to reconstruct prosperity, the inevitable solution became austerity. In contrast to the Global South, austerity in the United States has become the hegemonic policy in response to decades of restrictive economic policy, rather than as a cure for crisis-driven ills. Rather than imposed by powerful external institutions, austerity in the United States has been driven by a number of academic departments, foundations, and think tanks whose influence has grown over time.

How are recent experiences in the Eurozone different from previous impositions of austerity? Chapter 6 addresses the 2008 global economic crisis and its aftermath and how that window of opportunity was quickly closed by the quasi-religious conviction of neoliberalism: market fundamentalism. In much of the Eurozone, despite the claims that profligate states were at the root of the crisis, the crisis of debt was generated by the private sector (Blyth 2013). This chapter examines the experience of Greece and Spain to demonstrate how the recent global economic crisis provided an impetus for austerity to be imposed, and how the generation of the crisis differed from those in the Global South. Greece served in similar ways to the developing world as a target for low interest loans. Yet desire to join the Eurozone enticed Greece's policymakers to falsify and fudge its public deficit statistics to gain entry (Lynn 2011; Manolopoulos 2011). Spain, by contrast, was a stronger economic power, but in the years prior to the crisis its economy depended heavily on real estate, with subsequent heavy loans to developers. As a result of the country's mortgage laws, the bursting of the real estate bubble left behind inescapable debts. However, the Greek and Spanish cases are similar in that austerity continues to be used by dominant international actors to protect the interests of creditors. We also examine the experience of the United Kingdom as an early and permanent adopter of austerity, and as a way to understand the imposition of austerity within an economic giant. As in the US case, national economic power and democratic history prove little match for the seeming inevitability of austerity. Ongoing austerity in the United Kingdom demonstrates that economic power and a long history of democratic governance fail to withstand its policy hegemony.

Chapter 7 argues that austerity has consistently failed to create economic growth with equity; when growth has resulted, it is most often immiserating: characterized by increasing inequality, benefiting few and hurting many. Finally, different economic actors have played dominant roles in the imposition of austerity across time and place, demonstrating its role as a hegemonic policy even across different bodies of policymakers. This concluding chapter also raises the question of alternatives to austerity. The consistently harmful impact of the policy places its long-term hegemonic status in doubt. Its application to so many economic diagnoses further brings its future into question. The chapter argues that any attention to changed policy must also address the ideological demonization of the state that has accompanied austerity and other neoliberal policies. Reviving the value of the state, especially its economic regulation role, need not emphasize only human rights, or the need for a welfare state, although such discussions are helpful to displace current myths about the state. Recent discussions have reinvigorated the recognition that states are crucial not only to social protection, but also to innovation and creation (Block 2008; Block & Keller 2011; Mazzucatto 2013). But states will not reverse austerity in the absence of political pressure from both social movements and anti-austerity parties.

2

From Development to the Lost Decade in Latin America

This chapter focuses on experiences of austerity in Latin America that preceded the 2008 global crisis. Latin America was the laboratory for austerity policies, which were imposed largely because of the seeming danger of unsustainable national debts. Then as the rhetoric of dangerous debt spread, and as debt burdens grew in the 1970s and 1980s, IFIs, primarily the IMF and the World Bank, joined the United States in responding to Latin American governments' requests for debt renegotiation by demanding they impose austerity policies. These conditions protected the creditors, but brought substantial social costs to debtor nations; the pain of those years was demonstrated by the often-used term the "Lost Decade of the 1980s," during which the advances in social and economic development of previous years were reversed (George 1992; Portes 1997; Stiglitz 2002). Despite the time-limited implication of that term, austerity in Latin America continues, along with a number of structural reforms that have built on austerity and been called second-wave and third-wave neoliberalism. Indeed, the application of austerity accelerated after the "Lost Decade." After that period, the "Pink Tide" transition, during which many Latin American nations elected leftist governments, diminished, but did not eliminate, the reach and depth of austerity. Recent electoral turnovers have meant many of the "Pink Tide" nations have returned to neoliberal governments. What began as an experiment became hegemonic policy, denounced by many political opponents until they came into office and saw no other course but to continue austerity.

We examine this moment of austerity by looking at key historical examples that fit our descriptive variables. Chile, Ecuador, and Mexico provide examples of austerity trajectories in differing political environments from the 1970s through the 2000s. This chapter demonstrates the disciplinary nature of austerity policies on less developed and newly industrializing countries. Governments in Latin America were criticized for taking on inappropriate levels of debt or exercising undue government intervention in national economies that fueled their overspending. The external locus of power is clear as the IFIs and the United States remained the dominant policymaking actors throughout these impositions of austerity, prioritizing debt repayment over social needs. The cases addressed in this chapter varied from dictatorship, to emerging democracy, to one-party populism, and from an economic power like Mexico, to a nation with a thriving middle class like Chile, to a very poor nation like Ecuador. This chapter further demonstrates that neither variety of political system nor economic strength could successfully resist the early imposition of hegemonic austerity.

The Path to Austerity in Latin America

Beginning in the 1940s and continuing through the 1970s, import substitution industrialization (ISI) provided a development roadmap for much of Latin America (Green 2003; Hershberg & Rosen 2006). Following the Great Depression, policymakers sought to become more independent from global economic forces during both good times and bad, and advocated a form of protected indus-trialization. With some of their international consumer markets disrupted by World War I and later by global depression, Latin America's economic dependency on more powerful nations was brought into stark relief (Schoultz 2009).[1] Like many crises, the period from the Depression through World War II offered Latin American policymakers an opportunity, this time to step away from strictly externally focused economic policy. The shortages suffered during the war drove production and so nurtured industrialization as Latin Americans were able to supply not only raw materials, but also manufactured goods (Cardoso & Helwege 1992). The new intention was to protect domestic industry; the war supplied further flexibility to governments: "[W]ith the interruption of international finance, they naturally suspended debt payments and engaged in deficit spending. There was little incentive to follow free-market doctrine to attract foreign investment, since there was virtually no investment in the offing" (Drake 2006: 30).

Intellectuals from CEPAL[2] encouraged ISI as a resolution to long-term problems of dependent economies, including over-reliance on low-priced primary commodity exports and higher-priced manufactured imports, and the need to protect national economies from the unpredictable cycles of the world market. ISI requires an activist state in economic and social policy alike. In order to nurture manufacturing, the shift in the economic base required new infra-structure, educating and often subsidizing labor, and protectionist trade policy so that infant industries did not lose out to long-established international competitors (Green 2003). Many key industries were created or controlled as state enterprises in order to prioritize investment. Because it advocated manufacturing more consumer goods, ISI also required the creation of a larger middle class and a more prosperous working class, both to produce the new manufactured goods and to consume them (Cardoso & Helwege 1992; Dussel Peters 2000).

For much of the period in which they were used, ISI policies were successful. In Latin America and the Caribbean, real per capita GDP grew at an annual rate of 4.5% between 1940 and 1968, slowing to 3.7% from 1965 to 1973, and then further to 2.6% from 1973 to 1980 (Cardoso & Helwege 1992; World Bank 1990). Nations like Brazil and Mexico achieved substantial increases in industrial output, with Brazil becoming the world's seventh largest industrial producer. Imports dropped, one of the policy's intentions, while working people enjoyed some gains of improved salaries and welfare state provision.

Despite this substantial growth, however, ISI evolved in a contra-dictory context, which led to paradoxical outcomes. On one hand, ISI sought greater economic inclusion, especially of urban popula-tions. On the other hand, the policy was often carried through by authoritarian governments, or those that used labor policy for control rather than full participation. Argentina, Bolivia, Brazil, Chile, and Mexico, among other nations, had governments that ranged from military juntas to oligarchies operating under a façade of democracy. Where organized labor was strengthened, it was often under the political control of the state, and expected to support state policy and ruling parties. ISI also often brought increased quality of life by expanding welfare state expenditures on housing, healthcare, education, and other social protection, yet the political systems often remained exclusionary.

Industrial development was coordinated to diminish dependency, but the legacy of dependency meant that foreign capital was still crucial to the loans that ISI required. National policymakers intended to increase working- and middle-class consumption, but ISI was often captive to capital-intensive industrial growth, so limiting the amount of workers employed. Growth in aggregate measures such as GDP per capita was strong, but large sectors of the continent continued to suffer from low wages in agriculture, thus often leaving a poor majority's needs unaddressed. Governments protected nascent industries through tariffs, import controls, or nationalization in order to nurture production and compete with global predecessors with established production routines and markets, but at times these firms fell victim to poor quality or inefficient production. Then such industry required further investment, which meant governments had to loosen monetary expansion, resulting in inflation that swallowed some of the gains enjoyed by working people (Green 2003; Hershberg & Rosen 2006). Overcapacity at times proved to be a problem, as production outpaced salary increases and subsequent consumption. The urban bias of investment also shrank credit availability in the agricultural area, paving the way for increasing imports of food, while price controls meant to aid urban wage earners further hurt domestic farmers (Green 2003). Moreover, the expectation that key industries would have "positive spillover effects" with factories purchasing a variety of materials from domestic suppliers was stymied at times when entrepreneurs could not find secure material supplies. Finally, the coming globalization of production and the commodity chain supply model that began in the 1970s diminished the need for local suppliers.

Portes (1997) wrote about how the debt crisis supplanted the period of ISI, bringing austerity and other neoliberal measures first as a way to discipline indebted states and later as a development doctrine (see also Walton & Seddon 1994). Even this short discussion must recognize the influence of the Organization of the Petroleum Exporting Countries (OPEC), both in oil price hikes that leveled increased costs on production of all kinds, and in the enhanced revenue the price hikes brought member nations. Most nations suffered from the increased oil prices of the early and late 1970s, but the rising costs hurt much of the developing world in a way that played out over years. Banks simultaneously faced Western recession amid large OPEC deposits, and began to loan to developing world and socialist nations. Loans became newly and aggressively marketed with little regard for security because nations were not thought liable to bankruptcy (Drake 2006). During a time of global loan explosion, Latin America and the Caribbean accounted for half of the international loans (Walton & Shefner 1994: 98). The growth in lending did not alarm the IFIs, however, who saw no danger in more money going to the developing world, and even took comfort in the economic growth of those nations undertaking high debt. The share of the debt loaned by private banks continued to increase until it reached over half the debt load to developing nations by the mid-1980s (World Bank 1985).

Debt increased dramatically over the 1980s. In 1981, Latin America's external debt was $288 billion. By 1991, that sum had reached $456 billion, with much of the increase due to interest rates rising in the late 1970s. In human terms, the per capita debt in 1988 was $877, roughly 1000% over that sum in 1970. Many nations began to borrow to cover already-incurred debts, a pattern that has now been repeated for decades. In addition to increasing debt load, debt service became unsustainable. Not only did new credit become more expensive, so too did existing debt, since much of it was accompanied by variable interest rates (Sachs & Williamson 1985; Walton & Shefner 1994: 104). Per capita GDP declined from 1980 to 1988, and recovered only slightly between 1989 and 2000.

To make matters worse, the prices of many of the commodities on which nations based their repayment projections decreased. Although some of the money loaned was lost to corruption, rising interest rates, increasing oil prices, decreasing export prices, and the new wave of globalization-induced competition were much more important to the increase in debt. Consequently, more debt reschedulings occurred as nation after nation found it impossible to pay their debts. Debt rescheduling and renegotiations brought expectations of austerity. The reach of the IFIs into domestic economic policy became longer, as they sought structural economic change.

One nation preceded others in Latin America, a true pioneer in austerity. That nation's experience was driven by the 1973 coup against its elected government, and subsequent decades-long domination by a military junta that looked to the "Chicago Boys," the neoliberal economists who pushed for austerity as the avenue to structural reform. Chile proved a test case for Latin America, as Latin America proved a test case for the world.

Chile: Austerity at Gunpoint

Much has been written about the Chilean junta that toppled democratically elected President Salvador Allende, and the savage repression that followed. As important as it is to remember those experiences, we focus here on the austerity policies imposed during that junta.

On September 11, 1973, the Chilean military under the leadership of General Augusto Pinochet attacked and toppled the elected Socialist government of President Allende. US support for the coup was consistent with the Cold War rationale of its foreign policy in Latin America. From the 1950s on, the United States was directly involved in coups against legitimately elected leftist governments in Guatemala and Chile, and the propping up of right-wing juntas and dictatorships in Argentina, Brazil, El Salvador, Nicaragua, and elsewhere. The point of this case, however, is not to remind readers of the decades of misguided US foreign policy, but to demonstrate how the coup in Chile provided a laboratory for neoliberal policies, including austerity. We focus on the early years of Chilean neoliberalism to emphasize that, in addition to being a laboratory for austerity, the importance of the Chilean case rests in the new economic policymakers' relationship to the state. The hypocrisy of neoliberalism's attack on the state, arguing that less state intervention is better for the free functioning of an economy, could nowhere be more stark than in Chile. The military launched a coup against the state to implement neoliberalism, and imposed fierce state repression to avoid the protests that austerity elicited elsewhere.

Chile's economy was long based on its strong mining sector, where first nitrates and then copper predominated. After the devastation of the Great Depression, when foreign investment and mining production plummeted, the state's role in the economy increased. The government actively nurtured a "diverse industrial base in textiles and light manufacturing, producing goods for a rapidly expanding domestic market" to augment the traditional mining economy (Collins & Lear 1995: 14). Despite these efforts, the Chilean economy in the 1960s remained overly concentrated on copper, which was owned by US multinational corporations Kennecott and Anaconda. The presidential administration of Eduardo Frei, which immediately preceded that of Allende, bought back 51% of stocks in both nitrate and copper mining (Collins & Lear 1995).

Allende came into office amid a political environment split among left, right, and center. The right had fiercely resisted the previously attempted agricultural reforms of Frei's Christian Democrat government, while Allende's interests in redistributing income were seen as even more threatening to entrenched economic interests domestically and abroad. Allende immediately increased wages and froze prices, which made his government more popular with the poor, and much less so with manufacturers. He followed with a decision to nationalize the copper mines and much of the financial sector; these policies proved controversial, as did agricultural reforms. Allende's supporters among the rural and urban poor occupied farms and factories without legal permission, and citizen expropriations of land and productive facilities started to outpace the government's more controlled reforms. In response, the US administration of Richard Nixon cut off all bilateral economic aid, and blocked loans by IFIs, which previous Chilean governments had relied on for infrastructure projects (Sigmund 1977; Collins & Lear 1995; Kornbluh 2013).

By the time of the coup, inflation had reached 800%, commodities of many sorts were scarce, and many industries had suffered from the political conflict. Internal policy decisions, US propaganda launched as part of its pre-coup economic attacks, and the cutoff of international aid all contributed to Chile's economic distress (Valdés 1995; Kornbluh 2013).

Extensive violence accompanied the coup. After the storming of the Presidential Palace on September 11, 1973, thousands of those linked to Allende's government were rounded up and forced into the national soccer stadium; many of them were tortured and killed there or elsewhere. The political parties affiliated with the toppled government had their offices ransacked, their records burned, and their very existence outlawed (Sigmund 1977). The junta further outlawed organizations of peasants and the urban poor, as well as the national trade union confederation, and the military took over the universities. Over time, the junta killed between 3,000 and 10,000 people, while thousands more were tortured, exiled, or escaped.[3] The junta denied ongoing repression, or rationalized it by repeatedly announcing the discovery of arms caches, thereby maintaining the appearance of threat (Sigmund 1977).

The US government was clearly complicit with the junta, supporting the coup and other actions against the Allende government even before its election (Sigmund 1977; Kornbluh 2013). Indeed, the US had been long involved in Chile; the CIA and multinational allies spent twice the amount per voter to defeat Allende in 1964 than both US presidential campaigns spent that year.[4] After the coup, economic assistance was immediately offered through the "Washington Special Action Group," an interagency group working in the Nixon administration. The United States reversed its earlier course by immediately ending the "invisible blockade," which had frozen bilateral and multilateral assistance, and offering food and housing assistance.

In December 1973, the US government agreed to reschedule Chilean debts, and the junta began to discuss compensation with multinational mining corporations for the copper industry assets that had been expropriated. In February 1974, the multinational lenders' cartel the Club of Paris followed up on the United States' newly favorable economic policy and rescheduled Chile's debt. The World Bank joined in the love fest by making the first loan to Chile since before Allende's presidency. Also that same year, the IMF made available $95 million as a standby loan, which brought with it the kinds of conditions soon known across the developing world, and previously rejected by Allende (Sigmund 1977; Valdés 1995).

The newly preferential treatment was driven not only by favorable reaction to toppling the socialist government, but also by the entry of the "Chicago Boys," alumni of the University of Chicago Economics department, a bastion of neoliberal thought. From 1957 to 1970, around 100 Chilean students studied economics at the University of Chicago (Valdés 1995: 13). Many of these worked at the Universidad Católica de Chile before coming to lead economic policy for the junta and Pinochet government. The "Chicago Boys," too, were fully complicit with the coup. On the night of the coup, they feverishly photocopied their plan, known as "the brick," "a 500-odd-page plan for reversing the economic policies of Chile implemented over the previous half century" (Collins & Lear 1995: 255). Sons of Chile's conservative elites, the "Chicago Boys" had been working on this document at the behest of the Chilean Navy and business owners for months, anticipating the coup. Although it took some time to convince the junta to adopt their ideology, the neoliberals moved forcefully to replace both the previous model and policymakers who continued to argue for continuing the traditional role of the Chilean government in the economy. The economists soon devised the "shock treatment" that made Chile a laboratory for austerity and neoliberalism.[5] The only concern, as voiced by neoliberal champion Milton Friedman, whose followers were brought to Chile to advocate for their neoliberal policies, was whether the new plan "would be pushed long enough and hard enough" (Collins & Lear 1995: 29).

With the might of the military squarely behind them, over time members of the "Chicago Boys" became Minister of the Economy, Undersecretary of the Economy, Finance Minister, and Minister of Planning, as well as staffing influential offices within the Central Bank and the Budget Office (Valdés 1995).

The imposition of austerity lasted until at least 1980. During that time, the junta eliminated price controls and privatized banks and other companies. Under Allende's government, over 500 banks and other productive firms were controlled by the state; by 1980, that number had declined to 25. Strikingly, some of the privatization affected firms held by the government since 1939. Many of these firms were sold at cut-rate prices, and buyers were allowed to carry large debts over time. The government also sold off the pension system and part of the national health service (Ffrench-Davis 2010). Such measures facilitated significant private ownership of formerly public wealth.

With the exception of increased spending on the military, the "Chicago Boys" jettisoned government jobs while cutting social welfare spending, both signal policies of austerity. Thousands of government jobs were eliminated; one estimate found that a third of government employees – 265,000 workers – lost their jobs (Larráin & Vergara 2000, cited in Taylor 2006: 58). The junta also cut health spending by 17% and education by 11%. Interest rates were allowed to rise without limit. The government severely curtailed labor unions' rights, both as an economic measure and as a component of the repression, and kept wages under tight control despite rising prices. By 1975, wages had shrunk by a third from their 1970 level (Valdés 1995; Young 2006; Ffrench-Davis 2010). As one close observer summarized: "[T]he traditional role of the state, as entrepreneur and promoter of investment and industrialization, was to be curtailed as quickly as possible so that those functions might be fulfilled exclusively by private agents in liberalized open markets, under the 'neutral' rules of a free-market economy" (Ffrench-Davis 2010: 11).

These measures returned economic growth to 1970 levels, and inflation was eventually brought under control. Neoliberals touted the new model, much of which was based on substantial loans from the United States and IFIs, and the myth of the "Chilean miracle" was born. Yet the miraculous recovery was found to be illusory with the crash of 1982–4, and subsequent economic difficulties later in the 1990s. The social costs of the policies proved substantial over time (Collins & Lear 1995; Valdés 1995; Cypher 2004; Taylor 2006; Ffrench-Davis 2010).

Despite the economic fallout, the IMF and other neoliberal champions touted the Chilean transition as the model to follow. What they conveniently ignored, of course, was that it took both fierce repression and substantial external aid to shrink the Chilean state's welfare apparatus. The reforms carried through from 1973 to 1982 "faced neither criticism nor opposition since they were carried out in a framework of total deprivation of public liberties and citizen's rights" (Ffrench-Davis 2010: 10).

Chile provides a case of a largely middle-class nation deeply integrated into the global economy that was forced into austerity by internal repression and strict external guidance. Chile is unique in that it could not have been pushed into such economic restructuring without a long-lasting repressive military state, one that reversed decades of democratic civilian rule, and that was supported by the United States. The military force that brought austerity was complemented by internal actors who were more than prepared to reverse Chile's social democratic course with the newfound doctrines of neoliberalism. Despite its relatively unique position as a nation with a thriving middle class and democratic history, Chile provided a model for austerity policies that many Latin American nations were forced to follow.

Mexico: Austerity in the One-Party State

Mexico helped replicate that model across Latin America. We cover mostly the period from the late 1980s through the 1990s, when austerity was imposed under a single-party state undergoing glacial democratization. First, we provide some background useful to understand Mexico's experience during the debt crisis and beyond.

Like many nations in the developing world, Mexico's economy expanded during the 1960s and early 1970s. At the time, the country's population was composed of a small, wealthy, and politically powerful elite, a sizeable and prospering middle class, and a larger poor urban sector. People also remained tied to the land, ranging from smallholders, to participants in collective farms that were a legacy of the Revolution, to wage workers – most of whom, like their urban counterparts, were poor. Yet poverty in Mexico meant something different in the 1970s than it did later – the salary of one worker was then enough to provide for the survival of that worker and their family (Escobar Latapí & Roberts 1991).

During the 1960s and 1970s also, Mexico was roiled by political contention. The government responded to student unrest in 1968 with a massacre in Mexico City that left untold numbers dead, possibly into the thousands. Independent unions and community organizations in poor neighborhoods emerged to address their unresolved needs and protest the corruption of the predominant political party, the PRI (Partido Revolucionario Institucional, or Party of the Institutionalized Revolution), adding to the political turmoil. Mexican officials responded to political unrest with a mixture of strategies: cosmetic electoral reforms; clientelist strategies aimed at keeping neighborhood organizations quiet and tied to the PRI by buying votes with jobs, infrastructure installation, and incorporation of squatter communities; and selective repression (Ward 1986; Foweraker & Craig 1990; Shefner 2001).

The Mexican government paid for both economic growth and its maintenance of political power by borrowing heavily on the world capital market in the 1970s. The discovery of oil reserves in the Gulf of Mexico led to overly optimistic estimates of the riches that the nation would enjoy. When interest rates rose, oil sales provided the largest source of debt service, but a fall in oil prices diminished the potential for payback even while more infrastructural investment was required to exploit the resource. In 1982, Mexico, a giant of the developing world, shocked investors by declaring it held a debt it could not pay, and entered into debt renegotiations with the IMF (González de la Rocha & Escobar Latapí 1991).

Conditions for Mexican debt renegotiation included austerity measures that decreased governmental spending on citizens' needs. By then, academics and policymakers in the field of economics were under the sway of the increasing hegemony of neoliberalism. But Mexican policymakers, and their link to the neoliberal economic thought that had penetrated US higher education and policy, reinforced the power of the IFIs (Centeno 1997; Babb 2001). Many of those who served in the Miguel de la Madrid administration (1982–8) and the Carlos Salinas de Gortari administration (1988–94) were products of US graduate schools in economics and policy, fully indoctrinated into the new orthodoxy of neoliberal austerity. One-third of the cabinet members in the de la Madrid and Salinas administrations had postgraduate degrees from abroad (Centeno 1997).[6] The education in Ivy League schools, Stanford, and the University of Chicago ensured a shared ideological position that Centeno terms "international intellectual isomorphism," culminating in "a free-market revolution ... and the dawning of neoliberalism" (Centeno 1997, cited in Babb 2001: 171).

De la Madrid soon agreed to the IFIs' requirements to double gasoline prices, devalue the peso, cut government consumer subsidies, freeze wages, and privatize some of Mexico's state-owned enterprises. In return, he received quick disbursements of IMF- and World Bank-controlled loans and credits, along with the financial support of the US government. The relationship with these powerbrokers lasted the length of de la Madrid's six-year presidency, with meetings held to keep Mexico on track every six months.[7] By the end of the de la Madrid administration, austerity policies had cut public spending by 32%, with public education and health budgets reduced by half, as were wages. Unemployment besieged much of the Mexican labor force, leaving 5 million out of work (Larmer 1989; Middlebrook 1991; Woods 2006).

Carlos Salinas de Gortari faced a host of economic and political problems when he ascended to the presidency in 1988. During the election, a coalition of small leftist parties, social movements, and defectors from the PRI launched a significant challenge against his campaign. These new contenders were motivated by the painful austerity policies, a seeming betrayal of the PRI's previous efforts at economic inclusion, and the party's ongoing refusal to open the political landscape to democratic contestation. Early in the vote count, the leftist coalition the National Democratic Front was winning – and then the computers counting the votes mysteriously broke down. When they came back on line some days later, the PRI had won the presidency despite the earlier advantage to the leftists. This precipitated charges of fraud and a crisis of democracy to which Salinas responded over the course of his presidency.

The economic policies pursued by Salinas, a Harvard Ph.D., were even more closely tied to the expressed interests of the US government and the IFIs.

> [E]ven prior to the 1988 elections, the World Bank had become involved in preparing a series of short briefs on major policy issues for Salinas. … [I]mmediately after the elections [but] before Salinas took power, the World Bank organized a workshop for Salinas and his prospective cabinet … [and] … it became clear that these people wanted the World Bank's involvement in everything. (Woods 2006: 96)

The government tried to assuage the damage to the most vulnerable sectors through targeted social welfare programs, implemented largely through Solidaridad, Salinas' key social welfare program. Yet Solidaridad required co-investment from local and state governments, as well as local communities, in order to leverage federal funds, further stressing states and opening the door for more clientelist manipulation. The targeted relief offered by Solidaridad could not compensate for the IMF-imposed austerity mandate of large reductions in social spending. In addition to reducing funding for education, public health, housing, social services, and welfare, the Salinas administration imposed cuts in subsidies on milk, tortillas, sugar, and beans, staples on which the poor and working class relied. Subsequently, nutritional and health levels declined (Dresser 1991; González de la Rocha 2001; Shefner 2008).

Like other nations that prioritized state-centered development policy, Mexico had an economy long characterized by a significant amount of state ownership of productive capacity. During his presidency (1988–94), Salinas did much to open the economy to private control, selling state enterprises like airlines, mines, steel mills, and the telephone company. He additionally "permitted imports to surge to pressure Mexican producers to become more efficient; liberalized foreign investment regulations; [and] overhauled the tax system" (Rohter 1990). Because much of Mexico's union strength was in these publicly controlled firms, Salinas' privatization efforts required the quiescence of unionized labor. He used labor and business partners to provide cover through a series of "Pacts for Economic Stability and Growth." Making some minimal compromises with labor to give him cover, these pacts allowed the government to freeze wages, devalue the peso, and reduce public services. For a time, the pacts successfully imposed some discipline on unions that might otherwise have been much more contentious. But union activism increased as PRI policy diminished their favored status, and as state resources for patronage declined. Teachers, steel workers, miners, and oil workers all challenged the pacts the Salinas administration had signed with union federations, in which, despite them being touted by government as balancing austerity with agreements on wage and price increases, labor always came up short (Middlebrook 1991).

As the Salinas administration negotiated what was to become the North American Free Trade Agreement (NAFTA), unions found even more reason to worry, and teachers went out on strike to protest legislation that reduced pensions and increased retirement ages. The changes to another state-run enterprise, PEMEX, Mexico's oil industry, further hurt union workers, with tens of thousands of layoffs.[8] By 1996, government plans to privatize parts of PEMEX brought enormous political opposition. Dozens of protests ensued across the nation, forcing the government to postpone the sales.[9]

In general, Mexico's privatization inflicted great damage on organized labor, as unionization rates decreased from 22.4% in the early 1990s to 13% in 2012 (Roman & Velasco 2014: 25). By 1993, "several thousand" government-owned firms were privatized, including telecommunications and airlines (Green 2003; Reygadas 2006: 133). But austerity aided others; the number of Mexican billionaires surged as privatization provided wealth for those in a position to take advantage of the selloff frenzy.

Mexico's austerity measures met with international approval, at least among the funders of agreements. The IMF's acting manager Stanley Fisher "said in a statement that it welcomed 'the substantive measures adopted by the Mexican authorities to strengthen their economic program.' The White House issued a similar stamp of approval from President Clinton" (Farah 1995). Elites approved in spite of the expectations that 1995 would see the loss of 1 million jobs, according to Mexico's Labor Minister. US supporters of austerity no doubt noted that the Mexican negotiations required receipts from export petroleum sales be placed in an account held by the Federal Reserve Bank of New York, so that US bankers would have first claim in case of loan default.

The 1994 transition in presidential power to another PRI President, Ernesto Zedillo Ponce de León, was followed by an immediate deval-uation of the peso. But even before the newly declared economic crisis, indications of persistent problems remained evident, as Mexicans suffered large increases in loan defaults and saw reposses-sions of varied kinds of property. Annual wages dropped from 1982 through 1997, averaging between 7.7% and 12.3%, and the number of households below the official poverty line increased from 34% in 1970 to 43% in 1996 (Friedmann et al. 1995; Robberson 1995a; Lustig 1998).

President Zedillo's policies mirrored his predecessor's, as his administration increased gas and electricity prices, raised taxes, and imposed limits on pay raises. The devaluation of the peso led to soaring interest rates. The base rate reached nearly 90%; and mortgage and credit rates topped out at 150%, "[t]hreatening the closure of hundreds of thousands of businesses, the creation of millions of new unemployed, and repossession of homes, cars, and tractors" (Davison 1995).

Mexico's banks suffered a crisis analogous to those later seen in Europe only after austerity failed to bring economic order. In addition to surging interest rates, loan defaults reached into the billions of dollars, and the government was forced to seize three mid-sized national banks owing to overextension of credit. A newly emergent debtors' organization, El Barzón, joined other organizations in strikes uniting loan recipients, credit card holders, and small and medium-sized businesses, all of whom suffered from the recent wave of austerity and bank crisis (Robberson 1995a).[10] Skyrocketing food prices added to citizens' daily misery (Farah 1995).

Despite the protests and the declining quality of life, the administration continued to cut government jobs: by March 1995, Zedillo announced he would eliminate four ministries (agrarian reform, energy, tourism, and the comptroller general's office) that together employed 20,000 government workers. Mayday 1995, a day typically defined by the celebration of PRI unions' ties and gratitude to the party, found the festivities canceled for fear that union leaders could not control their angry rank and file. Independent unions marched instead, expressing their anger at the loss of wages and jobs. By May, the peso had lost half its previous value compared to the dollar, the number of strikes expected increased as over 750,000 workers expected to lose their jobs, and inflation continued to surge (Golden 1995).

Social conflict continued, with crime increasing and constant clashes between protestors and riot police. By mid-1996, a new guerrilla army, the Ejercito Popular Revolucionario (Popular Revolutionary Army), joined the Ejercito Zapatista por Liberación Nacional (Zapatista Army for National Liberation), which had engaged in brief fighting in early 1994, as a threat to the government. Both guerrilla fronts denounced the government's neoliberal policies, as well as the longstanding undemocratic national politics (Robberson 1995b). But cities continued to be the main locales of anti-austerity protest. Threatened privatization of the largest Mexico City public transportation line, and the expected firing of over 10,000 workers, elicited street protests and even more dramatic demonstrations such as planned crucifixions. Teachers from across the nation – whose daily salary, after years of austerity, only bought half of the basic food basket – convened in Mexico City to strike. El Barzón also continued to voice opposition to austerity-linked debt policies. With devaluation of the peso, debts climbed if they were borrowed in dollars, a common practice in real estate purchases. The injustice of debtors' economic travails stood in marked contrast to the government's decision to spend approximately $16 billion in 1995 – about 5.5% of the nation's GDP – to bail out banks (Anderson 1996; Gunson 1996).

President Zedillo planned to repay the US loan early in June 1996. Loans from international investors and government bonds sales supplied nearly half of the repayment to the United States. Thus the solution for debt was more debt, forcing the Zedillo administration to continue with austerity budgets. The budget announced in 1999 cut more government welfare programs while hiking prices on a variety of consumer items. At the same time, the Zedillo government bailed out more of its banks still suffering from loan defaults in the wake of the peso crash. By early 1999, the government eliminated the subsidy on tortillas that had been part of the Mexican poor's tools for survival since 1951. It also planned to raise tuition fees on subsidized higher education at the National Autonomous University of Mexico, an institution known for creating social mobility for the middle class. More than a quarter of a million students responded with a nine-month-long strike (Sheridan 1996; Preston 1999; Smith 1999).

By the beginning of the Vicente Fox presidency in 2000, the first won by a non-PRI candidate since 1929, the entire nation had been affected by an unceasing period of austerity. Over 40 million Mexicans lived on less than three dollars a day. Poverty increased from 1981 through 2000, touching 80% of Mexican citizens. Real wages in 1998 were 57% of real wages in 1980; the minimum wage in 1998 was 29.5% of the minimum wage in 1980. Between 1992 and 1996, the number of workers receiving workplace benefits dropped from 56% to 51%. Globalization brought increased industrial production to Mexico for a time, but the new factories paid wages 60% lower than established factories, and offered less union protection. The proportion of part-time workers increased from 17.4% to 28% of the workforce, an indication of the decreasing availability of full-time work (Lustig 1998; Dussel Peters 2000: 72; González de la Rocha 2001; Damián & Boltvinik 2006: 153; Cypher & Delgado Wise 2010).

Austerity policies also increased hardships for the urban middle class. Between 1988 and 1997, real salaries of middle-class professionals such as teachers and healthcare workers declined between 35% and 50%. The firing of state workers eliminated many white-collar middle-class positions. Additionally, interest rates increased substantially, making it difficult for both middle-class small business owners and consumers. Not only did money become expensive to borrow in the wake of austerity, it became difficult to find (Roman & Velasco 2001).

As a result of austerity, income inequality increasingly divided Mexican society, with "the richest 10 percent of the population earning 55 percent more in real terms in 1992 than in 1977 while the real income of other social groups declined" (González de la Rocha 2001: 82). In addition to the various hardships felt across so many Mexican households, aggregate measures showed the cost of the debt. For example, Mexican debt service in 1998 amounted to 59% of its annual budget. Mexico's progress had reversed. Once among the top Latin American economies by growth between 1951 and 1980, it fell to the bottom of growing nations between 1991 and 2000 (Green 2003).

One additional measure demonstrates the costs of austerity and subsequent neoliberal measures in Mexico: the unprecedented immigration flow into the United States. From the early 1980s to 2000, the flow of Mexican migrants increased significantly. There were approximately 2.2 million migrants in the United States at that initial date; those numbers increased to approximately 9.8 million by the year 2000 (Pew Research Center 2015). This flow of people suggests that austerity's economic hardships led many to flee Mexico in search of better wages.

Mexico provides us with an example of a nation with a diverse and growing economy that used some of its wealth for social development needs. The country was nominally democratic when austerity policies began in earnest in the 1980s, but in truth it was a one-party state until opposition inroads in state and federal elections were won throughout the 1990s. Fox's election as opposition President in 2000 confirmed Mexico's democratization, yet neither its one-party-state history, nor its transition to multi-party democracy provided leverage to resist the global pressure to impose austerity. Mexican policymakers not only acquiesced to but welcomed austerity. Similar to Chile's "Chicago Boys," many Mexican elites learned neoliberal ideology from US academics, and followed policies put forward by the IFI leaders, who by then were true believers that austerity was the only answer to debt and development. Decades of austerity and neoliberalism inflicted substantial harm on most of the Mexican public, while creating opportunities for vast riches for a few, but administration after administration followed the path begun in the early 1980s.[11]

Ecuador: Revolving Presidencies, Consistent Austerity

Ecuador provides another example of austerity-driven policy, differing from Chile and Mexico in political system and economic strength. Chile's initial experiences with austerity were defined by a repressive, authoritarian junta's ability to impose its economic and political will, and Mexico's by the decreasing ability of a democratizing single-party state to walk a populist line while diminishing citizens' economic security. Ecuador, during the period discussed below, was a true multi-party system, although one with distinctly Latin American characteristics. That is, Ecuador's political system was governed by different parties that represented different elite factions, while the power of the working class was exerted on the streets. Unlike the fierce repression of Chile's potential for resistance to austerity, and Mexico's resistance intertwined with its democracy movement, Ecuador's political response was led by a coalition of labor and indigenous organizations. Ecuador also provides a classic example of economic dependency owing to the relatively minimal number of commodities it has offered to the world market for much of its history. Oil exports consistently provide up to one-third of governmental budgets, and price fluctuations during the austerity years fed Ecuador's economic and political crises.

Ecuador's oil boom subsidized the quality of life for a segment of its citizens, and kept tax burdens low during the 1970s and early 1980s, expanding both public services and jobs. Despite the locale of much of the oil in their tribal lands, Ecuador's substantial indigenous population rarely benefited from the nation's growth, and instead bore the cost of environmental destruction linked to oil exploitation (Sawyer 2004). By 1978, government expenditures in petroleum production, transportation, communication and utilities, and consumer and industrial subsidies composed nearly half of the federal budget (Gerlach 2003). Similar to other nations, expenditures outpaced income. With the fall in oil prices in the 1980s, Ecuador was poised for the kind of policy interventions seen elsewhere during the international debt crisis.

Austerity policies were implemented consistently, beginning in the 1980s and continuing into the new millennium. Ecuador's economic history, together with its attendant political conflicts, has not been driven by class struggles as much as has been the case in Mexico. In large part this is due to the nation's sizeable population of indigenous peoples,[12] and its long history of oppressing them. Indigenous people were not allowed the vote until 1979 owing to a variety of constitutional restrictions (Becker 2007; Lucero 2007). The high profile of indigenous resistance led to powerful coalitions that often used general strikes as the strategy of choice. Despite the romantic celebration by the international left of the Zapatista uprising in Mexico in 1994, Ecuador's indigenous-led mass mobilization in 1990 was an earlier, much larger, longer, and more impactful political event.

This case largely concentrates on Ecuador's experiences in the 1990s, a time during which it was under great pressure from international banks, the IMF, and the US Treasury. But austerity measures began in the country in 1982, in response to both debt and the falling price of oil. When the nation's foreign debt reached $6 billion, the IMF imposed conditions on loan renegotiations that were familiar across the developing world (Tinsley 2003). Throughout the administrations of the 1980s, governments tried to "abolish [wage and price] protections and subsidies, reduce price controls ... reduce public spending, devalue the currency, and foster increases in interest rates" (Zamosc 1994: 45). Until 1984, the policies were mediated by supplementary programs that softened the pain for the urban poor (Sawyer 2004), but these measures often left out rural and indigenous populations. Moreover, not only did policies such as price controls hurt peasant agriculture, but also further debt renegotiation conditions required increased oil exploitation on lands heavily populated by indigenous peoples. When they sought relief in the cities, indigenous people found that austerity measures had shrunk employment opportunities in both manufacturing and construction, as well as diminishing wages, which "decreased by almost 20 percent between 1980 and 1985 and even further at an annual rate of 8 percent between 1987 and 1990" (Zamosc 1994: 46).

By July 1989, inflation had reached 92%, while wages were frozen. Citibank took the unprecedented step of freezing Ecuadorian national accounts held in one of its US banks in lieu of debt payments, sparking national and international outrage. Labor unions mobilized for a general strike to increase wages, freeze prices, and expel the multinational bank from the country.

In June 1990, protest in Ecuador reached a new peak, with a week-long general strike effectively paralyzing the country. "Tens of thousands of Indian peasants stopped delivering farm produce to the towns and blocked the main highways, picketed on the roadsides, and marched en masse in regional capitals. In some places, demonstrators seized the office of government agencies, and in others, localized skirmishes reportedly broke out" (Zamosc 1994: 37).

This general strike in response to neoliberal-influenced agrarian laws set the stage for contention throughout the following decade. The increasingly mobilized indigenous organizations demanded a variety of government actions reversing their historical oppression, such as the expulsion of state and private entities that reinforced their marginalization, and the recognition of indigenous institutions and practices. But the demands similarly targeted new forms of economic extraction through debt; austerity measures provided consistent causes for political action. In February 1991, the government's currency devaluation led to price hikes. Responses came later that year, when government austerity measures prompted Ecuador's largest union, the United Workers' Front, to call for another general strike (*Miami Herald* 1991a, 1991b; Porras Velasco 2005).

By 1992, ongoing austerity further diminished state attention to citizens' welfare needs. In response, the mobilizations that year simultaneously prioritized "500 years of indigenous resistance" and opposition to austerity (Porras Velasco 2005). Labor and indigenous people's responses had reached such a peak of feverish activity that President Durán Bellén's September 1992 announcement of another austerity package was accompanied by his mobilization of the armed forces. Durán Bellén further reduced consumer subsidies, and again devalued the national currency. Gasoline prices and utility rates immediately doubled, as did costs of other public services. CONAIE (Confederacíon de Nacionalidades Indigenas de Ecuador – Confederation of Indigenous Nationalities of Ecuador), one of three indigenous coalitions representing different locales in Ecuador, had played a leadership role since before the massive 1990 march, and soon joined the United Workers' Front (FUT) labor confederation in opposing the austerity measures (*Houston Chronicle* 1992; *LAWR* 1992; Sawyer 2004; Lucero 2007).

The government forced deep cuts in healthcare and made additional cuts to the education budget. It also announced its efforts at privatizing additional parts of the state apparatus, driving teachers, health workers, and others onto the streets demanding salary increases and back pay, reversal of the budget cuts, and greater commitment to job security in anticipation of the pending privatization. Weeks of protest culminated in a one-day general strike. Despite the popular unrest, the IMF expressed optimism about the direction of Ecuador's reforms, expressing expectations of more agreements to come (*LAWR* 1993a). Creditor banks were less pleased as payments had not been forthcoming since mid-1992.

By May 1993, the government added further increases in electricity and telephone charges, as well as wage freezes, including to the minimum wage, which was only the equivalent of $30 monthly. Further details of the privatization to come revealed the planned selloff of "160 publicly-owned companies, including the strategic oil industry and basic services, with the possible loss of 120,000 public sector jobs," a reduction by over one-quarter. Other priorities for the privatization chopping block included the national airline, telecommunications firms, ports, electric utilities, and subsidiaries of the state oil companies. The coalition of CONAIE, FUT, and students and government workers again paralyzed the country with road blockades and occupations of public buildings, responding to a government whose austerity policies had shrunk its approval ratings to 15% (*LAWR* 1993b). Although many sectors ceased the strike after a brief period, teachers stayed out of work for over two months, returning only when the government declared a state of emergency and placed the school systems under military rule. Despite the ongoing national labor unrest, an IMF spokesperson declared the institution "satisfied" with the government's imposition of austerity, although she voiced concern at the slow pace of state restructuring (*LAWR* 1993c).

The protests against government oil price hikes continued to roil the nation into 1994. In addition to action on the streets, factories, and farms, Ecuador's constitutional court ruled the price increases unconstitutional, while four former presidents warned that unceasing austerity was making the nation ungovernable. For its part, the FUT marshaled data that showed the minimum wage had decreased by over 70% from 1980 to 1992. Regardless of the hardships its citizens were experiencing, Ecuador returned to its debt service payments to creditors as a result of negotiations with the IMF and the United States for more loans. By 1995, the back and forth of conflict over austerity policies led the government to pass a law that would prohibit public workers from the right to strike, which was intended to ease efforts to privatize (*LAWR* 1994a, 1994b; Colitt 1995).

Despite massive public opposition, privatization efforts continued as an important part of the Durán Ballén administration's austerity program. The attempt to transform the state-owned energy firm Inecel into a majority private firm continued in 1996, again setting off protests. Resistance drove the President to issue a decree forcing striking energy and health workers back to work. Policymakers also targeted the social security system for privatization, again leading to subsequent opposition by public workers and indigenous organizations.

August 1996 brought the election of Abdalá Bucaram, who campaigned on an anti-austerity platform. Those campaign promises notwithstanding, once in office he continued to impose austerity measures during his brief presidency. Increases in the prices of cooking gas reached 230%, and those of electricity and telephones both reached 300%, continuing the upward pace they had maintained under previous administrations. Bucaram's administration showed a schizophrenic policy orientation, following austerity orthodoxy by continuing to cut subsidies, while countering neoliberal suggestions by shrinking imports from the United States. These inconsistent policies included further privatizing of state holdings in telecommunications while issuing compensation for cooking gas increases to low-income families.

Bucaram's antics during his election, during which he dubbed himself "*el loco*" ("the crazy one"), continued into his presidency with a release of a rock video titled "A Madman in Love." But his foray into popular culture failed to help his political career. Instead, Bucaram's great success was in uniting major sectors of the country against him, from students and teachers to the military, and from organized labor to indigenous peoples. Charges that his administration's corruption led to the theft of millions of dollars from the national treasury compounded the anger against austerity. After only six months in office, calls for his ouster increased until the Congress voted for his removal for "mental incapacity" (Gogoll 1997; Schemo 1997; *LAWR* 1997a).

As entertaining as the President's foolishness was, it failed to hide the fact that, even though Ecuador's $13 billion in debt had been reduced by his predecessor Durán Ballén, payments on the debt still made up half of the federal budget (Darline 1997). By April 1997, Ecuadorian monetary officials were asking the IMF for a loan of $300 million to cover debt service, saying, "It is not that the country can't live without an [IMF] agreement, but it is much better to have one" (*LAWR* 1997b). Interim President Fabián Alarcón continued the austerity measures, followed by the predictable response from Ecuadorian society, which remained highly mobilized after years of protest. Alarcón temporarily backed away from cutting subsidies, remembering the earlier vast protests. This moderation lasted only until Jamil Mahuad ascended to the presidency in August 1998, however. By October of that year, Mahuad's administration again devalued the currency and cut subsidies on cooking gas, electricity, and diesel oil (Newsome 1998). This time, protest activity included setting off bombs at public service offices.

Just six months into his presidency, Mahuad's commitment to austerity measures led him to cut teacher wages amid governmental failure to pay local governments money owed them. Plummeting oil prices, surging inflation, and an ongoing heavy debt forced the government to devalue the currency again. In addition to President Mahuad's reinforcement of austerity, he announced new renegotiations with the IMF. The nation's debt-to-GDP ratio rose to

82%, the highest in the continent. Amid rising expectations that the coming negotiations would bring another round of austerity measures, public anger grew once again (Newsome 1999; Newsome & Lapper 1999). By March, the now-familiar pattern repeated: the government imposed more austerity measures, including doubling gasoline prices, closing banks, increasing taxes, and freezing savings accounts to avoid investment flight. Social movements followed with national strikes. In turn, the government responded by declaring a state of emergency and mobilizing the military, especially to maintain power and oil production. Rock-throwing protestors on the streets were met by police in riot gear shooting tear gas, while highway barricades paralyzed much of the nation. July 1999 brought further impositions of austerity, more protest, and some retreat on increases in fuel prices (Faiola 1999a, 1999b; Lucero 2007).

In January 2000, the previous year's tally of costs from austerity included: inflation reaching over 70%, the currency's value decreasing by half, and only one-third of the labor force being able to count on regular work. Government policymakers then implemented one of their most dramatic policies: the dollarization of the economy (Marconi 2001). The government's intention was to control the heights of economic fluctuations by adopting the US dollar as the national currency. Not only was this move seen as precipitous by critical Ecuadorian elites, and tantamount to surrender to international interests by protestors, it was not favored by the IMF, which was poised to loan another $250 million.

The next wave of protests proved to be too much for the military to bear. Rather than respond with more repression, military leaders forced the dismissal of President Mahuad by announcing the creation of a three-person governing junta, which included the head of the army. Shortly thereafter, Vice President Gustavo Noboa became Ecuador's sixth President in four years (Gerlach 2003; Lucero 2007).

The following election brought Colonel Lucio Gutiérrez, one of the plotters of the 2000 coup, to the presidency. Gutiérrez's participation in the coup and his campaign rhetoric signaled potential opposition to neoliberalism, which convinced integrated indigenous supporters to join not only his campaign, but also his government. But Gutiérrez's seeming detour from neoliberalism soon proved false as he signed yet another letter of intent with the IMF. The promise of more austerity led several indigenous members of government to leave and return to opposition organizing. By 2005, protests drove Gutiérrez from the presidency (Lucero 2007).

Over the course of Ecuador's austerity regimes, familiar policies such as cutting welfare state expenditures and consumer subsidies, as well as currency devaluation, yielded high costs for citizens across the decades. Additional neoliberal policies such as trade liberalization seemed to meet some of the IFI policymakers' intentions. By the end of the 1990s, Ecuador was "considered to have one of the most open trade regimes in Latin America" (SAPRIN 2004: 47). Yet the development goals meant to be achieved by trade liberalization were not met; indeed, efforts to diversify output were contradicted by results such as declining manufactured exports. Ecuador instead concentrated more heavily on the exploitation of natural resources, especially petroleum (Sawyer 2004). Again contrary to intentions, neoliberal policies yielded negligible per capita GDP growth over 20 years of IFI intervention.

Unemployment and poverty increased across the period of adjustment, especially among lower-income earners. "At the end of the 1990s, two thirds of workers were either un- or underemployed, with 66 per cent of the population living on less than two dollars a day" (SAPRIN 2004: 98). The average income of Ecuadorian employees dropped by 18% over a 10-year period, while income inequality, measured by Gini coefficients, increased from .44 during the 1970s to .57 in 2000. These reforms also forced thousands of small and medium-sized firms to dissolve. The Ecuadorian government decreased healthcare and education spending while cutting consumer subsidies. When interest rates rose as high as 70%, credit availability became limited for small and medium-scale enterprises, further reducing employment and pushing more workers into the informal sector of the economy. Debt continued to climb: by 2000, it stood at $13.7 billion, while GDP was valued at $14.5 billion, with debt service ranging from 43% to 52% of national expenditures in 2000–1 (Marconi 2001; Gerlach 2003: 42; SAPRIN 2004: 182; Acosta 2006).

Ecuador, like Mexico, provides us with a more democratic model of an austerity state. Although notably anti-democratic in its long prohibition of indigenous people from political participation, Ecuador's modern democracy evolved through contestation by parties allied with different geographic elite centers and their middle-class supporters. The country's system of party contention was certainly more democratic than the single-party history of Mexico, let alone Chile's coup and subsequent repressive overthrow. As a nation whose economy depends largely on oil extraction, Ecuador provides an example of a less powerful player on the world stage than Mexico or

Chile. It also provides a clear example of the increasing hegemony of austerity as a policy, as even those politicians who campaigned against it ended up implementing it. Mexico's PRI candidates did not engage in such fiction, and Chile's junta did not have to. In Ecuador, unlike Chile and Mexico, neoliberal economists did not occupy policymaking positions, but with the domination of neoliberalism in economics and policymaking by the late 1980s, and the predominant power of the IFIs, those pioneers were less necessary.

The Power of Ideas and the Power of Power

> The key to the "new dependency" of the debt was not the circulation of capital or commodities but the flow of knowledge. Those policy makers who had decided to pay back the debt, no matter the cost, simply could not imagine challenging the dictates of a model of international behavior.
>
> (Miguel Angel Centeno 1997: x)

In their masterpiece on the influence of Karl Polanyi, Block and Somers emphasize the power of ideas. The triumph of austerity and neoliberalism in Latin America would seem to confirm their position. The centrality of the state as an economic actor came to be overshadowed by the neoliberal triumph over economic thinking. As Block and Somers argue, the power of the idea of "market fundamentalism" has been triumphant, based in a "quasi-religious certainty expressed by contemporary advocates of market self-regulation ... that rel[ies] on revelation or a claim to truth independent of the kind of empirical verification that is expected in the social sciences" (2014: 3).

This chapter describes three cases during the evolution of that quasi-religious certainty. The power of ideas is clearly demonstrated as Chilean, Mexican, and Ecuadorian policymakers pursued policy that was at first untested, and then found severely wanting. Not only were the economic outcomes of austerity shown to be damaging, if policymakers had listened, they would have heard as much; decades of protest in Mexico and Ecuador and elsewhere made that point eloquently. From the 1970s on, we witnessed an evolving hegemony of a set of ideas that became concretized in neoliberalism and austerity. It is important to look at how that idea became hegemonic, as Babb (2001) and Centeno (1997) show us in Mexico, and Valdés (1995), Collins and Lear (1995), and Winn (2004) show us in Chile.[13] New policymakers were educated under the neoliberal model, which influenced them and the policy they implemented in very real ways. As Valdés notes:

> This elite conducted, organized, and exercised state power with great resolve: the group of "Chicago Boys" gradually occupied all the main state economic posts; it exercised increasing control over the intellectual reproduction process of its own theories, dispatching disciples to the various institutions of higher education for economics, thus imposing its particular view of "economic science" and marginalizing all others. The group built a system of links and personnel transfers between the public sector and Chile's main centers of financial and industrial power. It participated in an active press and television campaign to spread its own message on economic science and to reject views that had influenced the discussion on economic development in previous decades. (Valdés 1995: 10)

Valdés further quotes an interview with Rolf Luders, one of the University of Chicago team of economists that restructured Chile's economy as saying: "[T]hey all formed a single community – incremented annually by new generations of economists graduating from Chilean universities – sharing the same technical language, a rationalistic approach to problem solving and the eagerness to contribute through their efforts, to creating a prosperous, fair and free society" (Valdés 1995: 32).

We find in Chile a confirmation of the power of ideas, as internal elites across the globe have followed a hegemonic policy designed by external elites responding to what they saw as the errors of state-centered development policy and its links to debt in the developing world. This path was different in the developed world, as we will see, but similarly dependent on the singular economic theory pushed by those in power. But as important to recognize as the power of ideas is the power of power. It is no accident that austerity and neoliberalism had to be first attempted in Chile under a murderous military dictatorship. Only in this way, with the active state exercise of repressive power, were the hopes of socialist economies able to be destroyed and the gains of ISI to become seen as "exhausted." The coercive power of the military was joined to the propaganda tools of a willing conservative media in Chile, in which " a systematic indoctrination was carried out in the style needed to spread a dogma" (Valdés 1995: 32). The different histories of resistance against austerity and neoliberalism in Chile, as compared to Ecuador and Mexico, clearly show

how Chile provided a freer laboratory for neoliberals to learn their craft. Chileans terrorized by rampant state repression were unable to contest the economic policies that soon diminished their material quality of life.

Although neither Ecuador nor Mexico suffered under the same level of repression as in the neoliberal laboratory of Chile, the exercise of power was not missing in their implementation of austerity. Latin American nations are defined by long histories of dependency and world system disadvantage. International powers have long exerted economic and political pressure across the continent. The evolution of austerity and neoliberalism is just the recent moment in this trajectory of unequal power. Chile also demonstrates that the power of ideas emanating from the most powerful nation of the core was not enough to make the experimental case for neoliberal austerity. Instead, that early exercise needed to be backed up by repressive military might and murderous action against those who supported Allende's socialist program and who were most likely to act against austerity.

Approximately 10 years later in Mexico and Ecuador, such military action was less necessary. By the time of the Mexican and Ecuadorian impositions of austerity, two developments had made its implementation easier. First, the orthodoxy of Chicago School Economics had become hegemonic. Thus, the policymakers in Mexico did not have to be Chicago-linked innovators – that brand of economic thought had displaced Keynesianism across academia in the United States, including the universities where so many of the Mexican presidents and ministers had studied. Second, the IFIs were firmly within the grip of neoliberalism. The policies advocated by the IMF and the World Bank, as well as the US Treasury, were now accepted wisdom.

"Perhaps the most important international factor was the intellectual legitimacy of the Salinas reforms both within policy-making and academic circles and in general world opinion" (Centeno 1997: 25). As Centeno makes clear, the neoliberal/austerity agenda was maintained in Mexico even during crises. Government elites cohered around their values and background, the former fully consistent not only with the authority of a centralized presidential system, but also with a global ideology that denied any alternative policy.

It is not that repressive action was unknown across Ecuador and Chile, which is clearly not the case. But the intellectual playing field had changed so that the experimental formulas of austerity had transitioned from theory into accepted wisdom. It did not matter that austerity did not accomplish its articulated goals and had diminished growth and prosperity. What mattered was that over time it had become the singular alternative. As it spread to other nations, the power that enforced austerity in Chile transformed into a coercive, more structurally than visibly violent regime led by the IFIs and the US government, and exercised by technocratic policymakers educated in US universities. The neoliberals succeeded in creating a hegemony without beneficiaries.

Recognizing not only the power of ideas but also the power of power helps us uncover the myth of the neoliberal dictum that states should be removed from economies as much as possible in order to maximize the free operation of markets to achieve liberty and prosperity. Nowhere is the falsehood of this myth more obvious than in the Chilean case, where austerity and neoliberalism did not diminish the state, but instead relied on fierce state repression to bring them to bear and maintain them. Rather than interpreting the actions of states as contradicting the neoliberal ethos, the Chilean "Chicago Boys" welcomed an authoritarian state as the only way to remove economic issues from political considerations and place them firmly in the hands of technocrats (Young 2006). By the time austerity came to Ecuador and Mexico, the power of the austerity idea was hegemonic. But the powerful idea still relied on the structural violence of dominant economic actors who could threaten non-complying actors with cuts in credit, trade wars, and other obstacles to participation in the global economy.

3

African Austerity

Latin American austerity was predicated on the notion that the debt held by developing nations was unsustainable and keeping them from full participation in the globalizing neoliberal economy. Although debt was one of the components of the rationale pushing austerity in Africa, the push to diminish state-centered development was more important. Nations entering independence from minority rule did so with a history of state policy maintaining imperial and racial domination using a variety of racially and class exploitative practices. Pre-emancipation states, in addition to actively keeping black populations in positions of diminished economic and political power, imposed protective measures that reinforced foreign control through a racial hierarchy, in many places creating and privileging a white middle class and elite. African state-controlled development was in the sights of the IFIs even during freedom struggles. An early report by the World Bank blamed Africa's economic stagnation on "excessive and inefficient state intervention in the economy" (Harrison 2005: 1303).

As neoliberalism matured, it began to mean more things to more people: an economic philosophy; a way to address waste; a way to diminish state control over the economy; even a way to impose economic logic on social relations. As we move to our examination of two African nations, neoliberalism for us continues to be an economic ideology that prioritizes markets over all other social institutions. Its market focus means that neoliberalism has been championed by those interested both in bald profit-taking and in social justice-oriented national development, including those trying to emerge from racially based oppression. Neoliberalism has evolved from a set of policies imposed on nations in crisis to an expression of common sense, having reached a hegemonic status. In Africa as elsewhere, powerful officeholders, in global and national seats of power, used austerity policies as some of the tools aimed at imposing neoliberalism.

Post-colonial Africa is especially useful in examining the hegemony of neoliberalism and austerity policies because so many of the freedom movements that transitioned into governments voiced strong opposition to strictly market-oriented policies. Capitalism, according to the analysis of the liberation movements, bore some of the responsibility for racial oppression. The experiences of nations like South Africa and Zimbabwe show how, revolutionary pasts notwithstanding, austerity becomes the go-to policy in nations forced to compete in the global marketplace. Yet austerity was often accompanied by social policy that sought to upend longstanding manifestations of racial domination, such as attending to inequalities in primary education, health, and infrastructure.

Africa was not quite as early an adopter of austerity as Latin America, perhaps because its liberation and post-colonial struggles took more of both government and challengers' attention. By the late 1980s, however, the IMF and World Bank had negotiated over 80 loans requiring austerity implementation with Sub-Saharan African nations (Harrison 2005). As austerity and neoliberalism progressed in Africa, the intention seemed to shift away from diminishing the state's role in ameliorating inequalities intrinsic to earlier racist paths of state-centered development, to creating strong states that could instead pursue strategies in line with elite economic control, in the interest of both national and global elites. In truth, as we have noted, anti-state efforts have always been more rhetorical than real throughout austerity's reach. The aim of austerity as a tool of neoliberalism has never been to reduce the influence of the state, but always to impose the new market logic and reinforce the power of the class constituency to which it responds. Our African cases demonstrate that, far from diminishing it, the power of the state is harnessed to push neoliberalism through the tool of austerity.

The opportunity for austerity regimes in Africa to emerge resembles the path taken across the Global South. First, the historical focus on primary commodity exports placed developing nations at a disadvantage as the raw materials they produced for sale on the global market consistently cost less than the manufactured products they bought. This consistent disparity in production versus consumption values reinforces inequalities between poorer and richer nations. As we noted in chapter 2, many developing nations in Latin America tried to address this circuit of inequality through ISI, a strategy also followed by some African and Asian nations. Despite ISI-guided efforts, many nations were unsuccessful in disrupting this unequal trade until commodity chains began to characterize global production. Even then, however, the new form of segmented production did not benefit the developing world to the extent of the previous models of industrialization that built the Global North.

Second, when oil dollars were plentiful in Western banks, developing nations were encouraged to take on loans. When interest rates rose in the late 1970s and early 1980s, the production expected to repay those loans often proved insufficient, given the low commodity export prices. Simultaneously, the IFIs jettisoned Keynesian economic logic, instead adopting neoliberal rhetoric diminishing the state's role in protecting and regulating national economies, and adopting austerity conditions when negotiating new loans and restructuring old loans alike. Finally, the increasingly neoliberal focus of powerful nations like the United States and the United Kingdom further consolidated the pressure to establish austerity as the go-to policy when nations experienced seeming crises. But the definition of crisis is an issue of politics as much as or more than an economic issue. Debt service may be a burden, but at what point does it become a crisis, and who gets to decide?

Both of the cases we examine in this chapter address the question of crisis; here a crisis of equitable growth amid global influence that shrinks previous state alternatives while attempting to redress histories of oppression. Both South Africa and Zimbabwe emerged from a politically repressive system based on exclusion of the majority black population. In the South African case, we trace austerity in a rich, economically diverse nation that transitioned from apartheid to multi-party democracy. In the Zimbabwean case, we similarly trace austerity in a nation that is again economically diverse (although with a greater proportion of its economy based in agriculture) but that emerged from racially based authoritarian rule to transition to one-party democracy and, shortly thereafter, to one-party authoritarianism. Both nations' economic policy responded to global trends of neoliberal hegemony. Both also saw elites endorsing that hegemony early, and with results that diminished the socialist/social welfare goals that they advocated for during their respective emancipation struggles and transition to governance.

South Africa: From Apartheid to Austerity

South Africa provides an important comparative case because its own democratic transition was conducted under very different political and economic pressures than any of the cases already examined. Internal elites in the newly governing African National Congress (ANC) largely generated pressures to impose austerity during the early days of the transition. But those policy decisions were rooted in the global hegemonic turn, and supported by neoliberal institutions. In addition, the newly multi-racial government, elected in 1994, headed a nation that until then had prospered economically because of the extraordinary exploitation and oppression of the black majority. The newly freed black majority expected the state to now direct its development strategies to their needs. This expectation was even stronger because, under the apartheid stalwart National Party, the government provided generous protections from the free market to white workers. Additionally, many of the ANC leaders espoused allegiance to Marxism at various moments, and much of their analysis and rhetoric linked racial oppression to capitalism. Finally, the crisis to which neoliberal and austerity policymakers responded was a creation at least in part of South Africa's racist political economy, and the international economic sanctions it provoked. We examine the period from the democratic transition to the ANC government until the Zuma presidency.

South Africa emerged from apartheid in 1994 with massive economic problems stemming from a number of sources. First, the international campaign to weaken apartheid leaders' resolve through economic sanctions had proven successful, but left a no-growth economy in its wake. Decades of political instability also shrank private investment and spurred capital flight. But as important was the failure of the economic model itself. Based on a violently regulated black labor force, the economics of apartheid also limited domestic demand by paying impoverishing wages and restraining the expansion of skilled labor. Poverty, unemployment, and inequality rates were high, and concentrated largely among the black population (Marais 1998).

The democratic transition brought with it high expectations. In addition to decades of violence perpetrated by the government against the black majority, the apartheid system was built to benefit whites through the deep economic exploitation of the black majority. In 1994, three-quarters of the South African population were black.

Of that population, approximately 7 million lived in substandard housing, about 12 million had no access to water, 24 million had no access to electricity, over half suffered with inadequate access to sanitation facilities, and about 15 million were illiterate (Tshitereke 2006). In contrast to the exploitation of the black working class and poor by a white capitalist elite, a segment of white workers benefited from South Africa's state-owned enterprises and state-centered development. One indication of the economic divide in 1994 was that 84% of the Johannesburg Stock Exchange was owned and controlled by just five firms (Seekings & Nattrass 2011).

Those who had been oppressed and had engaged in resistance for years believed that political change under the ANC would bring substantial economic change, and that the new government would "immediately begin to implement socialist – or at the least, radically redistributive – social and economic policies" (Murray 1994: 158). The long-articulated ANC program included nationalizing segments of the economy, redistributing land and wealth, and prioritizing workers' needs; the leadership of ANC-affiliated unions and movements in the political struggle reinforced the expectations that the new government would pursue such ends.

The architects of the global political economy, as well as the national political powers, foresaw the coming political change, and put their efforts into motion long before the transition to majority rule. The National Party, the main representative of the apartheid white minority, saw the handwriting on the wall by the early 1990s. Yet the problem that concerned them as much as the transition to a one-person, one-vote, non-racist political system was how to continue economic growth. The IFIs, in turn, saw the need for economic reforms even before the transition to racial democracy. The National Party, under pressure from the World Bank, began to shift from ISI to a more neoliberal-friendly export-oriented development scheme (Peet 2002). With further reforms under the de Klerk government (1989–94), "the IMF, along with the World Bank, began to increase its visibility in South Africa, with increasing numbers of, and more broad-based, visits, including contacts with academics, labor movements and NGOs. It was clear at this stage that the IMF was concerned with the economic policies that would be followed by the new government" (Kahn 2000: 2). In response to the apartheid government's reform efforts, such as the strike against value-added tax (VAT) in November 1991, the ANC and its allies publicly positioned themselves against economic restructuring that would hurt the poor. But World Bank and IMF policymakers continued a slow cultural weaning of the ANC away from state-centered development thinking. The IMF and the ANC signed a secret letter of intent that oriented ANC economic policy toward "responsible management of the economy, interpreted as cutting state deficits, controlling inflation, imposing wage restraints, adopting outward orientation," all consistent with a neoliberal economic restructuring (Peet 2002: 73). The ANC's new stance was confirmed by September 1993, when ANC President Nelson Mandela negotiated for $850 million in aid from the IMF even before winning the nation's presidency (Peet 2002). Other indications of the creeping influence of neoliberals came in the slow rejection of nationalization by ANC leaders. Slowly but surely, the government began speaking about policy alternatives in ways that contradicted years of socialist-leaning rhetoric.

In part, the nurturing of some ANC leaders by both international and national neoliberal advocates explains the new direction. ANC leader Thabo Mbeki, for example, who would go on to become President (1999–2008), had been involved in a number of conversations that familiarized him with the needs and policy preferences of South African big business. Those contacts led Mbeki to forge more relationships with policymakers in the IFIs and among global financiers. He mentored other young ANC-linked policymakers to take on business perspectives beginning in the 1990s (Tshitereke 2006; Segatti & Pons-Vignon 2013). Throughout Mandela's presidency (1994–9), Deputy President Mbeki was usually the public voice who introduced policies such as privatization, while President Mandela worked to keep the political alliances firm. Additionally, several analysts note the impact of the ongoing multiple visits by IFI policymakers to South Africa, and how ANC officials learned the neoliberal ethos on their trips to IFI headquarters in Washington (Habib & Padayachee 2000; Narsiah 2002).[1]

Neoliberalism was also fostered by South African elites prior to the democratic transition, however. Various elite voices, such as the South African Chamber of Business, the South African Chambers of Industries and Commerce, and the Afrikaans Trade Institute, reinforced the global pressure by convening meetings and conferences that included dissidents. These entities and others also commissioned reports that continued to advocate for compromise with black liberation forces, but only within a neoliberal economic reform framework (Peet 2002).

By the time of the 1994 democratic transition, the ANC had established tight and enduring relationships with South African corporate power, in addition to the links to IFI policymakers. Both connections "were decisive in ensuring that business's key expectations were met on issues of private property, continuation and deepening of market liberalisation, particularly financial markets, and privatization of public assets" (Segatti & Pons-Vignon 2013: 544). These contacts and the hegemony of neoliberalism were key factors leading the new leaders to prioritize neoliberal interests (Habib & Padayachee 2000). Thus, the IFIs and local elites were able to successfully, if unobtrusively, push neoliberal ideology even in the absence of the direct punishing IFI pressure found in Latin America. Arguably, though, the threat of such pressure was always present. The challenges of creating a new political system in a weakened economy, with the threat of internal violence constant, may have also pushed ANC leaders more rapidly into neoliberal economic policy than they may otherwise have moved. The result was economic policy that soon focused on aggregate economic growth as the route to greater equity, rather than the redistribution many expected.

The 1994–6 period of the Government of National Unity was one of deep democratic transition punctuated by an ongoing dance between the ANC, national and international private investors, and the IFIs. Nonetheless, the pressure to supply some relief to poor black South Africans dominated immediate policymaking. Government officials designed the Reconstruction and Development Program (RDP) with clear intentions to redress the staggering economic inequalities resulting from apartheid. This initial strategy prioritized redistribution, in order not only to make the majority of poor blacks full political citizens of South Africa, but also to establish their greater viability as economic actors. The goals were laudable: creating 2.5 million jobs over 10 years, building a million homes in six years, and providing water and electricity to many of those lacking such services. The government initially succeeded in strengthening a welfare system that provided healthcare and food for the poor and needy, as well as expanding electric power to poor areas, while funding public works projects in which young people might find work (Harsch 2001; Tshitereke 2006).

Many felt the RDP, with its basic needs orientation, improved poor citizens' material wellbeing. The policy failed, however, to generate the growth needed to overcome the stagnation that was a legacy of economic sanctions and a decades-old elite-centered development orientation, as well as a lack of foreign direct investment (FDI). Like many governments experiencing neoliberal pressures, the ANC administration found "it could not attain an equitable balance between economic objectives and political imperatives"

(Tshitereke 2006: 110). Neoliberalism was ascendant, and austerity soon followed.

In response to ongoing economic stagnation, and the prevailing winds of neoliberal hegemony, in 1996 the government implemented the Growth, Employment, and Redistribution strategy (GEAR). The GEAR focus on liberalization seemed to betray the ANC's resistance and campaign rhetoric. The strategy's authorship further demonstrated the primacy of economic growth over equality, and the prominence of policymakers from the World Bank and the African Development Bank roused suspicion among advocates of state-driven development plans. GEAR was meant to impose "a 'competitive, fast-growing economy' through tight fiscal and monetary discipline, significantly increased foreign and domestic investment, further steps to open the economy to international competition and a "repri- oritizing" of public expenditures" (Harsch 2001: 13). Like many austerity programs, GEAR focused on "fiscal discipline, ... privati- sation and corporatisation of state assets, a flexible labour market, decreased levels of corporate taxation" (McKinley 2016: 270; see also Habib & Padayachee 2000).

As they did in other nations, the IFIs responded positively to the self-imposed austerity; by 1996, South Africa began receiving more assistance from the IMF. The Ministry of Finance became even more deeply involved in the entrenchment of neoliberal policy as a process of "technocratic capture," creating more division between the ANC's political intentions and economic policy. Opponents argued that the new policy revealed that the government was imposing austerity even without IMF urging (Habib & Padayachee 2000).[2]

Almost all the GEAR targets were missed for the period 1996–8. GDP declined from 3.2% to 0.1% despite predictions it would hold in the 3% range. Per capita income fell by 2.6%. Unemployment increased with job losses of 500,000 in contrast to GEAR-predicted job gains of 675,000. Private sector investment, one of the main goals of GEAR policymakers, plummeted from 6.1% to -0.7% instead of the projected growth to 9%. Economic growth resulting from GEAR ranged from negative to 3%, no more than prior to the policy's imple- mentation. Urban poverty, unemployment, and inequality grew as a result of the government's spending cuts. The loss of private sector jobs was rationalized by GEAR policymakers' advocacy of "greater labour market flexibility." Policymakers also sought to shrink public jobs through firings and outsourcing, while diminishing labor protec- tions on overtime and dismissals. Although the government touted its increased spending on social needs, critics found that rate much lower when controlled for inflation (Harsch 2001: 14; Lesufi 2002; Narsiah 2002).

Although government programs addressed some social needs, including greater access to potable water and electricity, as well as to healthcare and housing, by 2000 57% of black South Africans were still considered poor. The high rate of poverty, with the incomes of the poorest 30% of the population declining, coupled with the low rate of formal education and employment, meant that South Africa was regarded "as the most unequal society on the planet" six years after the transition to democracy (Husy 2000). Critics pointed to GEAR's austerity components for this stagnation, especially the limitation of resources to address social needs and redistribution. The program's prioritization of entrepreneurship similarly led critics to charge that "the focus of reform policy is on those who have the resources to accumulate – in this case existing farmers and wealthy urbanites" (Husy 2000).

Meanwhile, the poor continued to suffer disproportionately. Welfare programs only reached 3 million of the nation's 20 million poor. The poor also took on more work in the informal sector in response as jobs were lost, leading to a further diminishing of worker protection. Government efforts to privatize continued, while new land policy failed promises to address the needs of the poor black majority, as "less than 2% of land ... changed hands from white to black, and ... less than 1% of the budget [was] dedicated to land reform" (Mngxitama 2002: 45).

Privatization compounded the pain of state budget cuts. Like much of South Africa's history of austerity, privatization began before the democratic transition, and became even more widespread after. The government sold whole enterprises, such as stations of the South African Broadcasting Company, resorts, and airports, to private owners, while partially selling off others (Pitcher 2012). Other state-owned enterprises suffered closure, in many cases due to the lifting of protections on indigenous factories and industry, subsequently increasing poverty and unemployment.

The privatization process often followed redistributive strategies articulated as "black economic empowerment" (BEE). BEE was meant to "to support small and medium-sized businesses belonging to historically disadvantaged groups; to encourage and finance the purchase by black investors of equity stakes in existing companies; and to build a workforce that reflected the demographic make-up of the country" (Pitcher 2012: 244).[3] State policymakers meant to help some of those black South Africans with political power through

BEE. Such a policy seems to contradict the theory behind austerity aimed at limiting state economic intervention. But as we have argued, neoliberals have always exaggerated the amount they want to limit state power over the economy. The real point has always been to reconfigure that power for class advantage, and BEE was meant to grow a black middle class. From one perspective, privatization of parastatals nurtured that growth: government spending supporting them averaged 25% of total public expenditures from 2004 to 2007. From another perspective, however, BEE failed to redistribute capital to the black majority, contained insufficient sanctions to positively affect inequalities in employment and labor skills, and shifted the monitoring of such efforts from government to the private sector (Freund 2007; Ponte et al. 2007; Pitcher 2012: 249). In this way, BEE has been entirely consistent with austerity and neoliberal policies.

Even as middle-class actors gained some advantage through state policy, the costs of basic services increased and access decreased for the poor. Austerity began to define local economic action in addition to federal policy. As local governments privatized water, sanitation, electricity, and housing across South Africa, urban dwellers lost jobs or saw their salaries stagnate. Pain for the poor accumulated as those who owed on utilities were kept from buying privatized housing stock. Privatization of public utilities in big cities especially demonstrated the complex mixture of class-oriented policies. In some South African cities, the state moved toward recovering utility costs by contracting profit-driven private actors to provide water and electricity at costs that hurt poor urban households. At times, in cities like Cape Town, the dominance of local ANC political power moderated the effects of those policies. Elsewhere, however, such as in Soweto, Pretoria, and Johannesburg, increased electricity and water costs led to widespread service disconnections (Oldfield & Stokke 2007).

The population's longstanding poverty meant that installation of electricity was a high priority, and the parastatal energy supplier had set high goals of household connections after democratization. Yet the cost-saving logic imposed on utilities meant the removal of basic service provisioning subsidies as parastatal organizations were forced to adopt a short-term market-driven mission, rather than a public service orientation. By 2001, increasing electricity prices resulted in more households suffering disconnections because of their inability to pay their bills than new customers enjoying electricity hookups (Bond & McInnes 2007). The movement of public services to a cost recovery rationale, where all costs associated with provision are meant to be recovered, further pressured poor and middle-income households. While simultaneously touting the importance of equity in service provision, the central government limited payments for municipal infrastructural needs, and cost pressures on local governments grew (McDonald 2008). Indeed, "government expenditure on most basic services and social infrastructure declined between 1997 and 2000. In this period, spending on housing declined by 16.2 percent, on water by 7.5 percent, on education by 1.3 percent, and on welfare by .3 percent" (Lesufi 2002: 292), while income continued to polarize, and wage levels fell. The flow of resources from the national government to cities and locales diminished or stagnated during the GEAR years and later. The reduction in government spending stunted economic growth and failed to diminish either poverty or inequality. By 2001, government data showed that 65% of South Africans lived in poverty (Harsch 2001).

South Africa, unlike some other neoliberalizing nations, has relied more on public–private partnerships and outsourcing than on outright sales of state enterprises. Although this may seem preferable to full privatization, the continuing link of the state to basic service provision also maintains it as the target of communities that are either unserved or paying too high prices. The relatively high level of political mobilization in South Africa meant that austerity was often met with protest, especially in response to cost increases and diminishing availability of public services. Community organizations across the nation resisted and contested these policies in a variety of ways, from boycotts to marches including thousands of participants.

Government statistics show that between the end of apartheid and 2007, inequality in South Africa dropped slightly, but also that the income of the poorest 20% of the population declined from 2.7% to 2.3% of total income (Presidency 2009). The beginning of the Jacob Zuma administration (2009–18) coincided with the global economic crisis, making it hard to differentiate between economic hardships rooted in national austerity and the global slowdown. According to the Quarterly Labour Force Survey, total employment dropped by 475,000 in the first six months of 2009, and by a further 484,000, 3.6% of the workforce, in the three months that followed. At the end of September 2009, the unemployment rate, already high, had increased to 31.1% (once discouraged work-seekers were included). Because so many workers survived by participating in the informal labor market, it is likely that these statistics underreported poverty levels. Inequality also increased in South Africa during the Mandela and Mbeki administrations, driven by an increase in the top decile of income earners, while monetary grants became increasingly important to the survival of the poorest (Statistics South Africa 2009; see also Leibbrandt et al. 2012).

Voters elected Jacob Zuma President of South Africa in 2009. Despite his recent history of enriching himself, ANC rank-and-file members, dissatisfied with the relative lack of economic progress, helped usher him into office. Returning to a traditional rhetoric of redistribution, and despite years of corruption charges, Zuma was seen as a champion of the poor after Mbeki's image was tarnished by years of austerity amid his efforts at capitalist expansion. A new patronage push began, using rewards to government workers to gain support for the new administration.[4] This effort notwithstanding, austerity soon returned. In 2014, Zuma's Finance Minister, Nhanhla Nene, announced cuts in government spending and increased taxes, wage caps for government workers amid hiring freezes, subsidy cuts, and a new wave of privatization. But corruption continued to define Zuma's presidency, overshadowing austerity: "Key parastatals [had] become headed by Zuma cronies; family and friends [had] been awarded government favour; and Zuma's personal interests intrude[d] upon the governance of parastatals" (Southall 2016: 73).

By 2016, despite decades of austerity, policymakers had resolved few of South Africa's economic ills. Between a quarter and a third of the population remained unemployed, over half of the population was poor, and that number was even higher among the black population. Despite policies targeting the black middle and upper class, the "wealthiest 10% of the population own[ed] more than two-thirds of the country's household assets" and those "patterns [were] heavily overlain by race" (Southall 2016: 75).

Recently, the political domination of the ANC has faltered. The Zuma presidency and its corruption, the 2012 Marikana massacre of striking miners, and subsequent waves of labor activism have all tested the legitimacy of the former liberation movement. But austerity has clearly played an important part, especially as the ANC's tight link to trade unions has loosened.

The most important complexity of austerity in South Africa has been the government's effort to achieve some balance between building the economic capacity of the black majority while shrinking state spending. Although neoliberals have long espoused this latter goal, in truth state power has not been shrunk under neoliberalism. Instead, the character of state policy has changed, and the constituencies to which policymakers respond have changed as well. Social welfare states of varying types address the needs of the poor and the working and middle classes to some degree. By contrast, the constituency most important to neoliberal states is the capitalist class. But in a nation such as South Africa, the focus on the rich had to be supplemented by a nurturing of the middle class, as producers and consumers, but also out of political necessity to address the black–white economic divide. So it is not that GEAR and later policies diminished the state; it is more the case that the policy aims of the state were redirected away from distribution to the needy and toward the needs of capital – growth.

South Africa's history of austerity once again demonstrates the overwhelming power of neoliberal hegemony. Despite the fact that the ANC governments' most compelling need was to confront the racial divide and address black economic exploitation, the push to aggregate growth advocated by global and national economic powers predominated over other concerns. Policymakers tried to empower black capitalism by growing the wealth of both middle and entrepreneurial classes. These policies marshaled state power in ways that were consistent with austerity and neoliberalism, and growth in inequality proved to be the outcome.

The politics of emancipation forced the election of an enormously popular government in 1994. Although South Africa's entry into austerity was different from its counterparts in Asia and Latin America, with comparatively lower debt levels, the nation was still reeling from international sanctions. Indeed, South African policymakers largely imposed austerity even before the pressure of debt negotiations. They followed these policies despite the presence of powerful democratic forces standing against growth without redistribution. For a time the government followed simultaneous efforts to address social welfare needs and economic growth. But the new government's links to global and national neoliberals soon demonstrated the contradictions in pursuing those parallel policies. The subsequent prioritizing of austere budgeting left many in need.

The South African case tells us of the power of austerity in a relatively wealthy nation defined by its transition from a racist government to a democratic one. The pressure to address new citizens' needs was a national experience largely shared by ex-colonial nations in Africa. Apartheid's legacy might have given new policymakers significant space to design the social democratic policies that their earlier rhetoric would have led observers to expect. And the influence of US and other academic strongholds of neoliberal economics seems less coercive than in Latin American cases. The

United States was among the weaker international voices calling for racial justice, suggesting that its influence in South Africa post-apartheid might have been less than in other nations. Instead, the power of IFIs was exerted in quieter ways, as IMF and World Bank policymakers worked in tandem with local elites to entice ANC leaders away from social democracy even before they took power, and toward the increasingly shared global hegemony of austerity. In part, we can understand the movement in ANC policy as a response to this careful persuasion, and the outreach by both external and internal elites. But we shouldn't forget that by the time the ANC was elected to power, few alternatives were indeed available. The fall of the Soviet Union meant that no external economic aid would be forthcoming. After a brief period, policymakers embraced the neoliberals' advocacy of addressing poverty through austerity and aggregate growth strategies, rather than through radical redistribution of economic resources. Like Ecuador, South Africa demonstrates the hegemony of austerity as the policy of choice even in a nation defined by new democratic possibilities.

Zimbabwe: Austerity and Corruption

The struggle to liberate Zimbabwe from its history of racial oppression into a state effectively dominated by one party lasted from 1963 to 1979. During that time, the Zimbabwe African National Union (ZANU) established its dominance over the Zimbabwe African People's Union (ZAPU) throughout both the guerrilla struggle and subsequent political contests, until they merged and became ZANU–PF (Patriotic Front) in 1987 (Ranger 1985). ZANU emerged triumphant after a guerrilla war that cost 40,000 lives, but it was quickly challenged by its needs to establish legitimacy in certain rural areas where its competitor ZAPU had greater support, and in urban areas where the war had not been fought. The former struggle included violence and repression, and the latter included the formation of the Zimbabwe Congress of Trade Unions (ZCTU), which served the dominant party as its labor arm (Raftopoulos 2000). Like the ANC in South Africa, the liberation movements in Zimbabwe espoused socialist solutions to the problems they saw with racist capitalism. As Prime Minister from 1980 to 1987, Robert Mugabe consolidated power while following economic and political policymaking that was restrained by the emancipation agreement. By the time that Mugabe's ZANU–PF was freed from the war-ending agreement, the government had become a one-party state which began to take aid from the IMF, and move toward austerity policies. We focus here on the period from liberation through the 1990s; after that time, Zimbabwe's economic struggles became inseparable from its political troubles.

The emancipation agreement, signed in 1979 in Lancaster House, London, ushered in political freedom for black Zimbabweans by removing the Rhodesian government from power and imposing temporary control of the nation by the United Kingdom. Although it paved the way for elections in Zimbabwe, the agreement left essentially untouched the racialized ownership of wealth, especially among agricultural landowners. It also postponed key reforms and elevated the importance of the United Kingdom and the United States when those nations agreed to pay for some of the costs of land redistribution.

ZANU–PF, the most successful liberation force, captured the state bureaucracy and implemented some reforms that reduced exploitative treatment of rural and urban laborers, but few inroads were made into black ownership of property. Owing to agreement stipulations that maintained disproportionate white power in the legislature and the judiciary, further state reforms meant to increase the material wellbeing of the black majority were stymied until 1990. The civil service became one of the few secure avenues to social mobility, especially for educated blacks, and the expansion of those occupations created a constituency supporting the government as the bureaucracy transformed. Veterans of the war comprised another important constituency favored by the state. The pre-liberation Rhodesian state, like that in South Africa, had established parastatal firms that imposed some control over "agricultural markets, mineral marketing and mining, and a few industries" (Moyo & Yeros 2011: 88). New black officeholders became the caretakers of those firms. But for the most part, white elites maintained their monopoly control over the economy. Ongoing racial domination and the role of the United Kingdom and United States helped build support for neoliberal measures in the 1990s.

The fervor of Zimbabwe's emancipators reversed white rule, but the new government was forced to provide for minority political representation and follow strict controls keeping the government from challenging property rights, despite its socialist rhetoric. The Lancaster House agreement contained provisions that protected white settlers' control of a disproportionate amount of land in a land-hungry country, along with a disproportionate amount of political control, which made the agreement hard to disrupt. Again, despite revolutionary rhetoric, the Mugabe government followed the Lancaster House agreement, even though it restrained the level at which it could address the needs of the black majority. The Zimbabwean government prioritized state-led development policies, controlling the market to a large extent, while maintaining a relatively authoritarian political process. The early trajectory that the Zimbabwean government followed included standard developing nation policies such as provision of subsidies and protection of local firms. Yet neither the organization nor its leader had the history, leadership, or mythology of its ANC counterpart. Despite its victory in the revolutionary struggle, ZANU–PF needed to build legitimacy and support; the ANC had a much stronger lead in that area. Consequently, the government followed a corporatist path, including use of resources, to build support among the newly emancipated citizenry.

Like South Africa, Zimbabwe "emerged from its colonial phase with well-developed industries and capitalist firms, a modern proletariat, good state services, and relatively high per capita incomes" (Brett 2005: 95), along with a system based on exploitation and exclusion of the black majority, which resulted in deep economic inequality by race. ZANU–PF's entry into government was characterized by contradictions: although the new political elites were sincere in their socialist rhetoric advocating the social wellbeing of the black majority, their commitment to follow the Lancaster House agreement meant that initial policy continued to favor white domestic capital.

The inequalities to which the new government had to respond were deeply entrenched. Six thousand white farmers owned 39% of the land, which not coincidentally was the most productive land in the nation. By contrast, 4.5 million black subsistence farmers owned only slightly more "of the most arid land, to which they'd been removed or confined by a century of colonial rule. In the middle were 8500 small-scale black farmers," who worked about 5% of the nation's land (Mamdani 2009: 3).

Despite the limitations of the Lancaster House agreement, the Mugabe-led ZANU–PF government pushed ahead on some policies benefiting the black majority. The government wanted to build on Zimbabwe's economic strength while promoting "growth with equity," voicing its commitment to socialism, poverty reduction, and diminishing foreign control over the economy. It intended to improve material quality of life, redistribute income, and provide increased and better health services and education for the black majority. To achieve these goals, the state maintained economic protection policies, continuing to shelter both agricultural and manufacturing firms. But the Lancaster House agreement and the ongoing influence of the white economic global and national elites restrained both the voice and the actions of the new government. By the adoption of the Transitional National Development Plan in the early 1980s, the socialist rhetoric had already been tamed to recognize the need for a continued role for private capital. Mugabe's government further betrayed the socialist rhetoric in its relatively conservative economic policymaking as it sought foreign investment (Meredith 2002).

The government implemented some redistributive policies, increasing budget expenditures in education, health, and emergency food provision during times of drought, resulting in shrinking inequality during the early 1980s. In addition, the government "introduced a minimum wage and virtually removed the right to fire workers, and increased expenditure on health and education by 10 percent, public-sector employment by 60 percent, and expenditure on the civil service by 12 percent per annum over the decade" (Brett 2005: 96). However, less than half of the targeted population enjoyed the promised redistribution of land from white farmers to blacks.

Public expenditures targeting poverty reduction rose from 1980 to 1982, yet hit a limit in response to threats from South Africa's apartheid regime. Nevertheless, the government continued to increase agricultural subsidies and extension aid, especially to black small-yield farmers, and met one of its development goals: increasing non-traditional exports of manufactured goods. As the 1980s progressed, however, drought and violence took their toll, with years of strong growth offset by years of significant economic decline. Limits on foreign exchange forced borrowing from the World Bank, which subsequently shrank the loan program that nurtured manufacturing export growth. High state expenses contributed to an increasing public debt. Debt service, of course, rises with debt, and by 1987, it rose to 34% of export earnings. Limited foreign exchange coupled with low domestic investment owing to white business owners' concerns over potential political and economic transitions meant that Zimbabwe was unable to surpass an average 2.7% growth from 1980 to 1990. Over that decade, despite improvements in social services, some better agricultural yields, and expansion of non-traditional exports, unemployment rose while manufacturing wages decreased (Carmody 2001: 82, 88). Government policy also continued to favor white enterprise owners. This policy focus retarded the growth of a "genuinely entrepreneurial African business class," and slowly eroded the legitimacy of the ZANU–PF government (Brett 2005: 98).

The government's restrained efforts on the black majority's behalf did result in improving some aspects of citizens' social welfare. Enrollment in primary schools nearly tripled from 1979 to 1985, and secondary school enrollment increased by over six times during that same period. The government increased its expenditure on public education from just shy of $130 million to over $530 million, allowing free primary education for all until 1991. Spending on health increased in both real and proportional terms during that period as well (Dashwood 2000: 41, 43). Decreases in infant and maternal mortality and incidents of polio and other diseases showed the successful increase in access to healthcare, as did successful vaccination campaigns. Until 1991, the government made the very poor a targeted focus of health policy. Even though racial and class inequalities persisted, and there were "imperfections in the delivery of social services, the democratization of access to health and education constituted a major achievement of the new government (Dashwood 2000: 47). The government also sought to increase peasant farm productivity and prices, which yielded some success in diminishing rural poverty. After initial gains, though, other government efforts to combat inequality, such as increasing wages and policies meant to foster employment, in addition to limited land redistribution, were much less successful.

Zimbabwe relied on the IMF for loans as early as 1983, forcing the government into conditions such as "wage freezes, restrictions on government expenditures, cutbacks in subsidies" (Dashwood 2000: 65). Yet the government defied the IMF's conditions on drought relief spending and other restrictions, which led to a suspension of that funding stream. The World Bank continued to lend the nation money, notably to fund programs that fostered increased manufacturing production. Zimbabwe's relative economic diversity increased its economic resilience even in the face of drought and sinking commodity prices. The lifting of financial sanctions, and the nation's economic strength, added to policy restricting the taking on of more debt and controlling the allocation of foreign currency up through the mid-1980s. Up to that time, then, the government's aid was a mixed picture: some aid to the majority black poor while continuing to honor commitments favoring the white economic elite; some progress in addressing social needs even while employment decreased; and some policies reflecting obligations to IFIs while denying their influence elsewhere. That mixture of policies tilted more toward austerity as the decade wore on.

The World Bank established a mission in Zimbabwe in 1985 and began to release a series of policy papers. As the late 1980s passed, the World Bank and IMF found an increasingly open environment in which to persuade policymakers to adopt austerity: "[T]he World Bank/IMF line appealed to a small, but increasingly influential constituency within the government, as well as to a significant constituency among the entrepreneurial and agrarian elites" (Dashwood 2000: 180). By 1987, national policymakers felt increasingly pressured by the IFIs to implement austerity in response to ongoing economic need. During this time, policymakers more comfortable with neoliberal adjustments gained power. Although national elites and IFIs generally agreed on the neoliberalization of the economy, the latter pushed the process further and faster at certain moments.

The period after 1987 found the government increasingly moving toward austerity. For example, in 1991, it adopted the Economic Structural Adjustment Programme (ESAP), which, while still allowing some elements of state-centered development, demonstrated the triumph of neoliberals in Zimbabwe. The announced strategy diminished social service spending while investing in agricultural and manufacturing production, both broad strokes aimed at increasing aggregate economic growth. Specific spending cuts targeted education, defense, and government employment, while privatizing investment in some parastatal firms. In turn, the program increasingly diverted government resources with the goal of increasing the viability of export-oriented production. By 1992, the government lifted all price controls, even those on basic foodstuffs, although protests forced it to reintroduce price control on corn six years later.

Additional policies demonstrated the new state focus, including the phase-in of certain elements of the neoliberal program aimed at providing incentives to export production, as well as changes to investment policy. Like so many other austerity policies, officials sought to alter the scope and beneficiaries of the state rather than merely to diminish the size of government, and so its place in the economy. Privatizing parastatal enterprises demonstrated such intent: selling productive firms advantaged large buyers by providing them with new productive resources while allowing them greater leverage by reducing wage controls. Officials rationalized ESAP and subsequent policy, suggesting that the market would reduce inequality where government programs had failed to do so. The goal of socialism was now replaced by the goal of economic growth, the benefits of which were expected to trickle down to the workers and poor. The government's decisions clearly disadvantaged the poor, including the reversal of income distribution policies. Despite maintaining targeted assistance programs, both health and education budgets were cut drastically in the early 1990s.

Like many nations, Zimbabwe's experience with austerity yielded negative economic and political consequences. Wages in 1993 were only 62% of wages in 1980, and by 2000, wages were still below those at independence. Rising unemployment and currency devaluation added to citizens' pain. Inflation, including in food prices, led to soaring malnutrition, a dramatic contrast to Zimbabwe's history of exporting food. Manufacturing output fell by 24% as local small businesses that had thrived with the aid of subsidies and protection were disadvantaged when those protections were stripped and global businesses were able to enter in force (Dashwood 2000: 172, 175; Freeman 2014; Nyabereka 2017). Other social costs included a fall in "the share of wages in the gross national income ... from 54% in 1987 to 39% in 1997, while that of profits increased from 47% to 63% during the same period." By 1995, 61% of Zimbabwean households were living in poverty, climbing further to 75% in 2000. Fuel prices and unemployment also increased amid the decreased state spending, leading to rising political contention (Raftopolous 2000: 261). Foreign debt as a proportion of GDP tripled in the ESAP period.

Rising health problems provided another symptom of decreased state spending: infant mortality, death rates, and HIV all increased, while life expectancy drastically decreased, leaving Zimbabwe "in a far worse state than that of the 1980s, when the nation had been exemplary in Africa for the provision of social services and the reconstruction and development of infrastructure" (Nyabereka 2017: 119). Access to clean water and basic medical services also declined during the ESAP period as the government sought cost recoveries to diminish expenditures for these services.

From its emancipatory moment as a diverse and productive economy through the austerity period, Zimbabwe's entry into the global marketplace proved problematic for the nation and profitable for its debtholders. "From 1993 to 1998, 'Zimbabwe had paid US$910 million more in debt servicing than it received in new loans', yet its debt had increased 'from US$4.54 to US$4.72 billion'. Only Brazil had a higher debt–export ratio: in 1998 Zimbabwe spent well over two-fifths of its export earnings on debt" (Moore 2001: 915).

As in other nations, national elites in Zimbabwe willingly acquiesced to the IMF and World Bank pressures. A "core of senior decision-makers who felt that market-based economic reforms were necessary and desirable" supported the reforms (Dashwood 2000: 11). Indeed, the World Bank had to convince Zimbabwean policymakers to implement its Social Development Fund, linked to its World Bank Social Dimensions of Adjustment program, a poverty alleviation plan that acknowledged the human cost of austerity. This targeted safety-net program focused on job training, especially for civil servants who had lost their jobs, short-term assistance in paying for education and healthcare, and food subsidies (Dashwood 2000). Although the government finally implemented a Poverty Alleviation Action Plan in 1994 to accompany ESAP, the additional policy provided little buffer to austerity.

As in South Africa, Zimbabwe's leaders tried to balance a series of pressures: international and national capital, black entrepreneurs, politically (if not economically) empowered labor, and war veterans who expected certain benefits, all competing for the government's attention in the new neoliberal moment. The government used its resources to maintain support through patron–client strategies and increasing state control. These strategies and the growing fortunes of a black elite of ZANU–PF functionaries also led to increasing charges of corruption (Meredith 2002). Moreover, the end of the Lancaster House agreement in 1990 meant greater freedom to expropriate land owned by white farmers, some of which was distributed by land-poor blacks, while other seizures were dispensed as patronage to supporters and rewards to the black elite.

Yet clientelism, authoritarianism, land seizures, and corruption could only go so far to protect the ZANU–PF base. Between the impacts of structural adjustment, austerity, and the limits on land reform imposed by the Lancaster House agreement, as well as the party's political machinations, the state was under fire by the late 1990s. Public anger erupted in the face of austerity and political legitimacy began to unravel. The ZCTU, created in 1981, largely served ZANU–PF until the mid-1980s, but austerity threatened the alliance. In 1992, the government tried to diminish labor's power on the factory floor, while increasing the power of the Ministry of Labour over collective bargaining. By the 1990s, labor actively resisted the new austerity policies, and doctors, telecommunications workers, and teachers all staged walkouts (Raftopolous 2000). Privatization of state-owned power plants and telecommunications facilities in 1996, and of agricultural marketing the following year, further eroded state workers' loyalty.

In 1996, cuts in pay resulted in a mass strike by civil servants, including doctors, nurses, prosecutors, and firefighters. Mugabe's government first fired the workers, then reinstated them and settled the strike with a wage hike. Strikes again came after the government's failure to follow through on accords with labor. More resistance ensued with a general strike in 1997, and wildcat strikes a year later, all showing that one-party loyalty was fraying. A multi-sector opposition emerged in 1999, organized by the ZCTU and the National Constitutional Assembly of the Movement for Democratic Change. In response to increasing challenges, the state halted the austerity program in the late 1990s. Soon after this decision, the IFIs cut Zimbabwe off from various forms of financial assistance, refusing to resume funding "even after the government repaid a substantial part of its arrears" (Freeman 2014: 351).

In response to multiple crises, state officials returned to radical rhetoric and action, especially in response to land reform and dealings with donors. The new political opposition, inspired by the hardships generated by austerity, threatened Mugabe's administration, which turned to a more drastic land reform process, threatening the longstanding privilege of white settlers. Although the government pursued the land reform strategy to regain support and legitimacy, austerity clearly slowed the pace of land reform in the 1990s. When Zimbabwe prioritized austerity and debt payment, the government could not simultaneously buy land for redistribution (Moyo & Yeros 2007). As the state lost support because of declining resources as a result of austerity, it turned increasingly to stripping white settlers of land in order to maintain legitimacy. The 2000 election brought substantial challenges to ZANU–PF, but the Mugabe government maintained power using its now traditional strategies of patronage, violence, and corruption. Mugabe remained in power even after contested elections in 2008 and 2013 were seen as illegitimate, leaving office only after a 2017 coup replaced him with a former Vice President, Emmerson Mnangagwa, still from ZANU–PF.

The case of Zimbabwe offers us another case of a liberation movement becoming a government in an economically stable economy. It also provides another example of a nation with a legacy of state-centered development strategies trying to address racially based inequality. Zimbabwe's path differs from that of South Africa with ZANU–PF's efforts to maintain single-party rule, which became increasingly authoritarian. ZANU–PF also did not have the early contact with either IMF policymakers or white national elites that the ANC had because of two significant differences in Zimbabwe's transition to

black liberation. First, the guerrilla war precluded the kinds of conferences and contacts aimed at maintaining and building a neoliberal
economy that punctuated the final years of apartheid. Second, the
limits set by the Lancaster House agreement basically provided
analogous barriers to socialist policy to those established by IFI and
white elite contacts in South Africa. Despite the racial divide, the limits
on change imposed by the Lancaster House agreement actually helped
white elites' fortunes during the early period of economic growth.
The Mugabe government also judged the need for economic stability
outweighed the benefits to be won by nationalization of white-owned
business, just as it sought foreign investment. As the transition to a
planned economic redistribution was held at bay by the Lancaster
House negotiation, with some limited resources provided by the
United Kingdom and the United States, the IFIs did not have the need
to move as quickly as they did in South Africa. Neither did they have
the luxury of an extended transition to make their entry.

In addition, Zimbabwe's initial political transition occurred before
the neoliberal infrastructure was fully established. With elections
only seven years after the Chilean coup, and in the early days of the
debt crisis of the developing world, neoliberal orthodoxy and the
use of austerity as a hegemonic policy were not as well established
as at the moment of South Africa's liberation. Although Zimbabwe's
government borrowed from the IFIs in the early 1980s, and subjected
itself to some of their conditions, it also continued to address the
black majority's needs with some welfare spending, and access to
education and healthcare continued to grow. It was not until the
later 1980s that the strength of the IFIs grew in Zimbabwe, and
austerity was endorsed by white elites and then black government
officials. As public debt grew, the debt managers and elites pushed
austerity, culminating in the 1991 ESAP, which effectively closed
any opportunities to socialist redistribution policies. The popular
base of ZANU–PF resisted the new policies, and the government
occasionally rolled back harmful measures, but the hegemony of
austerity choked out other policies until Mugabe seized on mass land
seizures to re-establish legitimacy.

Maintaining Racial Inequalities

The South African and Zimbabwean cases make our point that
austerity has an overwhelming influence even over states that are
founded on struggles to upend histories of political and economic

oppression. Both nations can also be understood as economically more stable at the moment of entry into austerity than their Latin America counterparts. They can also be interpreted as strong states given their initial legitimacy. In both nations, austerity was used in dual ways: as a response to seeming crises and as a development strategy. Crises may be in the eyes of the beholder, as we have seen, and in both cases national policymakers had many reasons to prioritize reforms aimed at decreasing historical inequalities rather than accede to the economic will and diagnoses of neoliberal institutions. These cases demonstrate that the diagnosis of economic crisis may supersede clearly defined economic and political needs as neoliberal and austerity remedies became hegemonic. Yet using austerity rhetorically as a tool of development, to nurture growth and to use that growth to diminish racially based inequality, reinforces the policy use in ways that make it hard to dislodge. In fact, austerity was used to disrupt the strategy of state-run development in both South Africa and Zimbabwe, a strategy inherited from each nation's predecessor racist states.

Dashwood suggests that the declining commitment to the poor during austerity was due at least in part to the "embourgeoisement of the ruling elite," which "explains the failure to combine these reforms with measures that would protect the welfare of the poor" (2000: 4). We suggest in addition that Zimbabwe's history shows, like that of many other nations, that neoliberal pressures also facilitate anti-democratic economic policy. No doubt Dashwood is correct that political elites became economic elites in Zimbabwe, as Jacob Zuma's administration in South Africa also demonstrates. But the hegemonic position of austerity policy creates it as a tool to be used by such elites, facilitating greater inequality even in nations inspired by socialism and emerging from deep racial oppression.

The African cases also make the point that deep-rooted racial inequalities could not shrink while the pressures of austerity were imposed. Zimbabwe and South Africa were both defined by inequalities of land and industrial ownership that could not be ameliorated strictly by market processes given the ongoing and overwhelming wealth of white minorities. So market-oriented neoliberalism could not address the market-rooted inequalities. Both nations were confined by the structural inequality of white economic power despite the transition to black political power. Democracy, or democratization, was consistent with neoliberalism in the case of South Africa, as authoritarianism in Zimbabwe once again is clearly consistent with austerity. Despite the fact that reducing vast societal inequalities was a priority for both nations, austerity won out.

4

Austerity in Asia and Oceania

This chapter examines the historical and policy trajectories of austerity in the cases of Thailand, Indonesia, and Aotearoa/New Zealand. In some ways, Thailand and Indonesia are non-traditional cases when examining Asia, and New Zealand – as an Oceanic European settler-dominated society with a powerful, yet marginalized, indigenous population – certainly embodies strong cultural, social, and political distinctions from much of the region, which itself boasts incredible diversity on those same counts. That said, each of the three cases is an exemplary representation of one of two distinct forms of austerity imposition. In Thailand and Indonesia, austerity accompanied externally imposed (IMF) loan conditions following economic crises. In New Zealand, by contrast, austerity became more integrated into longer-term reforms, reflecting a more intrinsic and structurally integrated form of austerity.

In Thailand and Indonesia, austerity policies followed the regional financial crisis in the late 1990s after a period of liberalization in the 1980s. The collapse of the Thai baht in 1997 prompted a broader decline that quickly spread throughout the region in what became known as the Asian Financial Crisis. IMF-imposed austerity in the same year deepened the economic crisis and exacerbated hardship conditions in both urban and rural Thai communities. While Thailand is representative of a higher-income classification (upper middle income) according to the World Bank, the impact of austerity on middle- and lower-income communities mirrored those of Indonesia (classified as lower middle income). The severity of the Indonesian economic crisis and accompanying social protests resulted in significant regime change (along with democratization) that highlights the political challenges of austerity and the significant costs placed on financially vulnerable national populations. Indonesia provides an example of *crisis austerity*, the role financial crises play in imposing and expanding austerity in the developing world. Despite differences in levels of income and wealth, the experiences of Thailand and Indonesia reflect a commonality experienced by other developing states in the post-colonial Global South.

The New Zealand case is more reflective of an advanced capitalist society, albeit one with a somewhat distinct colonial past. As a resource-based economy that has recently begun to diversify, the country has experienced many of the same global integrative pressures as Indonesia and many of the same trade connections as Thailand. However, New Zealand's development makes it unique in the region owing to its infrastructure and social investment. Its legacy of welfare capitalism nevertheless failed to protect it from a rapid embrace of neoliberal reforms in the 1980s. The strategic implementation of austerity through alterations of legal and economic structures, which Pierson (1998) refers to as *permanent austerity*, and its roll-out in Asia, is particularly relevant not only for the region but also as we consider the varied paths to austerity.

The difference in austerity imposition illustrated by our cases is certainly rooted in massive wealth differentials and the choices such wealth provides with regard to external financial conditionality. We also highlight the foundational distinctions of colonial experience in establishing the base for underdevelopment among emerging economies in the Global South. The extractive context of both materials and capital defines the colonial experience of Indonesia and Thailand, despite the fact that the latter was never officially "colonized." Preferential trade agreements, territorial annexation, and legal subordination certainly highlight similarities between the "autonomous" Thai experience and that of Indonesia; the contrast with a colonial settler state such as New Zealand brings the disparity into more stark relief.

These cases highlight the ongoing impact of different colonial histories on the imposition and impact of austerity. The British colonized New Zealand in the early 1800s, while Indonesia was occupied by the Dutch in 1800, with Thailand serving as an autonomous buffer between British and French colonial territories. The sheer demographic and geographic disparities between affluent New Zealand and the far more populous, yet less affluent, Thai and Indonesian societies make causal assumptions for underdevelopment problematic. However, the granting of self-government for the Crown Colony of New Zealand in 1840 (despite the presence of only 2,000 British settlers) dramatically increased the ability of the colonial government to invest in infrastructure and build a more diverse economic base. Economic development strategies in Indonesia were largely extractive and allowed the Dutch exclusive access to agricultural and natural resource products produced by local Indonesian populations (Ricklefs 2008). Bilateral European–Thai Trade agreements and a long-term Chinese trading presence were similarly based on extractive exportation, and while these relationships were certainly preferred to abject colonial exploitation, the export orientation based on agricultural and natural resource extraction did little to encourage economic diversification and reinforced the structural pressures of colonial conditions (e.g., Harrison & Jackson 2010).

We recognize the key role of racialization in the colonial experience and in the sustained legacy of colonial supremacist logic in New Zealand's development and the legacy of underdevelopment in Indonesia and Thailand. Multiple causal factors help explain New Zealand's (or other similarly positioned white settler colonies') development, but race and how it contributes to wealth accumulation is crucial. The policy space available for early New Zealand infrastructure development, more equitable trade relationships based on its Crown Colony status, and the capacity to develop economic diversity all contributed to this differential colonial experience. This policy space, not made available to either Indonesia or Thailand, reinforced the differential colonial experience based significantly on pre-existing assumptions of racial superiority.

The wealth disparity is not simply a colonial remnant; it helps us understand different paths to austerity. International lending institutions respond not only to differential wealth but also to differential status positions, and this helps to explain differences between imposed austerity and assumed austerity.

The Path to Austerity in Asia and Oceania

In many ways, austerity imposition in Asia follows a well-worn path: early market liberalization efforts, purportedly in the name of development and growth facilitation, create adverse conditions that are met with demands to institute requisite public spending reductions and "budgetary discipline" indicative of austerity reforms.

Significant state intervention drove economic development in the post-World War II era. The Cold War and the recent emergence of much of the region from direct colonial control created a context in which state-led development capitalism flourished, especially in response to significant developmental needs. Soviet influence throughout the region offered one such developmental approach, while Western capitalist alternatives provided a creative blend of market liberalization and central planning with substantial authority housed in the "developmental state" (Johnson 1982). Neoliberal proponents were unable to fully challenge state-led development until the 1980s, when crisis conditions provided them with the pretext to do so. The Thai currency crisis in the summer of 1997 provided one such opportunity. Although specific to Thailand, this experience resembles those of developing countries, especially Indonesia, South Korea, Malaysia, and the Philippines. The role of financial crises as a pretext to deepen austerity measures is both a common global strategy for austerity imposition and a common experiential condition of many Asian societies.

The Asian region is also home to several significant outliers in the emergence of both austerity imposition and resistance. Obviously, China, with its substantial size and unique approach to capitalism, is the most significant of these outlying examples. The centralization of Chinese capitalist policies allows the state the ability to address growth within specific productive and labor sectors, not to mention to utilize massive capital reserves for various growth-inducing initiatives. Austerity initiatives have been intermittently employed as a means of regulating rapid overall growth in the Chinese economy (Huang 1999). As such, the context of austerity within a deeper neoliberal model is far less relevant in the context of Chinese capitalism – to the point that Chinese "austerity" largely describes anti-corruption and anti-graft reforms. Quade (2007) argues that these anti-corruption initiatives serve as state-led mechanisms to control inflation and manage the deleterious effects of rapid growth.

Similarly, the Indian experience has been somewhat unique in the global context. The legacy of India's state-led economic planning created a particularly extensive bureaucratic infrastructure that continues to play a significant role in the country's economic life. Yet liberalization initiatives were undertaken in much the same way as in other developed countries, as a purported response to economic crisis in 1991 (Kohli 2006). Various proposals to reduce government spending have come and gone with little real staying power (Sen & Dasgupta 2014). Recently, the Modi government has renewed efforts to reduce state spending in areas such as scientific research and government largess. While Modi's proposal to cut spending by

10% to reduce budget deficits is certainly reflective of austerity, India has been reluctant to implement "structural reforms" indicative of traditional neoliberalization (Anand 2016). In fact, austerity implementation has been matched by a significant emphasis on social welfare initiatives – albeit often in the context of financialization and privatization of such services (Kar 2017).

Despite strong evidence that austerity implementation is varied and nationally distinct, there are two significant patterns of austerity implementation evident in Asia. The first, crisis reform, is the most common as it pertains to imposed austerity. Fiscal crises inevitably occur as liberal capitalism is deregulated. When crises happen, economists and policymakers prioritize spending reductions, especially restricting public sector activities, in order to reduce debt burdens and budget deficits (Roubini & Mihm 2010; Galbraith 2015). In much the same way that neoliberalization was accelerated in Latin America in the 1980s through debt crises, austerity is a common mechanism for deepening private capital consolidation and weakening public sector and labor initiatives (Cassano & Dello Buono 2010). Indonesia provides an exemplar of this crisis-driven austerity.

The second form of austerity imposition in Asia reflects the disproportionate colonial histories and experiences in the region. While many, including India, Vietnam, and China, have experienced a more traditional extractive and exploitative colonialism, European settler societies rooted in efforts to overwhelm or even eradicate indigenous populations have carved out particular political economic spaces in the emergent global economy. The experiences of countries such as Australia and New Zealand are distinct in the Pacific in that their demographic histories are rooted in settler colonialism; the racialization of colonial power networks and sustained economic connections with European capital centers reinforced massive capital discrepancies between such states (e.g., Australia, Canada, the United States, New Zealand, South Africa) and their more universally exploited colonial neighbors, who, not coincidentally, are demographically non-European.

The racialization of colonial experiences helps explain differential development histories, but the evolution of these settler pasts has influenced austerity experiences as well. New Zealand followed a more European model of welfare capitalism, morphing into varied forms of neoliberal capitalism throughout the 1980s and 1990s. The country's austerity represents a slower implementation of targeted budget cuts and caps on taxation that indirectly mandate cuts in public services (such as education) when costs inevitably rise. This contrasts sharply with the "shock therapy" experiences of developing countries throughout the Global South and follows liberalization and austerity patterns found in Europe and North America. This condition of permanent austerity (Pierson 1998, 2002) is a distinct form of austerity in affluent countries. The particular context of differential colonial experience (settler versus extractive) is salient in Asia as well as Oceania and – in line with our goal for this book – highlights a different trajectory of austerity.

Thailand

Thailand posesses strong global economic connections born of a long history of international trade arrangements and recent global market integration. In this sense, it is quite representative of other South Asian countries. Thailand provides an example of two austerity paths: an early "shock therapy" austerity similar to that experienced by many developing countries, as well as the crisis-prompted imposition of austerity by the IMF experienced in more recent decades.

Thailand's long history of commodity trade with China encouraged a relatively robust export-oriented infrastructure and economic organization as well as the inclusion of Chinese residential traders in Thailand, likely expanding in the Ayutthaya period (fourteenth century). This long history also facilitated a unique set of arrangements with regard to European colonial pressure, beginning in the 1500s with a series of engagements with Portuguese merchants, resulting in trade treaties with both the Portuguese and Dutch by the end of the century (Baker & Phongpaichit 2014).

The emergence of French and British colonial powers in the following century manifested in territorial control by the eighteenth century and created a unique situation for Thailand. The country signed numerous bilateral trade agreements, including the 1855 Bowring Treaty with Britain, which went far beyond trade agreements by granting residential rights and consular protection to British citizens in Thailand. Colonial acquisitions of nearby areas by the British and the French essentially surrounded Thailand, which subsequently was able to maintain its independence through a combination of political agreements that maintained its status as an international center for trade while creating a boundary between competing European colonial territories. While this situation certainly demonstrates Thai political savvy, the agreements came with a clear delineation of regional political economic authority. As a result, Thailand reduced its territorial claims to the French in the east (present-day Laos and Cambodia) and to the British in the north (Burma) and south (present-day Malaysia) (Falkus 1991; Baker & Phongpaichit 2014).

Thailand's experience in the era of European colonization was simultaneously distinct yet typical for the region. Its history of export-oriented and bilateral trade agreements created diplomatic opportunities which prevented the extremes of colonial occupation. But its territorial losses, subordinated status in trade and treaty negotiations, and role as a "buffer state" between two colonial powers created very similar colonial status conditions to other Asian nations. Thailand's subordination to European powers reflects the experiences of other developing states. Its longstanding emphasis on external trade relationships would play an outsized role in its postwar growth and financial crises.

Postwar Import Substitution and Liberalization

Thailand suffered from its (post-invasion) World War II alliance with Japan. The British demanded that food reparations be sent to their Malaysian colonial possessions, which effectively eliminated any rice surplus in Thailand. Despite this economic setback, Thailand quickly recovered in the 1950s on the back of substantial state-led investment and industrial consolidation. Further development of state regulatory institutions occurred after the 1958 coup, with the post-coup government, led by Sarit Thanarat, bringing Thai economic policy in line with the international standards promoted by the World Bank. The new government created the first National Economic and Social Development Plan, promoting a comprehensive system of ISI alongside a liberalization of financial regulations, to encourage both domestic and foreign investment (Unger 1998). These reforms resulted in significant GDP growth at over 7% between 1958 and 1973 (Chiengkal 1983).

With the financial liberalization of the 1960s, the Thai financial sectors expanded, particularly commercial banking. This financial infrastructure was established as a conduit for foreign investment and quickly became engaged in both corporate and consumer lending with substantial connections to transnational financial capital (Lauridsen 1998). This link to global financial markets provided a substantial source of investment capital, but also subjected Thai finance to severe instability as a result of global market fluctuations, which, particularly in the 1970s, proved to be challenging for Thai banking and finance industries.

The precipitous effects of successive energy crises had devastating effects on the Thai economy. Massive inflation following 1973 gave way to commodity value stagnation and a more prolonged economic downturn from 1979 to 1982. The Thai government's deficit-spending stimulus efforts had little effect once energy prices spiked again in 1979. It subsequently embarked on three rounds of currency devaluation from 1981 to 1984. This downturn crippled domestic borrowing and led to a severe financial crisis in 1983 in which over $500 million in financial capital left the country, with foreign financial investment decreasing by $84 million in 1982 alone (Beja et al. 2005: 150). After currency exchange agreements stabilized the baht and financial liberalization infinitives were proposed in 1985, import substitution ended, and the Thai government shifted to export manufacturing funded by renewed FDI.

This increase in FDI led to investment booms in financial sectors (particularly securities) and real estate in the late 1980s as the Thai government shifted to a tacit liberalization and deregulation strategy. By 1991, the pace of neoliberalization had increased; deregulation and financial liberalization were extensive and included the removal of interest rate caps and foreign capital controls, facilitating international capital mobility. The IMF-enabled liberalization expanded foreign investment and offshore borrowing, intending "to turn Thailand into a regional financial center" (Lauridsen 1998: 1576). Attracting foreign capital investment became the primary growth strategy for the Thai government with the 1993 creation of the Bangkok International Banking Facilities, designed to create a local financial infrastructure to take advantage of deregulated financial markets. These strategies significantly expanded the amount of investment capital in Thailand, much of which was funneled toward urban development and the inflating housing market in Bangkok. New housing units increased from approximately 40,000 in 1984 to approximately 175,000 in 1994 and 1995, driven by a huge increase in private development of housing units (12% developer-built in 1984 compared with 83% developer-built in 1996), reflecting this shift toward the privileging of private capital (Renaud et al. 1998: 6).

The 1997 Financial Crisis and Austerity Imposition

The influx of foreign capital and domestic bank lending led to various investment bubbles, particularly in Thai urban real estate markets

(Quigley 2001). But a slowdown in Thai growth panicked financial markets, which depressed foreign investment – all of which was compounded by a dramatic collapse of the Thai real estate market in 1996. These financial crises were made worse by a combination of foreign and domestic selloffs of Thai currency, which forced the Thai government to abandon the baht-to-US dollar peg in 1997 (Anwar & Gupta 2006).

The oversupply of short-term foreign capital and the dependency on foreign investment resulted in several crises in 1997. Currency investors saw the baht as overvalued and its value shrank, which subsequently led to a depreciation of both real estate values and Thai state assets. These depreciations subsequently impacted several financial institutions, which struggled to service outstanding debt. Combined commercial and residential real estate values depreciated by 379 billion baht and the debt tied to vacant real estate holdings rose to 430 billion baht (Renaud et al. 1998: 11). The cascade continued with the dramatic decline of Thai stock values. The bursting of the real estate bubble caused a decline in the value of stocks, substantially tied to private development and construction firms, by 2,453 billion baht from 1995 to 1997 (Renaud et al. 1998: 20).

The dramatic decline of the Thai economy in 1997 sent shockwaves through the region, prompting the so-called "Asian Financial Crisis," which quickly spread to other foreign-capital-dependent, states including South Korea, Malaysia, and the second case study in this chapter, Indonesia. As a result of the combined currency and financial crises, the IMF intervened in August with a massive succession of bailout funding to restore credit markets in excess of $17 billion. These loan moneys, of course, came with austerity conditions that the Thai government readily accepted in accordance with its broad liberalization initiatives taken earlier in the decade.

The austerity conditions accompanying the IMF bailout were conventional: spending restrictions on the Thai government (a 100 billion baht reduction in the following year's federal budget); a 3% increase in VAT consumption taxes; state subsidy elimination; and a number of fiscal regulations designed to limit deficit levels (including deficit spending) and stabilize financial industries (Lauridsen 1998: 1583). These conditions were designed to "re-establish domestic and external confidence in Thailand's financial system" (IMF 1997) and recapitalize targeted investment banks. While the $17 billion stimulus was primarily targeted for such recapitalization, the logic of structural adjustment through austerity was expected to provide an underlying foundation for future financial sector capitalization and stability. The primary goal of Thai austerity became protecting the primacy of financial capital (certainly domestic, but particularly the infrastructure of Thai financial sectors for foreign capital investment) and maintaining that primacy by reducing state-led initiatives to expand social and economic access to the majority of Thai citizens and shrinking broader Thai consumption.

The effect of these austerity policies on the Thai population was immediate: unemployment increased from 1.5% in 1997 to 4.4% in 1998; consumer prices increased 9.5% in 1997 and another 5% in 1998 (IMF 1997). Rampant underemployment and wage theft were compounded by the lack of unemployment insurance for Thai workers. By the IMF's own estimates, the impact of inflation and unemployment on the Thai population would increase poverty by up to 12% (Lane et al. 1999: 74 n. 23). The social costs of austerity were disproportionately felt not only among the less affluent, but also by women, who experienced the majority of layoffs throughout the country (Bungarten 1999: 255). The impact of austerity on families also demonstrates the broad hardship conditions experienced in the wake of austerity imposition:

> State-run hospitals and welfare homes report a 9.7% increase in the number of abandoned children under the age of five, and a 34% increase in abandonment of children between the ages of six and eighteen. Malnutrition among children, which had decreased from 19.6% to 7.9% between 1990 and 1996, is up again and affects no less than 25.5% of all children in the poor Northeast of Thailand, and 8.4% of the children in Bangkok. (Bungarten 1999: 256)

These austerity policies exacerbated the already adverse conditions. The cuts also worsened conditions of social inequality by reducing spending on both healthcare and education – the Ministry of Health budget was reduced by 17.3% in 1999 and education spending dropped to pre-crisis funding levels (Chomthongdi 2000) – despite IMF proclamations that neither would be negatively affected (IMF 1997).

The impact of austerity imposition certainly created material hardships among broad swaths of Thai society. Additionally, the adjustment also deepened the existing financial crisis through its damaging effects on the local economy, with exports and private domestic investment declining significantly. Moreover, and consistent with its actions elsewhere, the IMF severely overestimated the growth prospects of following austerity policies. The IMF-produced estimate of 3.5% Thai growth for 1998 (post-austerity) was subsequently "revised to -5% and the realized GDP growth rate was -10.51%" (Chari & Henry 2015: 171).

Although the Thai economy eventually recovered, there is ample evidence to claim that it did so despite the implementation of austerity policies. In the longer term, the beneficiaries of the financial bailouts, financed, in part, by austerity impositions (e.g., VAT increases and spending reallocations), did achieve the goal of protecting and expanding their access to financial capital. Those without vested capital – the poor, working- and middle-class households – saw only deepened hardships through commodity price increases, consumption tax increases, consumption subsidy decreases, property value depreciation, and reduced public healthcare delivery. While some of these issues have been addressed (by, for example, the 2001 universal healthcare initiative and the actual implementation of unemployment insurance), the restrictive context of post-austerity development leaves many Thai citizens, particularly the majority of the Thai labor force who are engaged in informal economic activities, vulnerable to price increases that exacerbate persisting material adversities (Jitsuchon & Siamwalla 2009).

Indonesia

Indonesia's eventual declaration of independence in 1945 reflected the common experience of decolonization, while also illustrating the chaotic aftermath of World War II. Sukarno and Mohammad Hatta made the initial declaration of independence while the nation was still grappling with Dutch colonial control and Japanese occupation. Following the Japanese surrender, Allied forces (largely British, Dutch, and Australian) moved to assert authority over Japanese relocation and to maintain economic control over Dutch commercial interests in the archipelago. The nascent Indonesian Republic emerged in the violence of decolonization with various constituencies vying for control over natural and trade resources. These include lingering Japanese groups, Communists launching a short-lived counter-revolution (1948–9), Islamic nationalists engaged in a longer counter-revolution (1948–60), American petroleum interests, and, of course, Dutch efforts to sustain colonial authority (Vickers 2005).

The end of Dutch colonialism came with a bilateral agreement in the fall of 1949 in which the Netherlands recognized the "United States of Indonesia" in exchange for sustained authority in Papua

New Guinea (which was relinquished in 1962) and the Indonesian assumption of 4.6 billion guilders in Dutch debt (Penders 2002: 49). This assumption of debt included significant World Bank ($195 million) and US funds ($400 million through the Marshall Plan) that had been granted to the Netherlands in 1947–8 and used to fund military actions against the Indonesian independence movement (Rich 1994: 69–70). Indonesian independence and unification in 1950 thus occurred within the context of an already debilitating debt burden.

This combination of external debt demands, sustained counter-revolutionary challenges, and weak colonial infrastructure hindered economic development during the Sukarno presidency (1949–67) and contributed to a change in political leadership during a period of extreme inflation and financial crisis. The subsequent New Order government led by Muhammad Suharto upon his election in 1968 (after serving as interim President in 1967) instituted a number of liberalization initiatives combined with sustained nationalization of key industries, including petroleum extraction. The oil price increases resulting from the 1973 OPEC embargo played a significant role in expanding the Indonesian economy. During the 1970s, Indonesia followed the other dominant trend among developing countries by investing heavily in its domestic manufacturing and extractive industries through the implementation of import substitution policies (James & Fujita 1989). As energy prices declined, the extraordinary growth Indonesia enjoyed slowed from 7% in the 1970s to 4% in the 1980s (Schwarz 1994: 57–8).

Indonesia embarked on a series of neoliberal structural adjustments in the 1980s in response to the decline of commodity prices. This economic slowdown reflects the prominent role natural resources play in the country's economic fortunes, which is problematic in at least two ways. First, natural resource extraction, as a primary means of economic production and growth, is increasingly devastating in a neoliberal context. That is, as regulatory oversight weakens, the opportunities to expand extraction in unsustainable ways increase, as do extra-legal efforts to take advantage of the lack of oversight (Ross 2003; Gellert 2010). Secondly, and more directly related to the context of neoliberalization and austerity, natural resource dependency links national economic growth/perceived health to wild fluctuations in global commodity prices that inevitably lead to boom-and-bust cycles, manifesting as financial crises (Bond 2006; Auty 2007). The occurrence of periodic financial crisis creates policy opportunities for those pressing for increased market liberalization and/or austerity policies, and while these cannot be specifically predicted, they can be anticipated (Peck 2014). In this context, austerity becomes a normative prescription in the larger narrative of market liberalization.

Austerity and structural adjustment in the latter half of the 1980s was reflected by typical strategies promoted by the Washington Consensus: currency devaluation and financial sector deregulation. The weakening of the rupiah was designed to make export pricing more competitive, and financial deregulation was intended to attract foreign capital investment. Both strategies resulted in growth, with the expansion of export-oriented manufacturing, agricultural and natural resource exports, and an increase in FDI (Karseno 1997). While these adjustments did increase overall growth, it also exposed Indonesia to increased exogenous financial risk, which would prove disastrous in 1997.

The devaluation of the Thai baht in July 1997 (owing to increased debt resulting from excessive borrowing encouraged by Thai structural adjustment) cascaded throughout East Asia. The Indonesian government responded to the overextension of private debt by increasing the interest rate in an attempt to boost foreign investment and capital liquidity (Pincus & Ramli 1998). By October 1997, it turned to the IMF for an emergency loan of $5 billion. Accompanying austerity conditionality required an immediate increase in the interest rate, cuts to local subsidies, and reductions in government spending (Stiglitz 2000). As usual, these austerity measures did nothing to stabilize the Indonesian economy. In fact, the accumulation of private capital debt following deregulation in the 1980s sustained downward pressure on the rupiah, which forced nearly three-quarters of Indonesian businesses into "technical bankruptcy" (Francis 2003: 2).

The exacerbation of the financial crisis, coupled with Suharto's reluctance to reduce food and fuel subsidies in a country with a high relative rate of poverty, led the IMF to impose a second round of austerity in January 1998. These sustained demands for subsidy elimination, tariff reductions, and the elimination of foreign bank ownership restrictions while also further restricting Indonesian monetary policy (Lane & Schulze-Ghattas 1999). These austerity measures did much to deepen material hardships among the Indonesian population by causing immediate price increases in the midst of job loss, particularly in urban areas. Although IMF austerity conditions intended to target public debt, they did little to assuage the government's debt burden, even while transferring the ownership of Indonesian financial entities to foreign investors (Francis 2003). The subsequent "success" of a decline in public debt was merely due to the privatization of formerly public enterprises, not a reduction in the debt burden for the government. This, of course, further constricted the ability of the Indonesian state to invest in public infrastructure or address the adverse social effects of austerity imposition.

While the restriction of state regulatory capacities is a longer-term goal of liberalization initiatives in general, austerity imposition in crisis situations is designed to increase foreign investment. In the case of Indonesia, the IMF-imposed austerity measures were crafted for three specific purposes:

> First, structural reforms were intended to build confidence and staunch capital outflows. Second, macroeconomic policies were to be adjusted: in order to ease the private sector's burden of adjustment to the capital outflows, a modest fiscal tightening was planned; and efforts to limit capital flight were to be buttressed by tightened monetary policies. Third, large financing packages were provided to help restore confidence. (Lane 1999: 18)

The emphasis on "confidence" belies the skewed logic of austerity in that it creates tangible opportunities for financial capital while being satisfied by vague – and empirically false – promises of future prosperity for national populations.

The immediate effects of austerity implementation in 1998 neither led to stability nor worked to address immediate adversities faced by millions of Indonesians. In fact, the eventual reduction or elimination of food and fuel subsidies occurred at a time of massive job loss, which only served to deepen crisis conditions. Job losses following the crisis were estimated at between 2.2 and 6.8 million additional unemployed Indonesians and an unemployment rate above 10% (Bullard et al. 1998: 519). While the influence of austerity policies on unemployment can be either direct (in terms of enforced banking closures) or indirect (in terms of the burden of drastically increased domestic debt, more difficult borrowing conditions, or a dramatic decrease in domestic consumer spending, for example), the immediate inflation that resulted from reduced state subsidies for food and fuel created sudden hardship conditions for the 19 million Indonesians suffering in poverty as a result of the financial crisis (Utting et al. 2012). Following the initial austerity program in 1997, Suharto resisted IMF demands for additional subsidy cuts and bank closures – the former owing to massive protests and food riots, the latter owing to deep personal connections to bank owners and managers (Park 2013). The insistence of the IMF and the Clinton administration that the government fully comply with austerity demands sustained popular protests while at the same time failing to reinstill confidence in Indonesia's shattered financial sector (Sanger 1998). Bank closures, interest rate hikes, and subsidy cuts aggravated crisis conditions and led to further liquidity crisis as depositors and investors fled the Indonesian banking system (Pincus & Ramli 1998; Stiglitz 2000). In the context of joblessness, material deprivation, and increasingly violent confrontations with protestors, Suharto was forced to resign in May 1998.

The end of the Suharto regime ushered in a more liberal capitalist-friendly era as the *Reformasi* period saw a significant shift toward the implementation of IMF austerity demands. The eventual impact of austerity implementation following Suharto led many to the conclusion that financial stabilization and positive growth conditions were enabled by finally giving in to IMF demands (Roach 2012; Giles & Harding 2013). The sustained liberalization and austerity program indeed created significant foreign investment opportunities. FDI increased over 500% in the most recent post-recession era,[1] which coincidentally saw further rounds of austerity as post-Suharto administrations continued to accede to IMF liberalization initiatives. These austerity and liberalization pressures continued to prove detrimental to the Indonesian people.

Successive and sustained protests responding to the *Reformasi* government's subsidy reductions and cuts in services eventually led the government to seek an end to IMF-imposed austerity in 2003, the same year as the end of the Emergency Fund credit line (Francis 2003). In fact, the subsidy reduction protests in January 2003 resulted in the Megawati government shifting back toward the protectionism underlying the New Order government as a means of ensuring political legitimacy in a nascent democratic environment. This ebb in austerity would turn to flow once more in 2005 and 2008 when then President Yudhoyono dramatically cut fuel subsidies to pay for currency sales made to finance oil imports (in a country with massive oil exports). Despite weathering the 2008 recession and experiencing nearly 6% GDP growth following the recession, the pressure to deepen liberalization through privatization and using austerity cuts motivated further subsidy reductions in 2013 and 2015. The downward pressure of these cuts on populations susceptible to sudden price increases highlights the cost burdens of austerity in developing countries but also the motivations for political actors to resist austerity policies.

Crisis-led austerity clearly defined the initial reform attempts in 1997 and 1998, but the 1998 *Reformasi*, which ushered in an unprecedented period of democratic reforms, was also accompanied by similar calls for economic liberalization. As a result, from 1998 to the present, the political economic climate of Indonesia is best understood as a vacillation between liberalization (privatization, deregulation) and sustained protectionism (subsidies, state-owned enterprises), with austerity serving as the hammer of neoliberalization during periods of political economic opportunity. It remains to be seen whether the administration of Joko Widodo will follow a similar pattern, but the centrality of foreign investment in current Indonesian economic strategy implies a move from crisis austerity to more sustained or permanent austerity that typifies policy strategies in advanced capitalist societies.

That said, the natural-resource-reliant nature of the Indonesian economy makes it a highly desirable location for external investment. Low-cost, limited-regulation access to raw materials such as petroleum, minerals, and timber underlies foreign investment interest in the archipelago and thus interest in maintaining positive conditions for such investment. Austerity has served as a contemporary tool in maintaining the long-term interest in foreign exploitation of Indonesian natural resources. The legacy of colonial extraction and domestic neglect means that sustained austerity policies in a country with many impoverished citizens will create severe hardships and further hinder social development. Despite these realities, liberalization proponents continue to push austerity as a way to sustain the reduction of extra-market protections such as food and fuel assistance. We turn next to a very different case that may offer an interesting juxtaposition in terms of colonial disparities and the common problems associated with permanent austerity.

Aotearoa/New Zealand

The islands that make up the country of Aotearoa/New Zealand were settled by Polynesian navigators sometime in the thirteenth century (McGlone & Wilmshurst 1999). The emergence of an autonomous Maori culture continued until initial European contacts in 1642 (Tasman) and 1769 (Cook); European colonial settlement then intensified until the 1840 Treaty of Waitangi. While the Treaty established a form of binational colonialism, it clearly established British control over the islands and limited Maori property rights by restricting the right of sale to the British government (Orange 2015). Despite the appearance of binational legal protection, the Treaty encouraged British land sale abuses. After Chief Justice James Prendergast nullified the Treaty in 1877, there followed a period of European consolidation of land, authority, and capital (Kawharu 1989; Walker 1989).

The colonial settlement of New Zealand is important to illustrate distinctions between settlement colonialism and the extractive colonialism evident in the Indonesian example. The early New Zealand economy was certainly extractive in terms of natural resources (gold, whaling, agriculture), but these extractive activities were also combined with infrastructure development and foreign capital investment in the late nineteenth century (Hawke 1985: 113–15). This investment in the productive capacities of a colony, especially one dominated by the European-descended kin of colonial parents, creates a cumulative growth in domestic capital that stays in the colony, which can then be invested in local infrastructure and expand productive capacities (Rodney 1972; Good 1976; Acemoglu et al. 2001). The accumulation of wealth by European-descended settlers further encouraged the circumvention of the Treaty of Waitangi through land theft and undervalued purchases of Maori properties. As a result, colonial development in New Zealand moved in a very different direction than that of Indonesia (or other extractive colonies). Colonial governments emphasized New Zealand's domestic development, prioritizing infrastructure and institutions, which in turn allowed for more genuine social and economic progress to take place. The racialized inequity typified in early colonial New Zealand development reflects practices and experiences already chronicled in Africa, Asia, and Latin America.

The first social welfare programs passed into legislation in 1898, which was substantially expanded by the Social Security Act of 1938. The latter represented the establishment of broad public responsibility for those facing socio-economic challenges, including illness, age, and unemployment (McClure 2013). This investment in the social development of colonial New Zealand (and nation-building after dominion independence in 1907) again reflects a distinct settler colonialism, but also demonstrates a historical engagement with social welfare and public support dating back to nearly the beginning of its European colonial status. These efforts to sustain a state-led social welfare system continued until 1984, when the newly elected Labour government, led by David Lange, pledged to address inflation and an altered trade context since the entry of the United Kingdom into the European Economic Community (EEC) in 1973.

Roger Douglas, Labour Finance Minister, quickly instituted a number of neoliberal reforms that rapidly deregulated portions of the national financial sector and facilitated capital mobility. The government also imposed austerity policies, reducing subsidies and social welfare spending as a means of compensating for high-income and corporate tax reductions (Kelsey 2015). These liberalization initiatives led to inevitable overspeculation, nurturing the same kind of financial market investment and subsequent financialization boom experienced throughout the expanding neoliberal capitalist world. The predictable burst of the financial market bubble on October 19, 1987 was felt particularly hard in New Zealand, with the national stock market losing nearly a quarter of its overall value (Roll 1988: 21).

The market collapse combined with other underlying problems, including rising costs of living and increasing unemployment that pushed beyond 10% in 1991 (OECD Databank). The election of a National Party government in 1990 surprised few; however, given the passionate defense of the New Zealand welfare state by previous Prime Minister Robert Muldoon in the 1970s and early 1980s, the shift to deepen the neoliberal reforms initiated by Labour came as a shock. It was such a surprise to New Zealand voters that they subsequently voted to change to a more mixed-member proportional representational system in 1993, largely as a result of sustained liberalization efforts (Denemark 2001: 70–1).[2]

Despite the unpopularity of liberalization initiatives, the National government repeated its application of austerity policies to deepen liberalization reforms. Once again using financial crisis conditions as justification, it reduced social spending on unemployment, healthcare, and subsistence assistance as a means of freeing up capital to be injected into the failing Bank of New Zealand. This reduction in social welfare spending was coupled with long-term strategic changes in order to ensure austerity conditions and an attack on labor became the structural norm. Ruth Richardson, then National Minister of Finance, crafted the Employment Contracts Act (ECA) in 1991, eliminating collective bargaining and moving employment to an individual contract model (Evans et al. 1996: 1878), fundamentally altering the nature of labor relations in the country. While these were only two reforms out of many, both are reflective of the character of austerity in New Zealand. First, the deep reduction in social service spending as a means of reallocating state revenues demonstrates the crisis rationale associated with austerity imposition. Second, the accompanying political alterations linked to employment were put in place to create structural changes that would sustain liberalization by embedding austerity mechanisms as permanent features of New Zealand society. By fundamentally altering the context of employment in the country, neoliberal proponents were able to gain control over wage negotiations and create a condition in which austerity shocks were no longer necessary. Rather, the downward pressure on wage expenditures and the facilitation of profit growth, central to the logic of austerity, would become a permanent and normative condition of employment in New Zealand.

Austerity imposition and dramatic alterations in labor relations, dubbed "Ruthenasia" by the New Zealand press, again proved deeply unpopular. The National government suffered a dramatic reduction in its parliamentary majority in 1993 and a Labour majority was elected in 1999. Although the fifth Labour government continued previous policies of corporate and elite tax reduction in addition to encouraging free trade initiatives and attracting foreign capital investment, it did not implement new waves of austerity. In fact, its passage of the Employment Relations Act in 2000 replaced the ECA and strengthened the bargaining power of labor organizations and individual employees. The political viability of maintaining permanent austerity conditions was becoming more difficult to sustain. Nevertheless, the partial reduction of those conditions had little impact on employment and neither reinstated collective bargaining nor reversed the social spending cuts undertaken by the previous National government. The sustained role of liberalization in successive governments remained evident.

Austerity imposition returned as a prominent feature in the fifth National government, led by John Key and elected in 2008. Financial crisis again served as justification, with additional social welfare reforms designed to reduce the number of individuals and families collecting welfare benefits, instituting work-for-benefit requirements. Increases in consumption taxes and increased cost sharing for services (such as prescription co-payments) created hardships for lower- and middle-income citizens, while at the same time granting corporate tax cuts and accumulating state budgetary surpluses (NZ$4.8 billion in the 2017 fiscal year). While not the traditional "shock therapy" of other austerity experiences, this form of permanent austerity accomplishes the same goal, seeking to do so in a more lasting and transformative fashion.

The combination of crisis justification and strategic policy reform creates an environment in which austerity is a normative expectation and a perpetual condition. While the election of a Labour-led coalition in 2017 has certainly been accompanied by more protectionist rhetoric, thus far changes have proven elusive. The pledge to maintain austerity budget discipline questions how much will change even under a socialist government like the current one in New Zealand. The structural changes instituted by successive National and Labour governments have created a situation in which a move away from permanent austerity will require significant policy and structural shifts.

In short, the role of permanent austerity is to both sustain and deepen conditions that enable private capital consolidation and growth. This inevitably hurts national populations as work conditions and costs of living become more challenging. In addition to the shifts in labor legislation, policy changes diminishing the role of the state in housing regulation have enabled increased private control over rental markets in the country. According to Statistics New Zealand, rental affordability decreased from the 1980s through 2012, largely as a result of a nearly 20% increase in the number of rental units under private control (Statistics New Zealand 2013: 9). The use of austerity as a means of relinquishing state regulatory control over national rental markets was accomplished by the policy requirement that state-owned rental units marketize rents in the 1990s.

These changes in housing policy were matched by financial deregulation in the mortgage industry that led to the same housing price increases seen in North America and Europe from the 1990s until 2008. In New Zealand, these deregulation initiatives, as accompanying complements to austerity spending reductions, pushed "the median house price from 17 times median annual rent in the 1990s to over 20 times in the 2000s" (Statistics New Zealand 2013: 10). The role of marketization and deregulation in the rapid increase in the cost of living and decrease in affordability is clear; austerity has sustained these market fundamentalist goals. That is, the policy changes that work to minimize labor power and marketize housing through austerity shift governmental emphasis to protecting the upward distribution of capital – the source of that capital being the citizens of New Zealand as costs of living increase. Foreign investment is, of course, also a primary goal of austerity proponents, but FDI in New Zealand has fluctuated wildly, making it an unreliable source of capital growth.

The end goal of domestic redistribution of capital upward creates clear pressures on national populations to be able to afford these price increases. The broad unpopularity of austerity policies means that the democratic process is potentially hostile to sustained austerity, thus permanent austerity strategies seem to alter the political opportunities available to future political actors.

Conclusion

Across our Asian and Oceanic cases, we find how austerity experiences have differentiated between the Global North and South. Among richer nations with democratic traditions like New Zealand, crisis plays a role in the origination of austerity. For poorer nations, ongoing crises provide the contextual opportunity for external powers like the IMF to enforce austerity.

But crises came first: in all the cases we examined in this chapter, austerity is utilized as a neoliberal crisis management mechanism. In Indonesia and Thailand, austerity was preceded by neoliberal opening of the economy. When austerity appeared necessary, governments reduced spending to resolve financial overextension while defending the profits of financial speculators. This form of revenue generation at the expense of most of the population clearly resembles other experiences in the developing world.

The goal of limiting spending as a means of addressing structural economic vulnerabilities is, of course, central to the logic of austerity. All three nations increased consumption taxation as a means of perpetuating state revenues while protecting corporate entities by deregulating and decreasing tax revenues from them. Obviously, the extent of consumption taxation in poorer countries such as Indonesia and Thailand is limited, but in New Zealand, this form of regressive tax policy was especially useful in supporting state revenues.

Control over labor markets also features prominently. Crisis conditions have long served as a justification to reduce labor costs within the context of capitalism through layoffs or wage reductions. Austerity policies designed to weaken labor organization and facilitate wage control are also common outcomes within the context of crisis austerity implementation, especially in Indonesia and New Zealand. Both policies are designed to promote capital growth quickly and at the expense of broadly distributed capital wealth. Inequality and precarity are common austerity outcomes and both are clearly evident in these cases. But even beyond the securing of profits, attacks on labor also seek to control a potentially disruptive political opposition, helping to perpetuate austerity in a manner consistent with policies in both the Global North and South.

Political opposition across these cases differed somewhat. The hardships resulting from austerity in Indonesia led to large-scale protests and sustained opposition. The electoral history of New Zealand after 1984 also highlights the broad popular opposition to these initiatives. Thai austerity seemed to generate less protest after the 1997 crisis, perhaps because of military influence and later political conflicts. Opposition to austerity in Indonesia and New Zealand persists in different ways owing to varying levels of opposition and specific political economic conditions in each country. Difficulties associated with fuel subsidy elimination in Indonesia have certainly posed particular challenges to austerity adherents. Similarly, the broad popularity of social welfare programs in an advanced capitalist country like New Zealand makes it difficult for strict austerity imposition to move forward while being politically viable.

The cases in this chapter also differentiate between the influence of external and internal powerholders. The traditional powers of the IMF and other IFIs drove austerity in Thailand and Indonesia; New Zealand was certainly subjected to such influences, but it was succeeding governments that instituted what became permanent austerity there. Explaining divergent patterns of austerity implementation, particularly with regard to external imposition and voluntary promotion, necessitates more attention to historical economic development and strategic policy development. In terms of the former, we recognize the role of racialized colonial histories in all three cases. Indeed, those divergent histories influenced levels of economic development and legacies of both poverty and extractive production. The potentially more powerful opposition to austerity diverges primarily because social welfare was allowed to proceed in the New Zealand case, while the previous weakness of welfare states in Indonesia and Thailand prevented their resurgence. Permanent austerity could be implemented in New Zealand owing to its latter stage of capitalist development. While neither Indonesia's nor Thailand's economy has reached that stage, nor will they have similar paths for growth, the sophistication and globally embedded nature of Indonesian and Thai production encourages adherence to policies amenable to foreign capital investment and growth. The policy progression in New Zealand has made structural changes that may be difficult to reverse despite the current social democratic resurgence. The question then becomes: what deep structural changes need to occur in order for austerity to be dislodged from its increasingly fortified policy position? We take up this question, along with others, in our concluding chapter.

5

The United States and the Inevitability of Austerity

This chapter examines the lead-up to and normalization of austerity in response to a neoliberal economic transition in the Global North. It expands our analysis by examining policies that created the context for austerity in the United States, as creeping and cumulative scarcity came to define the environment to which state and local governments had to respond. This path was significantly different than those followed in the developing world, where austerity responded to debt and the policy inclinations of functionaries in the IFIs. Elsewhere in the Global North, austerity came as a response to a diagnosis of crisis. In both the North and South, austerity was imposed by powerful external actors in coalition with domestic actors following neoliberal ideology. The growth of debt often led to the crisis diagnoses that led to the singular cure of austerity. Austerity in the Global South has provided a venue for continued extraction of wealth, and a trajectory where developing nations have remained dependent on more powerful nations and IFIs for access to credit and the global economy. Austerity in the Global North, as we will see, perpetuates a continental unity benefiting a well-established national hierarchy.

Why examine austerity's path in the United States? The US provides a contrast not only to the debt-driven cases we've explored in the Global South, but also to the crisis-linked cases in the Eurozone. In contrast to other cases, we link austerity in the United States to several economic shifts that disrupted the post-World War II capital–labor accord. Policies that shrank government's abilities to address social needs exacerbated the hardships generated by these economic shifts. Together, these changes have led to at least 40 years of creeping and cumulative scarcity. These policy shifts have been imposed by internal actors rather than external ones, largely following neoliberal policy design. The policy choices themselves created economic problems to which the predominant political solution has been reduction of state welfare provision. That is, the only seemingly available answer to the economic problems that have stagnated wages and diminished security for most US households has become austerity. Rhetorically, these political actors defend their actions by claiming that the global economy has changed to such an extent that the United States can no longer compete in certain kinds of production, or with certain kinds of protections for its workforce. The results of both the policies that set the stage for austerity, and the subsequent austerity policies themselves, have included greater inequality and shrinking economic and political power of working people and communities.

Another difference between the imposition of austerity in the United States and elsewhere, we argue, is how the intersection of causes took so much time to play out. Debt, political transition, and equity needs in the Global South, or diagnoses of crisis in the Global North, provide a clear rationale for a fairly rapid imposition of austerity. In the United States, economic shifts such as deindustrialization provided a favorable climate for early neoliberal strategies, such as the attack on labor. Other policies, such as governmental efforts to lure industries or keep them within their boundaries, provided a policy rationale for austerity, so shrinking state resources, which further made austerity a seemingly inevitable policy choice. Thus, austerity and the conditions for its further imposition were contemporaneous and drawn out, as opposed to strictly sequential and rapid.

The impact of deindustrialization in the industrial North of the United States, and then across the country, provided an initial context for austerity. Since the mid-1970s, deindustrialization and offshoring had diminished economic wellbeing as jobs were cut, and tax bases were reduced when industrial firms relocated. Local governments responded to the flight of industry using policies that limited their future economic flexibility. Governments turned to tax incentive funds and other state expenditures to attract industry or keep it from fleeing, shrinking tax income that could be used to address social needs. Other policies familiar to those in the United States, such as tax reforms, similarly decreased public resources that could be used to resolve economic need, and simultaneously limited governments' policy options.

All of these policies, like those elsewhere, were political choices that demonstrated the interests of the powerful and the hegemony of austerity. In the presence of ideological cover that argued for decreased economic regulation, federal, local, and state governments faced a contradiction. Social needs increased, owing largely to changes in the global economy that disadvantaged working people. Inequality rose, exacerbating economic hardships. Yet policymakers enthralled with neoliberalism designed strategies that cut state flexibility either by shrinking the state's ability to address social and economic needs, or by committing resources in ways that again shrunk state prerogatives. Thus, the strategies with which governments could address growing needs were limited by prior and contemporaneous policymaking that diminished their resource base. With fewer policy tools ready to reconstruct prosperity, the inevitable solution and political choice became austerity. Austerity in the United States becomes the elite hegemonic policy in response to decades of restrictive economic policy, rather than as a cure for debt, as in Latin America, inequality and development needs, as in newly liberated African nations, or to address financial crisis, as in our Asian and European cases. The national economic power and democratic traditions of the United States proved little match for the slow but seemingly inevitable turn to austerity.

This chapter proceeds as follows. First, we discuss the appearance and impact of deindustrialization. Next, we turn to the policies that US politicians commonly chose to maintain the presence of industrial manufacturers. Additionally, we examine policies that further constrained policymakers' abilities to respond to social needs, such as taxation policies and deregulation of speculative industries and the support of the financial turn. Then we describe welfare reform, a signal policy of austerity in the United States, even when it was not labeled as such. Again, this narrative does not follow a clean chronological path, as some of the strategies to make austerity inevitable, like the attack on unionized labor, both preceded austerity and were part of it.

Deindustrialization

For US-based corporations, a quarter century of unparalleled postwar growth gave way, by the late 1960s, to unprecedented global competition. As a consequence, profits were severely squeezed. Companies might have responded by going "back to basics": improving product quality, investing in new technology, and fashioning more constructive relationship with their workers. Instead, they abandoned core businesses, invested offshore, shifted capital into overtly speculative ventures, subcontracted work to low-wage contractors here and abroad, demanded wage concessions from their employees, and substituted part-time and other forms of contingent labor for full-time workers – all in the name of "restructuring."

(Harrison & Bluestone 1988: xxviii)

As supporters of Bernie Sanders and Donald Trump recognized in 2016, the industrial and occupational base of the United States has undergone massive change. Manufacturing employed approximately 31% of all workers in the late 1950s; by 2011, this figure fell to 8.9% (Bluestone 2003; Mishel et al. 2012). Without romanticizing those jobs, it is important to recognize that manufacturing was the location of higher wages, benefits, and security for a large section of the US working class. As a result of deindustrialization, inequality in the United States has skyrocketed, not only because wages have stagnated, but also because the numbers of workers enjoying employer-provided pensions and benefits have diminished. Both as a result of these occupational shifts, and reinforcing them, union membership dropped from 26.7% of US workers in 1973 to only 13% by 2011 (Mishel et al. 2012).

As early observers Barry Bluestone and Bennett Harrison demonstrated, workers and business observers had already been experiencing this shift.[1] By the time of the publication of their influential book *The Deindustrialization of America* in 1982, capital stock crucial to manufacturing had been aging. Rather than upgrading production machinery, Bluestone and Harrison showed that industrialists sought lower-cost production locales or other higher-yield economic growth strategies. The search for the highest profits animated all these choices. Corporate profit rates sank from an average of 15.5% in the early 1960s to 12% later that decade and further to 10.1% by the early 1970s (Bluestone & Harrison 1982: 17). The choices US industrialists made in the wake of falling profits included abandoning certain markets such as electronics; reducing investment from previously productive industries; diversifying into other profitmaking ventures, including non-productive financial investments; reducing labor costs; moving to cheaper production locales; and pushing politicians to decrease taxes and regulations.

The costs of these choices have been substantial. In the 1970s, the United States lost between 32 and 38 million jobs as a result of various forms of private disinvestment. During that decade, "large, established manufacturing plants closing down ... exceeded 30 percent" (Bluestone & Harrison 1982: 9), affecting many of the mill-based industries in the industrial Northeast and subsequently cutting many working- and middle-class jobs. Although the US South and Southwest became new locales of the manufacturing shift, in addition to the Global South, those areas suffered from their own plant closings. The net outcome was a reduction of firms, and unemployment rates in the industrial South often rising to above 10% (Bluestone & Harrison 1982: 39).

The jobs that replaced those lost were often lower-paying, with fewer benefits and less security than in manufacturing. Many of the new jobs were in service industries, an overly aggregated category that contains both high- and low-paying jobs with varying status and security. The much-celebrated FIRE jobs (finance, insurance, and real estate) proved to be the highest-paying and lowest-employing subsector. From 1952 to 2002, for example, FIRE sector employment only increased from 4% of the workforce to about 7%, while other service industries increased their workforce from 15% to 36%. The relative share of the FIRE sector's corporate profits during that same time skyrocketed, however, from about 11% to 45% (Krippner 2005: Figures 1, 3). But from the perspective of most workers, manufacturing still continued to be a better employer: from 2000 to 2010, manufacturing jobs continued to be those with higher salaries than growing employment areas such as leisure and hospitality, administrative support services, and "other services." Of growing service sector jobs, only those in the FIRE subsector and healthcare exceeded manufacturing salaries (US Census Bureau 2012: Table 632).

The jobs lost to deindustrialization cost local governments tax revenues and subsequent popular support. Responding to industry's threat of exit, governments designed new strategies to diminish costs for industry to remain in place, or to entice them to relocate. Over the last 40 years, the choices policymakers have made to address these threats have diminished governments' ability to provide for social wellbeing, and so make austerity seemingly inevitable. The next section details some of the governmental policies that have catered to business needs.

TIFs, Tax Moratoria, and Other Incentives

If you were a mayor of a medium-sized city in the United States, and you were confronted with a threatened departure of a large employer in your area, what would you do to keep them from leaving? Or if you were a state governor who wanted to increase employment, or staunch a wound of unemployment, and a firm signaled an interest in moving to your state, what would you do to ease that relocation? Across the United States, the answer has been that you would spend tax dollars in various ways, doing all you could to keep or lure that business. Lost jobs mean hardships for your constituents, greater pressure on your tax base to support them, and potentially lost political support from those same constituents, while gained jobs likely mean the opposite. In the pursuit of maintaining jobs, however, government officials have contributed to a hardening of class politics, making business actors even more powerful than their workers and the communities in which they work. They have also reduced resources by which they might address the social needs of their constituents. What have US policymakers done in the face of these very real threats of exit?

US politicians have designed a myriad of policies to make it easier for business to stay in, or be lured to, various locales. A database created by the *New York Times* identified 1,874 programs mandated to incentivize businesses' location decisions across the United States over the period from 1997 to 2010. These programs included outright cash grants, corporate income tax credits, and sales tax exemptions or refunds. Governments have also provided infrastructure, property tax abatements, low-cost loans or loan guarantees, and free services like worker training. In devising these policies, local and state governments have devoted more than $80 billion a year to the companies that enjoyed government largess (Story 2012; Story et al. 2012).

As large a sum as this is, it appears to be a severe undercount, because "incentives are granted by thousands of government agencies and officials, and many do not know the value of all their awards," and "the beneficiaries come from virtually every corner of the corporate world, encompassing oil and coal conglomerates, technology and entertainment companies, banks and big-box retail chains" (Story 2012). Automakers appear to have paved the way, pushing cities and states to set up incentive programs for decades. For years, General Motors was the top beneficiary, receiving at least $1.7 billion in local incentives from 2007 to 2012, followed closely by Ford and Chrysler.[2]

A few examples are instructive.[3] Michigan, a former industrial powerhouse owing to its history of automobile manufacturing, spent at least $6.65 billion on 11,747 grants to companies through 46 separate state programs from the 1990s to 2012. The top forms of incentives include sales tax refunds, exemptions or other sales tax discounts, property tax abatement, and corporate income tax credit, rebates, or reduction. By far the largest sum was spent on manufacturing industries; the second was on filmmakers. The largest sum of awards was to the big three automobile manufacturers, with Chrysler at $1.3 billion, General Motors at $1.26 billion, and Ford at $1.21 billion. The next five biggest beneficiaries were chemical and battery companies.

Texas's legendary affinity for large things is confirmed in its corporate incentive programs: it spent at least $19.1 billion in 2,649 grants through 27 identified state programs from 1997 to 2012. Manufacturing industries are again the largest recipient, followed by agriculture, and then healthcare. The forms of expenditures resemble those in Michigan. The largest single recipient corporation was Amazon, followed by Samsung, and Andarko Petroleum.

Records for Tennessee's expenditures in this area were available only from 2010 to 2012. Within that time, the state spent $1.58 billion on 25 incentive programs targeting 143 companies. In Tennessee also, use of the incentives reduced the amount of taxes paid by relocating businesses, or those convinced to stay. Manufacturing, agriculture, and film industries were the top three beneficiaries of state generosity. The state and local governments gave large grants to such profitable companies as Electrolux, Dow Corning, Kroger Foods, and Mitsubishi, among many others. Between 2009 and 2015, Tennessee also provided Volkswagen with $637 million to first locate and then expand a manufacturing plant (Farmer 2015).[4]

Tennessee provides an example that demonstrates the normalization of state support for corporations. During 2016 budget hearings, Governor Bill Haslam asked for an earmark of $30 million for an undisclosed economic development project in the state. Although the state's Finance Commissioner was questioned about the blind spending, he declined to elaborate on the development prospect other than to describe it as an "exciting project" during a Senate Finance Committee meeting. The Commissioner's argument that the Governor was "not yet prepared to disclose who this is, but I can tell you that it has a very good payback and a strong return on investment," was sufficient to be included in the yearly budget (Schelzig 2016). This example shows how such incentives have become business as usual, even when cloaked in budgetary mystery.

States across the United States spend tax dollars this way; often the amount spent on incentives makes up a substantial portion of state budgets. Oklahoma and West Virginia give up amounts equal to about one-third of their budgets, and Maine allocates nearly a fifth (Story 2012). Indeed, tax incentives, a smaller subset of the policies examined by the *New York Times*, cost states and localities $50 billion yearly, and "are actually a drag on national economic growth" (ITEP 2013: 1). The costs to social services that end up unmet are not worth it: "If offering more tax incentives requires spending less on public education, congestion-relieving infrastructure projects, workforce development, police and fire protection, or high technology initiatives at public universities, the overall impact on a state's economy could actually be negative" (ITEP 2013: 2).

The social costs are clear. Incentive policies decrease public resources that could be used to resolve economic need, and simultaneously limit governments' freedom to address citizens' needs. "Nationwide, billions of dollars in incentives are being awarded as state governments face steep deficits. Last year [2011] alone, states cut public services and raised taxes by a collective $156 billion" (Story 2012).

Although these policies certainly influence business decisions to stay or go, it is less clear that they have had positive influences on job numbers or quality in either the short or long term, as policymakers "rarely track how many jobs are created. Even where officials do track incentives, they acknowledge that it is impossible to know whether the jobs would have been created without the aid" (Story 2012). We know that short-term decisions to stay owing to government incentives do not influence corporate decisions for long. General Motors, for example, chose to close 50 "properties" despite the fact that all had received incentives previously, and generally professed no more responsibility to plants in locales that gave incentives than others (Story 2012). Analysts indict these policies for contributing to a zero-sum gain in a competitive national environment, considering incentives "much more likely to reshuffle investment between geographic areas than they are to spur genuinely new economic activity" (ITEP 2013: 2). Subsequently, crucial social services and infrastructure and those who use them suffer.

If governments devote an increased share of revenue to helping corporations without increasing the tax base, the sum available to help struggling citizens declines. If citizens' security and benefits diminish, they require more from the state and contribute less to the tax base, initially shrinking income and sales taxes; over time, real estate taxes can shrink too. If state revenues decline, there is less to offset the increased contributions to private firms. Deindustrialization has resulted in increased power for business, as the incentives government officials have granted have strengthened corporations and weakened workers. Across the United States, scarcity has increased, slowly but surely, as state policymakers have come to believe they have no alternatives to help citizens other than catering to business. The overattention to business in turn has made austerity seem to be inevitable. The next section of this chapter addresses both federal and state tax policies, more measures that have cemented this seeming inevitability.

Tax Policy

Tax policies of multiple varieties have reduced the burden of taxation on certain actors within the United States, at both federal and local levels. The political rhetoric justifying these efforts is consistently anti-state and by now repetitive and familiar: governments cannot create jobs; people do better things with more control over their own money than do governments; allowing more money into the hands of previously highly-taxed wealthy individuals will "trickle down" to create jobs and prosperity for all; and in the case of taxes on business, the government should not be in the business of picking market "winners and losers." In addition to the rhetoric is the reality that once taxes go down, it is hard to bring them back, and resources with which governments address citizen needs again shrink. In the wake of shrinking resources and a rhetoric that is more pro-market and pro-individual, the choice to impose austerity appears to be inevitable.

Innovations in tax policy, and the subsequent impact on the resources with which governments can respond to citizens' needs, can be traced back to the 1978 passage of Proposition 13 in California. Middle- and working-class property owners voiced concern about their rising real estate taxes as property values in California exploded, and so supported the proposition, which limited tax increases until properties were transferred. Even early in this debate, critics voiced worries about how tax cuts would affect government welfare state spending. But the advocates for the policy prevailed, in part because they relied on conservative and neoliberal economic voices as champions, including Milton Friedman and William F. Buckley, both of whom argued for the legislation as good tax policy. Although

California's social expenditures may not have shrunk, Proposition 13 has shifted the burden. California

> has the highest top marginal income tax rate in the country at 13.3 percent, a corporate income tax of almost 9 percent, and the highest statewide sales tax in the country at 7.5 percent. But in 1978, California had the fourth highest overall tax burden, and today the state still has the fourth highest burden. Although one cannot say for certain that Prop 13 caused the other taxes to increase, Prop 13 at the very least failed to prevent high taxes and an expansive public sector. (Glyn & Drenkard 2013)

As important as Proposition 13 was for California's economy, it was more important for emerging neoliberals because it provided a high-profile success to tout. Using tax policy seemed to help citizens, and so became part of the neoliberal ideological and policy toolbox. Over time, however, tax policies of this sort constrained state expenditures to satisfy citizens' needs. So began a new set of policy interventions to limit taxes at different government levels.

For example, federal income tax rates have been reformed owing to criticism that they were too high and too complex. They were indeed complex, if complexity is defined by numbers of tax brackets. In 1956, there were 24 separate income tax brackets, ranging from 20% to 91%, the latter figure unimaginable now because of its height, but also because those taxes were supported by a Republican adminis-tration. By 1965, the rates of marginal taxes had started to diminish so that the top bracket was at 70% and the lowest at 14%, but the number of brackets rose to 25. Tax rates remained unchanged until 1977, when a new lower bracket was introduced, eliminating income taxes entirely for single incomes under $8,335 (in 2013 dollars). By 1979, the amount of different brackets reduced to 16, while the high and low points remained the same. The Reagan revolution brought the first reduction in the top bracket when that was lowered to 50% in 1982. Since then, the trend for top rates has been consistently down: the Tax Reform Act of 1986 reduced the number of brackets first to five and then to two, with the highest earners taxed at only 28%. The Clinton administration stabilized the number of brackets at five, with the highest marginal taxation at 39.1%, until George W. Bush's administration drove that down even further to 35% for most of that presidential regime. The Obama administration's American Taxpayer Relief Act of 2012 increased the highest of seven brackets back to the Clinton-era levels of 39.6%, while the lowest taxpayers paid 10%, a reduction from the 15% rate for the poorest passed in the final year of the Reagan administration. The most recent reduction under President Trump maintains seven separate brackets, the highest at 37% and the lowest at 10% (Tax Foundation 2013; Mercado 2018).

It's clear that income taxes have gone down proportionate to earned income, and the efforts of the Reagan, Bush II, and Trump administrations have been successful in reducing the rates for the wealthiest. But income taxes remain the largest single source of tax revenue for the US government, making up 47% of total federal revenue in 2013. By 2007, with the legacy of the Bush tax cuts, critics noted the "dramatic" cuts in progressivity of the federal tax code, with the very highest-earning families enjoying the largest cuts, while pre-tax inequality increased (Aron-Dine 2007). This critique is echoed now in the wake of the would-be populist Trump's cuts (Sherlock & Marples 2014; Aron-Dine 2017).[5] Various US states copied the move away from progressive tax codes, with swift repercussions.

In 2014, the state of Wisconsin reduced its income tax from 4.4% to 4.0% (Tax Foundation 2014; see also Henchman 2014). From 2011 to 2018, Wisconsin Governor Scott Walker signed 15 bills that cut taxes by nearly $15 billion; income and property taxes made up a large portion of these cuts, but capital gains and corporate taxes were also cut. Austerity loomed immediately: by 2015, the state had to cut K-12 schools' budget by $127 million, and that of the University of Wisconsin system by $300 million. As time and budgets revealed, the tax cuts actually cost Wisconsin almost twice as much as estimated, converting it from a state with a $1 billion surplus to one with a nearly $2 billion deficit (Ollstein 2015).

The state of Kansas provides another example, when in 2012 Governor Sam Brownback forced through the largest tax cut in state history, reforming the tax code from three brackets to two, with the top reduced from 6.45% to 4.9%, and the lowest from 3.5% to 3%. In answer to critics who worried that the cuts would decimate state services, Governor Brownback responded, "My faith is in the people of Kansas, not its government." By 2014, the state received $803 million less than in 2012, and had to resort to its reserve fund. The bond rating agency Moody's cut Kansas's debt rating, citing the cuts and a lack of confidence in the state's fiscal management. In that budget year, K-12 education budget was cut by 2%, while higher education's budget was reduced by 3%. Further cuts proposed at the time would have left school funding at 17% below pre-Great Recession spending.

Austerity was again swiftly imposed: the Kansas state government cut $3.7 billion in expenditures over five years, affecting government workers, business owners, and those who used state services of various kinds. Libraries, local health departments, state funding of welfare services through the Temporary Assistance to Needy Families program, and courts were all confronted with less funding. Social service resources were cut by 8%, and it was estimated they would shrink by a further 16% by 2019, with a cumulative social cost estimated to reach $5 billion. Like the previous Bush-II-era federal tax cuts, most of the benefits went to the wealthy: the highest 1% of earners saw 2% tax cuts, while middle earners saw only .5% tax reduction, and no cuts came to some low earners (Leachman & Mai 2014; *New York Times* Editorial Board 2014).

As a result of the cuts to programs that addressed social needs, Kansas became one of only five states to lose employment, earnings, and net business growth as others were recovering from the Great Recession. The pain continued as the 2015 budget year brought regressive solutions, raising sales and cigarette taxes under threats that without these increases, education and disability services would suffer more cuts. This proved to be only a temporary solution, as in March 2016, with Kansas tax receipts still down, higher education cuts of $17 million were announced. The pain of austerity finally forced Kansan legislators to reverse the policy, while still left with a $900 million budget deficit as a result of the failed "experiment" (Hobson et al. 2017).

These kinds of tax cuts consistently hurt states and their citizens. The biggest cuts since 2007 have occurred in Kansas, Maine, North Carolina, Ohio, Wisconsin, Arizona, Louisiana, New Mexico, Ohio, Oklahoma, and Rhode Island. Subsequently, these states consistently enjoyed slower income growth and created fewer jobs, contrary to the rhetoric accompanying these policies. Looking back over 40 years, none of the 12 big tax-cutting states have seen their economies surge since enacting tax cuts. Instead, states have paid for tax cuts by imposing austerity in state services, raising other taxes, or both. Tax cuts consistently yield *slower* job growth and declining share of national employment compared to the nation as a whole, with the exception of states that can rely on increasing oil revenue to offset other losses.

Tax policies, along with industrial incentive policies, were only some of the tools brought to bear in response to deindustrialization, or as a part of the extension of corporate abilities to make profits. The choice to shrink manufacturing in the search for greater profits also led business to financialization, increasing their strategic focus on making profit through investments rather than bricks-and-mortar industries. The lure of financialization led business to champion deregulation, allowing corporations to act in formerly restricted ways.

From Deregulation to Financialization

Deregulation weakened the bargaining position of working people, adding to the increasing power of business at the expense of labor and local communities. "The deregulation of everything from airlines and telecommunications to finance opened up new zones of untrammelled market freedoms for powerful corporate interest. Tax breaks on investment effectively subsidized the movement of capital away from the unionized Northeast and Midwest and into the non-union and weakly regulated South and West" (Harvey 2005: 26).

Deregulation of the financial industry specifically incentivized investment away from manufacturing. As US manufacturing declined, diversifying corporations sought new places to invest, and new financial instruments to generate profit (Krippner 2005; Foster & Magdoff 2009). With the spread of austerity and neoliberalism, new global investment opportunities opened: ownership restrictions were abolished concurrently with privatization of many state-owned industries; capital mobility increased as industrial protection policies were reduced; and new financial markets opened wider to international investors (Stiglitz 2002, 2006; SAPRIN 2004). Even the debt of developing nations went on the market in ways that benefited capital.

Government removal of controls on interest rates on consumer savings deposits facilitated the financialization of the US economy from the mid-1960s to the late 1990s. Credit became much more expensive for those manufacturers that wanted to remain competitive, and "more volatile interest rates contributed to a macro-economic environment that favored financial activities over productive investment" (Krippner 2011: 59). New financial instruments also became available, opening more opportunities for risky investments that became riskier with the reduction of consumer protections.

As elites pursued financialization, they pushed politicians to accommodate them in the same way that they pursued incentives. For example, Clinton's abolition of the Glass–Steagall Act in 1999 opened the banking and financial industry for further investment (Lessig 2011). Increased profits further generated expectations of even greater profit growth. In addition, with financial deregulation, "credit flowed freely across the economy, fueling a credit expansion that increased financial sector profits and provided further impetus to financialization" (Krippner 2011: 59). Making money betting on money began to make more sense than making money on production, especially if the government was making the former easier while globalization challenged the latter.

As profits from financial speculation accrued, US consumers responded to one of the available investment opportunities. Housing values increased, pushing people and brokers to turn to real estate as an investment strategy. Investment capital pursued real estate, driving prices above and beyond reasonable expectations of return. When bundled mortgages became investment sites, a vicious cycle ensued in which inflated values further inflated profit returns and expectation of returns. Homeowners took on more debt as the surging real estate market appeared a safe bet.

Internationally, deregulation of investment and ownership in other nations also increased capital mobility. But these additional financial interrelationships also increased vulnerability. When the US housing bubble burst, the result was the devaluation of a chain of loans, each linked to the other and all risky. Added to the financial meltdown, after decades of deindustrialization, the nuts-and-bolts economy, newly called the "real economy," was no longer able to protect the nation. The increased interrelatedness of national economies within a global economy meant that vulnerability was contagious, as was crisis. The increased opening to speculative investment that could move across national borders with a click of a computer mouse provided huge investment opportunities; it also meant that crisis moved quickly. As the costs of financialization mounted in the United States and elsewhere, governments took on more private liabilities through policies such as the Bush II and then Obama administrations' bailouts of troubled banks, investment firms, and other companies. The bailouts and subsequent recovery of financial profits stood in distinct contrast to the limited stimulus the US government provided, and demonstrated the ongoing political power of economic elites. Other policies demonstrated that power differential, including union-busting and the reduction of social welfare.

Union-Busting

Deregulation facilitated speculation and financialization, but it also diminished worker power. Among those industries that chose to stay in the United States, increased competition led capital to push governments to deregulate. Hours at work increased, wages decreased stemming from some of the deregulation trends, and many industries squeezed their workers. In the trucking, airlines, and telecommunication industries, "management demanded wholesale wage concessions from their employees and increased pressure on the job to squeeze out more productivity from them" (Harrison & Bluestone 1988: 14). Additionally, the squeeze came as worker protections became deregulated, with truckers working more hours, airline personnel making less money, and workers becoming generally less secure. These policies were implemented simultaneously with union-busting, weakening worker security, and enforcing worker discipline (Harrison & Bluestone 1988: 15). Diminishing the power of working people also meant shrinking their ability to resist austerity.

Attacking labor's right to organize is a consistent component of austerity policies. In the United States, these efforts both preceded and were a part of the shift to austerity. The Reagan administration came into office with clear intentions to tip the scale of power further in the favor of employers. Firing striking air traffic control workers signaled a new era for labor relations, one that continued through later presidential administrations. Employers' strategies to weaken or abolish unions include delaying union elections, propaganda campaigns aimed at weakening workers' affinity to unions, and "outright intimidation" (Clawson & Clawson 1999). Consultants were regularly brought in to make the anti-union case in elections, and supervisors were used in face-to-face meetings to assess and pressure individuals to oppose unions. Firms also fired workers who supported unionization campaigns with little fear that governments would support workers. "In 1980 the odds were one in twenty that a union supporter would be fired for supporting an organizing drive" (Clawson & Clawson 1999: 102), and employers retained the upper hand in mandated reinstatement processes addressing illegal firings for organizing. Active employer organizing against unions helped weaken organized labor just as governments were offering incentives for firms to stay or relocate. Even when multinational corporations were friendly to union shops, governments went to extreme measures to discourage union formation. For example, Tennessee's Governor Haslam and Senator Corker's falsehoods and intimidation tactics had a significant impact on discouraging unionization in Volkswagen's Chattanooga, Tennessee, auto plant (McKenney 2018).

In addition to fostering union-busting, the Reagan administration's labor policy allowed corporations to take on a number of new flexible employment practices. Firms forced organized labor to accept a number of wage and benefit concessions during negotiations held during the recession of the early 1980s, and this new trend lasted well beyond that period. Even after the Reagan recession's end, in 1985, "a third of all workers covered by new collective-bargaining agreements submitted to a total freeze or cut in wages" (Harrison & Bluestone 1988: 40). All of these policies were reinforced by Reagan's anti-labor appointments to the National Labor Relations Board.

The two-tiered wage system emerged as another facet of the attack, with industrial policy allowing new workers to be paid less than more senior workers doing the same work. Corporations also began hiring more part-time workers, often earning less, with fewer benefits and less security, in place of a permanent workforce. Both strategies diminished worker protection and solidarity.

The Reagan administration's attack on organized labor was followed by neglect under subsequent Democratic administrations, especially when they were obstructed by Republican control of Congress, while Republican Presidents renewed the assaults. For example, although President Clinton repealed the 1938 Hatch Act, which had previously barred federal employees from engaging in political activity, labor's hopes for additional support were soon dashed by his commitment to NAFTA, which resulted in the loss of an estimated 766,000 US jobs (Zieger & Gall 2014). President George W. Bush reinvigorated the attack on labor by repealing workplace safety rules, making it harder for unions to fund political activity, and ending the preference for unionized contractors on federally funded job sites. Although President Obama restored that preference, as well as stiffening penalties against federal contractors for anti-labor organizing, his power to address workers' needs was soon stifled by a Republican congress. The attack on unions, begun early, was sustained well into the Great Recession and its aftermath, as neoliberal public officials like Wisconsin Governor Scott Walker succeeded in pushing through legislation "depriving public-sector unions of bargaining rights ... even in traditionally progressive" states (Formisano 2015: 65).

As unions were being attacked, as good working-class jobs became scarcer, and as financialization provided new areas for investment while further shrinking worker opportunities, the protection provided by welfare also shrank, a signal marker of austerity policy. The US welfare system has never been generous compared to its counterparts in other wealthy nations, but the Reagan administration demolished relief even more savagely. The Clinton administration followed suit by changing US "welfare as we know it."

Austerity through Welfare Policy Changes

The welfare system expanded in the 1960s and 1970s, but came under attack during the Reagan administration. Voicing charges of cheating welfare queens and allegations of overcollecting to further stigmatize the US citizens receiving welfare, the Reagan administration painted the poor as undeserving, and so gained cover for attacks on social protection programs. Some of the welfare "reforms" won during the Reagan administration included making formerly tax-exempt unemployment benefits taxable and diminishing eligibility through administrative machinations. For most of 1984–9, "the proportion of the unemployed receiving unemployment insurance benefits set a record low" (Piven & Cloward 1993: 360). In addition, hundreds of thousands lost their public service jobs with the repeal of the Comprehensive Education and Training Act. Many receiving disability payments also lost that benefit, while the government reduced food stamp expenditures and access, and imposed work requirements on some welfare recipients.

Although the attacks on the poor and the imposition of austerity via welfare cuts began under a Republican administration, it took a Democratic President to comprehensively change the US welfare system for the worse. The Clinton administration's 1996 Personal Responsibility and Work Opportunity Reconciliation Act not only further imposed work expectations, it also imposed lifetime limits on recipients. In addition, the new law continued funding by the federal government, but moved responsibility for the administration of welfare to the states. States gained a flexibility that allowed them to diminish coverage, as they "could outsource the program, turn applicants away, give them whatever amount they thought was right, and so on. The only requirement was that no one could stay on the rolls beyond a certain length of time" (Frank 2016: 116).

The Clinton administration abolished a signature welfare program, Aid to Families with Dependent Children (AFDC). In its place, it created the Temporary Assistance for Needy Families (TANF) program, which provides minimal cash assistance to low-income families. The maximum time for which an individual can receive assistance shrank from an unlimited period under AFDC to 60 months under TANF, although many states adopted even shorter time limits as part of their own imposition of austerity. By July 2015, this cash payment program offered recipients much less than its predecessor. Even among those states giving the most generous benefits (Alaska, New York, Connecticut, and New Hampshire), the maximum benefit brought recipients only to 40.9% to 47.8% of the poverty line. Among the 33 less generous states, benefits for a family of three reached less than 30% of the poverty line. Sixteen of those states paid less than 20% of the poverty line.[6] States also received a flat level of funding for the new program, which has not increased in response to growing need.

Increased flexibility for states also means that many now use a much smaller share of the diminished TANF funds to help poor families than previously.

> In 1997, three of every four federal and state TANF dollars went to cash assistance for these families. Today, only one in four TANF dollars does. States shifted substantial portions of these funds to other purposes in the years when the economy was stronger, and need was less, and have been unable (or have declined) to shift funds back when need grew sharply as the economy weakened. (Schott et al. 2015)

Deindustrialization, politicians' choices in responding to it, and other economic changes yielded savage results in the United States. In the year 2000, 33.3 million US citizens were poor; by 2009, that number had increased to 42.9 million; and by 2014, it had increased to 47 million (US Census Bureau 2012: Table 709; Poverty USA 2016). Simultaneously, inequality rose dramatically. Between 1970 and 2009, the income shares of the lower-income-earning 80% of households declined; only the income of the top 20% increased over that time (from 43% of aggregate income to 50.3%), and it is the share of the top 5% of income earners (from 16.6% to 21.7%) that accounted for most of that increase (US Census Bureau 2012: Table 694). Throughout most of this period, US politicians chose to gut the ability of government to address citizens' material needs.

Welfare reduction is a key component of austerity. Such cuts not only diminish the resources that working people rely on; they make tangible the ideological position of neoliberalism: the market will resolve issues of poverty, wages, and employment if only government stays out of its way. The attack on welfare does not just reinforce the unequal power between labor and capital in strict economic terms, but also enforces labor discipline by shrinking worker alternatives, forcing them to work for ever smaller compensation. In addition, it becomes easier to diminish public relief institutions as welfare recipients are demonized. Those resources have been more difficult for states to build and citizens to obtain. Here the imposition of austerity preceded some of the ideological shift in favor of the policy, further reinforcing the ideological arguments against state intervention, even when the need for that intervention grows. Like deindustrialization and incentives to capital, tax policy and union-busting, the attack on welfare serves to curtail state flexibility either by shrinking states' ability to address human development and economic needs, by precluding it in better times (as we have come to think of the Clinton administration), or by committing resources in such a way that the same ability diminishes.

And if state resources are interpreted as shrinking, what becomes the inevitable economic policy solution? Austerity. Austerity in the United States became the hegemonic policy in response to decades of restrictive economic policy, rather than as a cure for crisis-driven ills. One additional difference between the US case and the others described in this book is the relative absence of protests specifically targeting austerity, even as austerity policies became less shrouded in mystery and obfuscation. Why has there been such little protest against austerity in the United States? Occupy Wall Street provides us with one of the few exceptions, but even that opposition was short-lived and with varied aims.

A variety of reasons explain this relative absence of protest. First, the creeping and cumulative hardships that have characterized austerity and the runup to austerity in the United States stand in great contrast to the sharp shocks suffered elsewhere. When one's bus fare doubles overnight, or the interest on loans quadruples in that same time, it is easier to mobilize against that clear policy target than if similar damage is imposed over years. Second, the simultaneous attack on unions served to demobilize a sector that might have served as a launching pad to organize protest. During this period, unions fought for survival as much of the industrial base in which they were rooted disappeared. Organized labor found it difficult to react to the slow-moving and bi-partisan imposition of austerity when addressing declining membership alone required so much focus and effort, and while it was confronting both government and corporate attacks. Third, the simultaneity of another globalization-driven shift, the increase of immigrant low-wage labor in the 2000s, provided the champions of austerity with a scapegoat on whom to blame the problems suffered by US workers. The high-flying industrial and government "architects of austerity" were less immediately apparent for many US working people than new immigrants, who were targeted by so many right–wing ideologues. Finally, the ongoing efforts of right-wing think tanks provided ideological cover for the slower-moving imposition of austerity. We address this briefly below. Foundations and think tanks in the United States had enormous influence on the policy shifts we detailed above.

Ideologues for Austerity

Placing the US experience of austerity within the scheme of our three variables is in some ways simpler than in some of our other cases. The issue of national affluence appears to be straightforward. The United States is clearly an affluent nation, ranking 13th wealthiest according to an analysis of GDP per capita and purchasing power parity. Of the 12 richer nations, only six of them have a population over 4 million, and the largest, the United Arab Emirates, had a 2017 population of 9.5 million. So the US level of wealth, with a population of over 326 million citizens, seems to be a simple evaluation. The United States is also home to 43% of the world's millionaires, another datum that suggests US wealth is unquestioned (Gregson 2019).

But perhaps the issue is not so simple after all. The United States is clearly an extraordinarily wealthy nation, but that wealth is very unequally enjoyed. In 2010, the ratio of the wealth of the top 5% of the population in the US compared to the nation's median wealth holders was double its closest wealthy competitor, the Netherlands. When examining the 1% of top wealth holders in comparison to other wealthy nations, only Luxemburg approaches the United States in terms of income inequality, a level that no other nations come close to approaching (Collins & Hoxie 2017). It's worth noting that these statistics predated the recovery from the Great Recession; the recovery of wealth among the richest further exacerbates that inequality.

In addition, poverty in the United States is among the highest in wealthy nations. The official poverty rate at 12.7% in 2015 offers a number of 45 million people. But critics have long found the official formula of assessing poverty yields a severe undercount. Thus assigning the United States a label as affluent is not an unambiguous exercise. Nevertheless, despite the disproportionately large number of economically disadvantaged citizens, it remains a wealthy nation, although with a significant polarization of that wealth.

The question of political regime form is similarly more complicated than initially appears, as the criticisms of US democracy are many. These criticisms include the ever-increasing penetration of money into electoral campaigns, the relatively minimal ideological differences between the two main parties, and the archaic voting structure manifested in longstanding voting obstacles and the Electoral College.[7] Despite these criticisms, all of which we share, we place the United States on the democratic side of our political regime continuum. As a comparison to some of our cases – junta-era Chile and Indonesia, for example – it serves not as an exemplar of democratic practice, but certainly as a political structure affording democratic possibility.

US politicians have imposed austerity as a matter of choice in response to many of the political economic pressures we note above. Yet as a globally hegemonic policy, even US austerity is linked to its membership in the "neoliberal thought collective." The Mont Pelerin Society, which was "constituted as a closed, private members-only debating society ... [and] consciously sought to remain out of the public eye ... to create a special space where people of like-minded political ideals could gather together" (Mirowski 2013: 44), inspired neoliberals across the globe. Despite the European origins of neoliberalism, specific US economics departments, such as the University of Chicago and George Mason University, among others, became key disseminators of the new ideology. Indeed, global ambitions defined the neoliberal network from the very beginning. After funding the initial 1947 meeting of the Mont Pelerin Society, the Foundation for Economic Education (FEE) went on to become one of the think tanks responsible for pushing neoliberal thought in the US (Plehwe 2009). Corporate elites soon found reasons to support foundations; for a time a "hardcore of nonunion firms such as B. F. Goodrich, DuPont, General Electric, General Motors, and Sun Oil Company" funded the FEE (Steiner 2009: 190). Other foundations, such as the Volker Fund, the Earhart Foundation, the Relm Foundation, and the Lilly Endowment, worked with international counterparts to help create a cohesive ideological framework of neoliberalism; influencing global politics and policy was their shared goal.

US think tanks enjoyed great influence, with an "impact far beyond Washington. They introduced doubt into areas of settled academic and scientific scholarship, undermined genuinely unbiased experts, and gave politicians a menu of conflict statistics and arguments from which to choose" (Mayer 2016: 128). Their influence is unmistakable: of nearly 130 specific policy proposals launched by the neoliberal Heritage Foundation, "the Reagan administration adopted 61% of them" (Mayer 2016: 142). Additionally, 27 members of the similarly neoliberal American Enterprise Institute came to work for the Reagan administration (Bair 2009).

Conservative businesspeople showed great foresight as they created think tanks that nurtured neoliberal thinkers well before the triumph of neoliberalism and austerity. In addition to the FEE, the American Enterprise Association (later the American Enterprise Institute) devoted itself "to articulating an economic philosophy centered on the idea of the free market and disseminating this vision to intellectual elites – journalists, politicians, businessmen, and academics. ... The partisan thinktanks functioned almost like a political party, in terms of developing and refining ideology and relating it to matters of immediate concern" (Phillips-Fein 2009: 282). Over time, a division of intellectual and policy labor emerged. The Olin Foundation concentrated especially on influencing academics, while the Heritage Foundation departed from other groups such as the American Enterprise Institute in its groundbreaking role as "purposefully political, priding itself on creating, selling, and injecting deeply conservative ideas into the American mainstream" (Mayer 2016: 120).

Think tanks in turn nurtured legislative groups such as the American Legislative Exchange Council (ALEC), in which business-people and legislators met together and crafted neoliberal-friendly legislation. In ALEC, "thousands of business and trade groups paid expensive dues to attend closed-door conferences with local officials during which they drafted model legislation that state legislators subsequently introduced as their own. On average, ALEC produced about a thousand new bills a year, some two hundred of which became state law" (Mayer 2016: 554). Direct advocacy groups were also linked to the think tanks, such as Americans for Prosperity, a group funded by the billionaire Koch brothers in response to perceived threats of business regulation. As politicians responded to changes in the US political economy, billionaire funders such as the Koch brothers, the Olin and Bradley families, and Richard Mellon Scaife possessed ready-made answers to problems often of their own making, all the while nurturing neoliberal ideology and austerity policies.

Thus, in the United States, the power of ideas again merged with the power of power. The network of neoliberal stakeholders in foundations, think tanks, academia, and advocacy organizations strategized to provide answers to politicians confronted by a new global political economy. Similar efforts explain the emergent hegemony of neoliberal ideas as Keynesianism seemed to fail the Global South. But because of the difference in political systems and economic dependency, the pattern of austerity in the United States followed a delayed ideological and policy transition. In the Global

South, the imposition of austerity followed the pretext of debt, development and inequality, and financial profligacy; in the United States, austerity followed and contributed to political and economic changes that yielded scarcity, making it seem that austerity was inevitable.

6

Austerity Lands in the European Union

After two devastating world wars, European nations recognized more than ever the need to create deep and lasting bonds to forestall more violence. The economic devastation of Europe added urgency to the unification project, which was facilitated by massive Marshall Plan spending and the efforts by the then EEC at economic cooperation as a means of enhancing growth opportunities. The EEC formalized several multilateral initiatives to enhance political and economic cooperation, perhaps the most notable of which was the elimination of customs tariffs between European countries in the 1960s. The formation of the contemporary EU was laid in the 1986 Single Europe Act, which provided the exploratory framework that would later result in the 1993 Maastricht and 1999 Amsterdam Treaties. These treaties integrated the union members by creating uniform rules concerning finance capital, goods and services, as well as eliminating intra-EU immigration controls.

The Stability and Growth Pact, a direct product of the common economic planning goals of the EU, helped create indirect spending restrictions through debt and deficit caps for member states (Debrun et al. 2008). Beginning in 1999, the newly created ECB took on the task of maintaining annual oversight of member state deficits (not to exceed 3% of GDP) and central debt (not to exceed 60% of GDP). Should a member state exceed either cap, the ECB must recommend a structural adjustment (i.e., austerity) strategy that will bring the violating country back in line with EU standards (Hallerberg et al. 2007). This policy emphasizes the ECB's role in promoting austerity as a means of pacifying the anxieties stoked by financial capital and credit rating agencies, and has had significant implications for many EU members following the 2008 crisis.

The cases we examine in this chapter diverge from our other case studies because these nations experienced austerity as members of a union, despite the United Kingdom's special (and now changing) status. We continue to investigate how austerity is experienced differently according to the political and economic strength of states. Our European cases demonstrate how states' capacity in relation to others shapes experiences of austerity, but in different ways from our previous cases. First, membership in the EU limits the prerogatives of domestic economic policymaking among member states. Second, in some ways these nations represent relatively stronger states than in our other cases, with the obvious exception of the United States, but Greece and Spain still rank among the weaker partners within the EU. Third, as members of a union, individual nations (such as Greece and Spain), in the absence of national central banks and with the existence of a common currency, were unable to print money on their own. Finally, the long history of differential power across European nations also meant the ties of dependency, manifested as relying on credit to purchase exports from wealthier EU members, reinforced the weakness of both Greece and Spain. Our cases also provide some differences in origin and urgency. Austerity in Greece and Spain emerged as a response to the global fiscal crisis of 2008; the United Kingdom's experience long preceded the crisis, as we will see. Both Greece and Spain differed from the United Kingdom as they explored early and brief efforts at Keynesian stimulus before they were forced into austerity. Greece's role was interpreted as key to the wider Eurozone financial crisis; the EU was motivated to take quick action due to the fear of contagion the country seemingly posed (Varoufakis 2016). In both Greece and Spain, austerity was triggered by the halting of low interest loans and replaced by tight credit and much higher interest rates.

Greece: The Fear of Contagion and Austerity

Austerity is not really an economic policy at all. Austerity is a morality play pressed into the service of legitimizing cynical wealth transfers from the have-nots to the haves during times of crisis, in which debtors are sinners who must be made to pay for their misdeeds.

(Varoufakis 2017: 40)

Greece offers a particularly complex "crisis" case, because it highlights a mixture of origins and actors both during the period preceding austerity and in the austerity experience. These included the lies Greece's leaders told about its financial stability during its bid to join the EU, which were not uncovered owing to the EU's overenthusiasm at its expansion. Critics targeted Greece's welfare state as the root of state debt, but the country's commitment to its citizens was not dramatically unlike many of its EU neighbors. As occurred elsewhere (Della Porta et al. 2017), an anti-austerity opposition came to power, then soon capitulated to the austerity pressures it railed against during its electoral campaign. Finally, the EU's actions demonstrated a hierarchy of power within that union, even while credit agencies exerted greater influence than in earlier moments of austerity.[1]

Greece formally joined the European Union in 1981 and the Economic and Monetary Union (EMU) in January 2002. As previously noted, the Greek administration lied about its public deficit in order to win acceptance into the Eurozone, a prevarication that became evident after the 2008 global financial crisis forced the issue (Lynn 2011; Manolopoulos 2011). But the lie was matched by the failure of the EMU to perform due diligence in examining Greece's debt claims. Italy was earlier admitted with debts violating those limits, setting a precedent for Greece the following year. The desire to expand, it seems, outweighed the willingness to investigate Greece's economic claims.

Greece's leaders wanted to join the union because, like many of the union's poorer partners, entry provided the nation access to low-interest loans from more powerful EU countries. These loans were often used to purchase and import commodities produced by those very same richer nations: France, Germany, the Netherlands, and Luxembourg (Lapavitsas et al. 2012; Perez-Caldentey & Vernengo 2012). Richer EU nations' desire to sell their goods is key to understanding the relative negligence in checking Greece's books upon its application for entry. Despite the EU's overall agenda striving for economic and political unity, Greece remained among a number of poorer nations in the union. This power imbalance reveals itself in entrenched current account deficits in those poorer nations, consistent current accounts surplus for core countries, especially Germany (Lapavitsas et al. 2012), and the selective imposition of austerity.

EU investment in Greece drove a credit boom, which was accompanied by apparent economic growth. Artificially low interest rates and subsidies of exports paid for by loans from powerful European nations drove working people's seeming high standard of living (Varoufakis 2016). But the cost of that illusion, and indeed entry into the EU, was to be found in the nation's deteriorating trade balance and increasing public debt. Greece's trade deficit of 7.2% of GDP in 2001 more than doubled to 14.9% of GDP by 2008 (IMF 2014). The country's increased imports could only be sustained by additional heavy borrowing from the same foreign sources that contributed to the trade imbalance. Subsequently, its external debt increased from 42.7% of GDP in 2000 to 82.5% in 2009 (Manolopoulos 2011).

The globalized nature of investments led the 2008 crash in the US housing market to quickly become a worldwide crisis. The Eurozone initially experienced the crash as problems with liquidity; in Greece specifically, the crisis precipitated an economic slowdown (Lapavitsas et al. 2012). The Greek government first responded to the economic recession with a short-lived Keynesian effort to stimulate its economy through government spending. It provided a 28 billion euro package to rescue the banking sector in December 2008. But additional responses by EU institutions demonstrated Greece's limits on its domestic policymaking flexibility. In an attempt to boost liquidity and ease pressure, the ECB reduced borrowing rates and provided unlimited liquidity to Greek banks at a fixed rate in May 2009. These measures soon added to the rationale for austerity because the state intervention increased Greece's public debt (Papadopoulos & Roumpakis 2012; Pasiouras 2012).

The interpretation that Greece's recession exposed the rest of the Eurozone to harm emerged when the truth was revealed about Greece's previous representation of its economic status. Then Prime Minister George Papandreou's announcement that Greece had been falsifying its public deficit statistics since at least the mid-1990s shocked international financial markets. Greece's debt, according to the October 2009 announcement, was not the previously stated 6% of GDP. Instead, it was over twice that at 15.8% of GDP (Karagiannis & Kondeas 2012). By late 2009, media and global institutions began to fear that the financial troubles in Greece held dire implications for the wider Eurozone.

The Standard & Poor's credit rating agency reacted to the news by downgrading Greek debt in early December 2009. Other major ratings agencies, such as Fitch and Moody's, soon followed suit with their own subsequent downgrades. The EU's concern about the implications of the Greek crisis had yet to lead to suggestions of bailouts. The increasing vulnerability of Greek bonds drove further downgrades of Greek creditworthiness, which immediately increased the costs of borrowing and fueled speculative attacks. As Greek debt became more risky, capital fled, just as it previously did in Asian and Latin American nations (Lynn 2011; Manolopoulos 2011; Papadopoulos & Roumpakis 2012).

The decline of Greek government bonds, which had lost 82% of their value by 2010, joined with the flight of capital, and further drove fear of contagion. As owners of Greek debt, French and German banks were heavily exposed. The first bailout loan, argued to be in Greece's interest, ended up as "the largest loan in history of which the bulk, more than 91 percent, went to make whole the French and German bankers, by buying back from them at 100 euros bonds whose market value had declined to less than 20 euros" (Varoufakis 2016: 157). The loan was meant to avoid bankruptcy, based on the expectation that more money would follow the loan restructuring. Avoiding bankruptcy would also maintain the illusion that the crisis was due to Greece's poor economic management, with no blame assigned to either global creditors or the neoliberal model.

To add insult to injury, the bailout came with austerity conditions, to be supervised by the ECB, the European Commission (EC, the executive arm of the EU), and the IMF. The specifics of austerity became clear when, in February 2010, George Papandreou announced the details of the first of many packages that would attempt to cut the ballooning budget deficit and debt. The package especially targeted the state, limiting the hiring of public sector workers and cutting back their benefits by 10%, and their overtime pay by 30%. Additional measures included increasing VAT and the petrol tax. Greek people took to the streets in angry response to this austerity package, a sign of things to come (Lynn 2011). During April 2010, Fitch downgraded Greece's credit twice, resulting in a grade that made the country's credit rating effectively junk (Lynn 2011; Manolopoulos 2011). As a result of this increasing pressure, on April 23, 2010, the Greek Ministry of Finance sent a letter to the EC, the ECB, and the IMF, soon collectively labeled the Troika, officially requesting financial assistance. The Troika swiftly agreed to a rescue bailout package worth 110 billion euros, accompanied by a push to further austerity (Kotios & Roukanas 2013). Had the Troika policymakers bothered to examine the history of austerity in the Global South, perhaps they would have reconsidered. But austerity policy had become hegemonic by the time of the 2008 crisis.

Greek private consumption and growth declined in 2011, the former by 7.5%, and the latter by 7.1%. Debt increased, reaching

170.32% of GDP in 2011 (FIER 2012; IMF 2014). The spiral of bad news continued, with Fitch and Moody's downgrading Greek credit again in 2011. With these ratings well into junk territory, the credit agencies sent a clear signal to international financial markets that Greece's financial crisis persisted, and so too did the EU's fear of contagion.

In spring 2011, the EU designed a five-year economic strategy for Greece called the "Medium-Term Fiscal Strategy" (MTFS), to be implemented until 2015 (Directorate-General for Economic and Financial Affairs 2011). The MTFS intended to reduce the public deficit and debt, and so generate surpluses for future government budgets to address Greece's needs. The cycle of aid and austerity resumed in July 2011 when the Troika agreed to a second bailout of 130 billion euros ($173 billion). This forced Papandreou's government out; it also hurt Greek citizens, making them responsible for debt restructuring by canceling the debts the government owed to their pensions and bondholding. As before, Greek banks and Greece's foreign private creditors enjoyed priority as the new bailout money was divided among them, and used to service the first bailout loan.

The MTFS also created several institutions that increased the dependence of Greece's economy on foreign actors not only for credit, but also for direction, removing the authority of Greece's parliament over banking practices, and replacing it with the Troika. But the institution most important to austerity oversaw privatization of Greece's infrastructure, putting up for sale everything from "the nation's ports and railways to pristine beaches and small islands" (Varoufakis 2017: 46). Throughout the bailouts, the Greek state took on, as public debt, the losses and near-bankruptcy of the country's banks. The heightening of debt from both additional loans and assuming bank debt continued to force austerity with each subsequent bailout. Despite the influx of cash, the credit agencies failed to change the low credit ratings (Schoenbaum 2012).

Once again, this program relied on austerity policies as the cure for the financial crisis. But austerity exacerbated social and investment needs, as the plan sought to cut 14.32 billion euros of state spending and raise 14.09 billion euros through tax increases. Austerity policies imposed spending cuts that again hurt state workers as the Greek government was forced to shrink its budget by 15% between 2010 and 2012 (Varoufakis 2017: 34). Over the life of the plan, 20% of government employees were to be sacked, while public sector wages were intended to be cut each year. The MTFS further targeted state workers, cutting and freezing pensions, and raising the retirement age and the number of years employed before they could claim a pension. Added to other social benefit cuts such as social security funds, the punishment of Greek citizens proved too much to bear and more protests ensued.

The MTFS advocated other cuts that would make economic recovery more difficult. These ranged from slashing operational expenditures of public institutions, to further shrinking healthcare and education expenditures, as well as public sector investment. The revenue-gathering component of the MTFS also followed austerity designs, with increases in the VAT rate accompanied by other increases in tax rates, new taxes, and abolition of several tax exemptions. Finally, the MTFS additionally relied heavily on privatization. The Greek government agreed to sell a variety of public assets, including ports, airports, railways, the water supply and energy, as well as public land. Greece committed to raise 50 billion euros by 2015 through the sale of these state assets, but the privatization revenue consistently missed its goals (Petrakis 2014).

Between 2008 and 2012, austerity policies shrank Greece's economy, with a 30% drop in GDP. Unemployment tripled, with long-term unemployment reaching 14.4% (Kentikelinis et al. 2016). Nevertheless, the Greek government again passed austerity measures in July 2013, resulting in another 15,000 layoffs in the public sector, mostly among teachers and municipal workers. For three days, Greeks protested outside of parliament, to little effect (Gatopoulos & Paphitis 2013). Later, in early November 2013, the Troika and the Greek government held talks that again led to the implementation of austerity measures as a condition to receive the next bailout installment of 1 billion euros. In response, unions staged a 24-hour general strike to protest the measures. Doctors and medical staff also joined a 24-hour strike against planned health cutbacks that would eliminate at least 3,000 jobs in the medical sector (Agkyridou 2013; Becatoros 2013).

Despite popular condemnation, the Greek parliament again traded bailout monies for austerity in March 2014. Even before receiving funds, the Greek government passed a bill containing further attacks on public and private sector workers. Once again, public sector workers suffered reduced pensions, while the unemployed saw their benefits reduced. Additionally, the new measures reformed the labor code to drastically curb workers' right to strike. In response to these threats, thousands of Greek workers held a 24-hour general strike on April 10, 2014 (Ekathemerini 2014; Martin 2014; Stevens 2014).

By 2014, austerity policies had yielded both macroeconomic and household damage. With the cuts in wages, benefits, and worker security, domestic demand continued to shrink by 31.3% from 2009 to 2014, while the economy declined by an additional 3.9% in 2013 (Tzanetaki 2013; IMF 2014; Papachristou 2014). With shrinking domestic demand and growth rates, Greece continued to rely on financial support to avoid a total default. Yet that support further harmed it, as the bailout mechanisms piled even more debt on the Greek state (Weisbrot 2014).

The social costs of years of austerity have also proven substantial. Greek unemployment rose from 9.5% in 2009 to 26.5% in February 2014. The effect on youth unemployment was especially devastating, rising from 21.9% in 2009 to 58.3% in 2013 (Eurostat n.d.-d). The proportion of people at risk of poverty or social exclusion increased from 27.6% in 2009 to 36% by 2014 (Eurostat n.d.-b), while the proportion of severely materially deprived people rose from 11% in 2009 to 21.5% in 2014 (Eurostat n.d.-c). Healthcare access dropped as hospital budgets suffered extensive cuts (Marmot et al. 2013). Cutbacks to the health sector and welfare meant that "the proportion of individuals on low incomes reporting unmet medical need due to cost doubled from 7% in 2008 to 13.9% in 2013" (Karanikolos & Kentikelenis 2016). The diminished pension and services cuts also yielded a fall in life expectancy (Varoufakis 2016). Other social costs included rising suicide, homicide, and theft rates.

Credit rating agencies' downgrades perpetuated the cycle. Although Fitch finally upgraded Greek credit from B- to B in May 2014, still remaining well in junk territory, that action reflected their expectation that Greece would remain committed to austerity (Chua & Papachristou 2014). The same unwavering allegiance to austerity is what allowed Greece to return to the international bond markets in April 2014 (Alderman & Thomas 2014).

Hardships and widespread protest fed an electoral rejection of austerity. The growth of the left-leaning opposition party SYRIZA was due to its emergence as a fierce challenger to the unceasing imposition of austerity demanded by the Troika. SYRIZA's landslide victory in the January 2015 elections appeared to place Greece on an imminent collision course with the Troika and Greece's private lenders. Conflict seemed all the more likely with the elevation of Yanis Varoufakis to the Greek Ministry of Finance. Varoufakis, a well-known economist and outspoken critic, had earlier voiced his opposition to austerity in "A Modest Proposal for Resolving the Eurozone Crisis" (Varoufakis et al. 2013: 11). This proposal sought to avoid violating any existing treaty, finding alternatives to austerity within the existing European institutional infrastructure itself.

Varoufakis's debt renegotiation efforts started taking shape with SYRIZA's election when he asserted the goals of new policy must include uncoupling the state's public debt from that of private banks, relieving citizens from responsibility for loans they had neither taken on nor benefited from, and relieving state and banks from the burden of each other. He also advocated freeing banks for foreign purchase once the Greek state stopped propping them up. SYRIZA also challenged the EC, stating that repayment of debts had to wait on the recovery of the Greek economy (Varoufakis 2017).

As the possibility of another bailout without relief loomed, the SYRIZA government put it to the electorate in a citizen's referendum – with the hope that citizens would reject it. In response to its plan to consult its citizens, the Eurogroup, one of the EU's "informal" economic consultation bodies, barred Greece from further negotiations. Without further agreement to negotiate on the Troika's terms, Greece was threatened with expulsion from the Eurozone.

As the second bailout agreement ran out, banks were forced to address shrinking liquidity by limiting daily withdrawals. Party leaders initially argued that a no vote would provide the government room for further negotiations that would strengthen its hand against further austerity and the subordination of Greece's economic policy to the Troika. But as the referendum drew closer, splits within SYRIZA's leadership obscured its earlier coherent and unified message, and false messages about the dangers of leaving the Eurozone superseded the party's earlier position.

Years of hardship elicited a no vote that exceeded 60%, but the SYRIZA government decided to follow the lead of the Troika rather than resist. Even though SYRIZA was elected owing to its political and economic opposition to austerity, and its search for alternative policies had been reinforced by the referendum vote, the government chose to subject the nation once again to austerity. Against the advice of its Finance Minister, SYRIZA's Prime Minister Tsipris agreed to bailout conditions that would once again require 10 years of austerity from Greece.

By late summer 2015 and the passage of Greece's third bailout, the government's resistance to austerity seemed at an end. As a result of the accompanying austerity package, taxes increased on most of the population even while a program aimed at catching elite tax evaders was dismantled, pensions were slashed, and a new wave of privatization ensued, with the resulting revenues "to be controlled directly by the troika" (Varoufakis 2017: 478).

Further pension cuts came in 2016 and 2017, along with more privatization of utilities, railways, and airports, and another increase in VAT. In 2018, Greek lawmakers approved new actions demanded by international creditors, including cuts to benefits for large families and restrictions on trade unions, again spurring protest as 20,000 demonstrators gathered in Athens (Kitsantonis 2018). Austerity has continued to define Greece's economy.

Early in the crisis, Eurozone leaders and the credit agencies blamed the Greek state for an exorbitant public debt rather than examining a wider set of dynamics as we do. Internal economic problems certainly added to Greece's crisis, including a history of political corruption, an uncompetitive and inefficient economy combined with a bloated public sector, and an inefficient tax system (Lynn 2011; Manolopoulos 2011). This problematic history, however, did not stop EU nations from allowing Greece entry. When crisis appeared, this history was turned against the nation, and became part of the rationale for austerity.

Greece presents similarities to and differences from our other cases as it suffered through austerity. First, Greece was clearly a less economically powerful actor than its EU counterparts; this relationship was similar to Latin American nations and the United States. That weakness was hidden by Greece's false claims made to enter the EU, but the failure to investigate those claims led to risky loans, again similar to the flurry of haphazard financing of Latin American governments in the late 1960s and early 1970s. Second, like the cases we've examined after Chile, and despite Greece's post-World War II history, the nation had transformed into one of democratic norms. Third, the protest resistance to austerity led to the creation or increasing prominence of critical electoral activity, but once elected, those critics folded in the face of powerful actors pushing for austerity, just as governments did elsewhere.

Important differences help us understand how the hegemony of austerity had been forged by the time of the European crisis. The powerful actors responsible for imposing austerity differed from earlier experiences, as credit rating agencies possessed more power to define the crisis situation, and in effect protect creditors at the expense of citizens. Austerity itself was championed and pushed by a European-led Troika in which the IMF was slowly becoming a less enthusiastic partner, rather than a leader. Finally, Greece's very membership in the EU limited its policymaking flexibility, providing a new kind of dependency on powerful economies. Another difference, replicated in Spain, was the state's taking on of private debt, bailing out creditors while the very rationale for austerity increased.

The Pain in Spain

Spain's path differed from other post-World War II European nations because its priority was to recover from the anti-democratic fascist government led by Francisco Franco from 1939 until 1975. Shortly after Franco's death, a new political structure evolved, decentralizing power as political alternatives recalibrated. With these changes, Spain sought entry into the EU.

Spain's entry into the EU opened access to cheap loans, sparking higher property prices and a construction boom. Like the Greek experience, access to easy money masked some domestic economic problems in Spain, such as a dual labor market, which benefited some workers while others had access to only insecure, low-wage, and unprotected work, with less social welfare coverage than their more privileged counterparts. Those latter benefits only brought recipients to half of the poverty line, and only 20% of the unemployed qualified for unemployment benefits, although older workers and pensioners enjoyed better coverage than younger workers (Kickert & Ysa 2014: 453). Like elsewhere, Spain's entry into the Eurozone required it to reduce its public deficit, from 6% to 3%, which was done by cutting "social public expenditures rather than by increasing taxes. ... The popular classes were the ones who paid, by the weakening of their welfare state, the entrance costs into the Eurozone" (Navarro 2013: 190). The government's subsequent response to strong growth was to continue to reduce taxes, especially corporate taxes, making the economy more vulnerable when the housing bubble burst. But until the Great Recession, Spain was seen as a powerful economic actor; its economic growth from 1997 to 2007 often outpaced that of other member nations, with deficit and debt well under the levels prescribed by the EU.

Unlike elsewhere in Europe, rather than the bank crisis causing a general economic crisis, it was the bursting of the housing bubble that hurt Spanish banks that were overinvested in property and construction (Kickert & Ysa 2014; Della Porta et al. 2017). The size of Spain's economy may have sheltered it a bit more than Greece's, providing it more leverage than Greece in negotiations regarding austerity. "Italy and Spain ... were seen as too large to bail out, while default by either would spell the end of the Euro" (Perez & Matsaganis 2018: 194). But, as we will see, Spain's economic power did not save it from austerity and hardships.

After the fall of Lehman Brothers in September 2008, things went downhill quickly. The Spanish stock market fell, and the banking sector collapsed. Spanish banks differed from other European counterparts as they "were primarily meant to support and stimulate regional economic development and ... had an explicit social task of funding regional social and cultural projects. ... Commercial profitmaking was not the only or primary task of these public bodies" (Kickert & Ysa 2014: 454). The Spanish government responded to bank failure with a 71 billion euro bank guarantee, and created a stimulus package offering funds to local governments, prioritizing small infrastructure spending with the intention of providing employment, and even putting a small amount of money in taxpayers' hands through a refund. The stimulus helped 410,000 remain employed, but only temporarily (Conde-Ruiz & Marín 2013; Kickert & Ysa 2014). Unemployment soon increased, as did mortgage defaults.

These initial bows to Keynesian strategies were swiftly overshadowed as austerity was imposed. The Socialist Workers' Party-led government of Prime Minister José Luis Rodríguez Zapatero found itself unable to resist credit rating agencies' and German Chancellor Angela Merkel's reactions to high budget deficits. Germany forced Spain to prioritize its creditors in part because its banks' exposure to Spanish debt, at $146 billion, was greater than any other country (Chorafas 2013: 152).

In 2010, Prime Minister Zapatero cut 15 billion euros of state expenditures, much of it targeting public workers, reducing their wages, laying off civil servants, and freezing pensions. Zapatero's government also raised the retirement age despite promises not to do so. In addition, it passed a Labor Bill against the objections of organized labor, which led to a general strike at the end of September 2010. But accommodating factions within the labor movement soon agreed to the increase in age when workers would receive pensions. Although this package took some by surprise, Zapatero later revealed the heavy hand of European powers in the decision: "Chancellor Merkel wrote a confidential letter to him saying that if he wanted to keep counting on European support he had to improve Spain's fiscal credibility with harsh fiscal austerity" (Kickert & Ysa 2014: 456). Zapatero's government also ushered in reforms to the constitutional guarantees to labor, on which we focus more below.

By December 2011, Spain's unemployment was among the highest in the EU at 23%, but this did not soften the push to austerity. The EU expected that Spain would further cut its budget by 50 billion euros by 2013 (Salmon 2017). A 2011 constitutional reform, pushed by the EU and the IMF, eliminated state and regional budget deficit flexibility; further cuts "included increased duty on tobacco, … subsidies on renewable energy, and the partial privatization of the airports group Aena and the National Lottery" (Salmon 2017: 242).

The right-wing People's Party replaced the Socialists in 2012. Mariano Rajoy pledged not to continue austerity and quickly betrayed the Spanish people: only 11 days after promising otherwise, the new Prime Minister announced new taxes on income, savings, and property. The government moved quickly to diminish protections on job security for workers, and increased firm power over wages and collective bargaining. Rajoy's People's Party government followed with cuts in health and education spending and other harmful measures: mortgage relief was included in the 2011 package, but revoked in 2012 (Kickert & Ysa 2014; Salmon 2017).

By the fall of 2012, Standard & Poor's had downgraded Spain's bond ratings to close to junk status. The credit raters responded to the unmet goals of deficit cutting, and ushered in further austerity measures. Unemployment had risen to 25%, the economy was continuing to contract, and citizens took to the streets in protest (*The Economist* 2012). Spain's government responded to the downgrading of Spanish banks and debt by asking for European aid. The entry of the Troika brought further bailout of the Spanish banks with a 100 million euro loan. The loan also meant the elevation of the Troika in its role in the Spanish economy, as it made the transition to monitoring and controlling the banks in addition to demanding conditions for its loans.

The way the government was forced to take on public debt was especially harmful to homeowners. In 2012, the Troika mandated the creation of the SAREB (La Sociedad de Gestión de Activos Procedentes de la Reestructuración Bancaria, or Bank Restructuring Asset Management Society) as part of the third bailout of Spanish banks. SAREB covered the mortgage assets that became unpayable. Funded by taxpayer money both through direct state investment and investment by nationalized banks, SAREB was another way that foreign creditor banks could be protected from mortgage failures while the state and taxpayers were instead made responsible. As a result of the new policy, "there were between 2008 and 2015 at least 500,000 evictions, out of which at least 250,000 are the result of mortgage repossessions" (Berglund 2018: 807) even though 3.4 million homes already stood vacant. Obviously, the high rate of evictions became a burden that was mainly borne by homeowners, owing to Spanish bankruptcy laws that protected creditors (Berglund 2018: 807). SAREB further served to export Spanish assets as it only sold to large investors like the Blackstone fund. As global capital gained ownership over more Spanish real estate, including housing, the longer-term political control of housing policy also accrued to these global actors.

The Rajoy government's other austerity measures were consistent with efforts elsewhere. They increased VAT even while reducing corporate taxes. Public workers suffered wage cuts, hiring freezes were imposed, and hours extended. Education and health cuts followed, including an increase in pharmaceutical costs to citizens (Conde-Ruiz & Marín 2013)

Its relative economic size did not spare Spain pain, nor did the fact that economic growth returned in 2013. Instead, "Spain was one of the worst hit countries during the Great Recession, having lost about 15% of its gross domestic product … between 2008 and 2013" (Ramiro & Gomez 2017: 110). Additional costs included the rise of unemployment to 27% by 2013, second only to Greece in the EU. The increase of youth unemployment to 55% was especially painful and drove much subsequent social movement action. Inequality also rose, with an income loss to the bottom decile of households of 34% from 2007 to 2014. Median income also fell by 11% during that time (Matsaganis & Leventi 2014; Perez & Matsaganis 2018).

Public investment and education spending fell as well, the former by 58%, and the latter by 19%. The character of poverty, moreover, changed with the housing evictions with the "new poor … considerably poorer than the old poor had been … includ[ing] significantly more unemployed workers … and significantly fewer pensioners" (Perez & Matsaganis 2018: 197). Child malnutrition also rose in 2013 owing to austerity, and national charitable foundations categorized "21.8% of the population as living in 'relative poverty' (defined as earning less than the average costs of living), and 6.4% as experiencing 'severe poverty'" (Barbero 2015: 271; see also García Rada 2013). By 2016, 30% of all Spanish children were poor, the second highest in the European Union (Verde-Diego et al. 2018).

In 2015, Spain's GDP was still "5% lower than in 2008, and ha[d] recovered only 30% of the jobs lost during the crisis. After reaching a peak of 27% in 2013, the unemployment rate was still 21% in the fourth quarter of 2015" (Uxó & Álvarez 2017: 1002). By 2017, observers were assessing Spain's austerity decade as a period of "lost growth," characterized by an "explosion of public debt ... from 36% of GDP in 2007 to 98% of GDP in 2018 ... [and] a loss of 3.7 million jobs ... [leaving] 20.8 million unemployed" (Salmon 2017: 253–4). As austerity in Spain reached its 10-year mark, the nation had become one of the most unequal countries in the EU (Miley 2017: 264, 265).

Indeed, the toll of austerity would have been calculated as even worse if out-migration numbers were taken into account, as well as the significant shift to part-time work and the subsequent costs not only of lower wages, but also of less job-related social protection of workers (Black 2014). Finally, the effects on Spain's health have been long-lasting. For example, cuts to the healthcare system included increased waiting times for elective surgery, significantly decreased access to most medical care for undocumented migrants, and increased out-of-pocket spending for all (*The Lancet* 2018).

The pain did not go unnoticed by external powers as both the IMF and the Organisation for Economic Co-operation and Development (OECD) acknowledged the unexpectedly high costs of austerity (Perez & Matsaganis 2018). The additional intrusion into constitutional guarantees also bore significant costs in reduction of wages and workers' hours. As important, the new workforce legislation increased the power of capital in collective bargaining, and in ability to outsource.

Several elements of Spain's experience with austerity are similar to Greece's. First is the important role played by external actors. The credit rating agencies' downgrades increased the interest rates on Spanish debt, further providing impetus for the EU's demand for austerity. The accompaniment by intrusions into constitutional guarantees on worker protection further cemented the importance of the new austerians: the EU, of course, but also the credit rating agencies, who played an increasingly important role in Asian and European austerity experiences compared to the Latin American cases. The think tanks and US-educated economists so important to the US and Latin American experiences of austerity were unnecessary in the Spanish and Greek cases. Even the IMF increasingly questioned the propriety of austerity. The new champions were the EU institutions and the core EU states, especially Germany.

Also similar across Europe and Latin America was the way opposition to austerity led first to social movement opposition and then to new partisan alternatives.[2] General strikes in Spain in 2010 and 2011 responded to the labor market reforms, attacks on public workers, and pension reforms (Salmon 2017). Massive protests broke out in May 2011 in response to austerity, and the *indignados*, or M-15 (May 15), movement occupied public spaces across the country. Soon this movement was voicing the anger of youth in the face of their dramatically high unemployment numbers. Radical trade unions increasingly collaborated and coalesced with anti-austerity movements from 2012 on. The heterogeneity of protestors, in which older pensioners, middle-aged homeowners, and unemployed youth all participated, demonstrated the wide assault of austerity on Spanish society. In 2014, Podemos, a new radical left anti-austerity opposition party, emerged to challenge not only austerity, but also what was seen as lackluster opposition by the established leftist Izquierda Unida (Ramiro & Gomez 2017; Della Porta et al. 2017). Podemos "aimed at translating the electoral arena to the demands of anti-austerity forces, and, in particular, of the 15M movement" (Díaz-Parra et al. 2018: 83). The elections of 2015 and 2016 showed the growing power of a coalition of leftist parties, including Podemos, who become the third biggest electoral power.

As noted above, the political opposition austerity generated in Spain is similar to experiences elsewhere in Europe, and of course to many Latin American nations. However, two components stand out as distinct in the Spanish experience. The first is the link to the housing bubble. It's important to recognize that financialization pushed speculation in housing construction, which subsequently fed the construction boom. State policies supported this speculation: "[I]n 2005 Spain began the construction of 800,000 buildings, bypassing the rates in France, Germany and the UK altogether – countries not only with larger populations than Spain, but also with significantly higher incomes" (Díaz-Parra et al. 2018: 71). The push to take on mortgage debt further nurtured the boom. But these policies made Spanish citizens even more vulnerable when the construction/housing bubble burst. To repeat, however, this was a failing of private capital, which in turn influenced the Spanish state. The push to austerity accelerated because the government took on the responsibility of the private housing-linked debt. Revenues of local governments also fell owing to falling property taxes, which meant that locales were further pressured in their ability to deal with social needs. Additionally, because so much of Spain's economic life was tied to the housing bubble, overall economic activity slowed.

This component of austerity also influenced the political response. When the housing bubble burst, evictions skyrocketed, creating a certain character to the political resistance not found elsewhere, or at least not to the degree it was in Spain. The Plataforma de

Afectados por la Hipoteca (PAH, Platform for the Mortgage-Affected) emerged, working both inside and outside the traditional political system to push the cause of those harmed by evictions, and advocating for change in housing and debt legislation. The strategies of the evicted include squatting, chaining themselves to their properties, and occupying bank offices, all aimed at forcing their grievances into public view. The movement also used "name and shame"-type protests against those profiting from evictions, especially contrasting the citizen harm caused by the evictions to the rescue of rich creditors in the bank bailouts. In addition, PAH created a Citizens' Legislative Initiative, which called for "immediate suspension of evictions; the conversion of mortgages into social rent; and a number of other measures that would ensure decent housing for people who have been evicted" (Barbero 2015: 275). The movement found some success when the rights of those evicted in Spain were supported by the Court of Justice of the EU and the European Court of Human Rights.

The second distinct characteristic of austerity in Spain is how deeply and immediately linked it was to attacks on labor protections. We have seen how attacks on labor have accompanied austerity in the past, but the pace and breadth of the attack seemed particularly fierce in Spain. In 2011, the Socialist government pushed through constitutional reforms that weakened workers. With the election of the conservative People's Party, the attack went further. In 2012, a new employment law "enabled employers to introduce 'internal flexibility' without the need for trade union or works council consent; created a new form of employment contract, [allowing] 1 year's probation without employment security; reduced compensation for dismissals; increased the priority of a company over multi-employer agreements; and enabled employers in certain cases to reduce wages without union consent" (Fernández Rodríguez et al. 2016: 271). Additionally, the requirement of "advance notices for economic dismissals were shortened and the use of special 'employment-promotion' open-ended contracts with lower severance pay, easier dismissal proceedings (so-called 'express dismissals') and lower compensation for unfair dismissals was facilitated" (Picot & Tassinari 2017: 470). The overall effect of these reforms has been to increase employers' power by diminishing those protected by collective bargaining agreements, increasing the proportion of the working poor, reducing conditions of work, and generally making workers more vulnerable (Fernández Rodríguez et. al. 2016; Picot & Tassinari 2017). Additional changes in the Spanish welfare system during austerity compounded the harm to working people, including: "reductions to pension arrangements; the implementation of measures aimed at curtailing health expenditure, including long-term care; unemployment benefit reductions; and changes to child benefits" (Ornellas et al. 2017).

United Kingdom: Early and Repeated Austerity

> It is now very clear that austerity does not promote growth or reduce deficits – it is bad economics, but good class politics. ... It is not an exaggeration to call it economic murder.
>
> (King, quoted in Matthews-King 2017)

In many ways the modern use of austerity was born in Britain following the decimation of World War II. Facing both infrastructural rebuilding needs and a financial crisis in 1947, the postwar Labour and Conservative governments simultaneously attempted nationalization and austerity programs in the hopes of stabilizing the pound and expanding the postwar economy. The government prioritized producing domestic goods for export, reducing local availability and raising prices, while devaluing the currency, resulting in rising prices and product scarcity. This so-called "Age of Austerity" resembled contemporary efforts in that it was state-designed and intended to achieve macroeconomic goals despite the cost of broad social hardships.

These austerity measures remained in place until 1954, when rebuilt infrastructure and production increases throughout Europe began to fuel large-scale economic recovery and growth (Frieden 2006). As recovery took hold, Britain expanded in the same Keynesian-embedded liberal economic strategies as much of the rest of the advanced capitalist world. These state-led approaches were facilitated by the nationalization initiatives undertaken in the immediate postwar period alongside the establishment of the British welfare state. The construction of social welfare programs in 1946 (health and unemployment insurance) and 1948 (subsistence assistance through the National Assistance program) alongside deep austerity measures seems counterintuitive, but was necessary due to the adverse effects of the austerity measures themselves. In essence, austerity created the explicit need for the expansion of the British welfare state.

Wealthy class interests reacted to the expansion of social spending within Britain just as they did in the United States (e.g., Harvey 2005).

The desire to wrest control of economic policy decisions back from the state popularized the emerging "neo-classical" economic ideologies. Academics and policymakers championed the autonomy of market mechanisms from state control, save for central management and control over the supply of money in a respective economy (i.e., Milton Friedman's monetarism). These ideological platforms soon coalesced into a collective policy platform that would inform neoliberalism. In the United Kingdom, this ideological platform would come to transform government and society.

The British system of public service provision continued to define social life into the 1970s. The change came with the energy crisis of the 1970s, which was accompanied by ongoing decline in mining and manufacturing sectors, and subsequent wage stagnation, all of which enabled neoliberal supporters of Margaret Thatcher's Conservatives in 1979 to win power. Thatcher's liberalization initiatives, consistent with austerity policies, aimed at macroeconomic growth and privileging financial capital. These policies were matched by a renewed hostility to labor unions (as demonstrated in the failed 1984 Miners' Strike), privatization of public assets such as British Airways and British Petroleum (often at below market value such as the case with the Royal Mail), and eventual decreases in tax rates for corporate and high-income earners. The tax decreases were again consistent with austerity-based approaches to growth: decreased revenues from income taxation were replaced by regressive increases in VAT and the controversial Community Charge or "Poll Tax," whereby a single flat-rate tax was levied on every adult (O'Hara 2015). Thus, not only was financial capital privileged, but so also were affluent citizens.

The articulated goal of Thatcherism was to minimize the authority and control of the British state over economic and social matters. Deregulating capital was meant to foster innovation and increase profit, while opening privatization opportunities were designed to promote the marketization of state services. Private individuals and corporate investors increased their profits simply because of the opening of new market opportunities. However, the Thatcher government did not achieve all of its promised spending cuts when unemployment increased as a result of substantial privatization and public sector reorganization.[3] But increases in private ownership drove a push for greater efficiency, which further contributed to a significant increase in the number of British citizens joining the ranks of the unemployed. These policies had long-lasting effects: British unemployment peaked at around 8.5% in late 2011 as a result of significant public employment reduction before gradually decreasing after 2014. The changes in tax policy also facilitated capital growth by quickly allowing the same private capital interests to transform tax revenues into investible capital. The British state was able to maintain spending levels through the shift to consumption and flat-rate taxation through the Poll Tax. Clearly, the burden of austerity was to be borne by those not likely to have disposable investment capital.

The resignation of Margaret Thatcher and her replacement by John Major in 1990 did little to change broad-scale neoliberalization in Britain, but austerity measures associated with taxation were reduced. The Poll Tax, in particular, proved so unpopular that it was eliminated in 1993 and replaced with the Council Tax, which returned to a more progressive tax valuation based on property value. The Conservative Party eventually lost its majority in 1997 with the election of Tony Blair's Labour Party. The UK's neoliberal trajectory was by this time firmly established. In fact, one could look at Blair's "Third Way"[4] as a necessary legitimation strategy to maintain the unpopular neoliberal project. The very promotion of Third Way politics was a means of deepening neoliberal reforms through rhetorical shifts that maintained the ethos of market fundamentalism while appearing to remain sensitive to the adversities experienced by citizens. The same phenomenon occurred throughout the advanced capitalist world, perhaps most strikingly in the United States as the Clinton administration undertook the most extensive dismantling of American social welfare with its TANF reforms in 1996 (Abramovitz 2006; see also chapter 5 in this volume).

The implementation of Third Way politics is another step in the creeping hegemony of austerity politics. The United Kingdom's embrace of neoliberal ideology, regardless of political party or traditional constituency, remained firm despite demand for political redress of the hardships such policies had caused. The UK government not only implemented policies during the 1990s that shifted it away from the protectionism inherent in traditional labor/social democratic platforms, but also ushered in the reality of permanent austerity with spending and revenue restrictions now common and rationalized in the name of "fiscal responsibility." Underlying these shifts was the structural reality of a growing dependency on debt and financial institutional control over access to debt-borne capital. Streeck (2014) explains this shift in state revenue generation as one from a "tax state to a debt state," in which governments decrease tax revenues while increasing borrowing as a means to maintain requisite state institutional operation. Thus, another irony (of many) inherent in austerity is the vilification of debt simultaneous with policies expanding dependence on debt as a means of state funding. UK government debt increased from 41.9% of GDP in 2007 to 88.3% of GDP in 2016 in part because of taxation policies (Eurostat n.d.-a).

The political and structural shift to conditions of permanent austerity in the United Kingdom coupled with increased reliance on financial sector pacification set the stage for the government's response to the 2008 bursting of the real estate price bubble. The (re-) emergence of crisis conditions prompted Gordon Brown's Labour government to return to austerity by conceding an inability to punish "irresponsible" behavior on the part of the financial industry. Then Chancellor of the Exchequer Alistair Darling undertook a substantial initiative of banking bailouts funded by tax increases and spending restrictions designed to "show the City and foreign investors that Britain had a clear plan to restore prudence to the public finances" (Giles & Parker 2008). Once again, market liberalization contributed to crisis, and provided ample opportunity for policymakers to turn to austerity, which then exacerbated upward capital redistribution.

A succession of bank failures in 2007 preceded the collapse of the UK housing market. These failures quickly led to a panicked realization that careless investment and overextended lending would lead to substantial defaults. The run on Northern Rock in 2007 was the first in a steady stream of financial strains that eventually contributed to the resurgence of the Conservatives, who ironically campaigned in 2009/10 on a promise of protecting British citizens from creeping Labour Party austerity. But once the Conservative Party regained power, Britain would experience some of the deepest austerity reforms in the advanced capitalist world. In June 2010, Prime Minister David Cameron and Chancellor George Osborne inaugurated an austerity program intended to balance deficit spending budgets through public spending reductions and reduce the overall state debt burden.

The 2010 austerity budget coupled substantial cuts to social service spending with increases in both progressive (capital gains) and regressive (VAT) taxation (Hay 2010). The program froze both public sector salaries and family benefits; Cameron boasted that further spending reductions would achieve a £14.3 billion cut in the public sector (Merrick 2017). The impacts were both immediate and broad, impacting nearly every aspect of British social life. Despite claims that healthcare and education spending had been "ringfenced" (or protected from austerity spending reductions), both sectors experienced reductions in funding either directly (Karanikolos et al. 2013) or indirectly as a result of devolved funding strategies and operational responsibilities (Lowndes & Gardner 2016), which then contributed to declines in quality of service. This kind of devolution, under the rationale that local governmental authorities are better able to utilize resources in ways that benefit local communities, was by then common in both Latin America and Africa.

These decreases in care, whether the result of funding decreases or constraints on delivery, are more dramatic once economic inequality – itself a product of austerity – is taken into account. Significant disparities in UK health have grown since 2010 in terms of both physical (Barr & Taylor-Robinson 2016; Loopstra et al. 2016; Hiam et al. 2017) and mental healthcare (Barr et al. 2015), and have been blamed for declining life expectancy. Austerity's contribution to inequality has added to other harm to individual and group health (Cervero-Liceras et al. 2015; Ifanti et al. 2013; Reeves et al. 2014).

Similarly, funding for UK education is also being restricted and educational opportunities are being limited. Even in instances of limited or no reductions in spending in supposedly protected sectors, cost increases outpace annual budgets, which creates pressures to reduce services (Lawrence & Andrews 2018). UK public education budgets were projected to decrease by 4.6% between 2015 and 2020 (*The Guardian* 2018). Policymakers have protected some higher education sectors such as mathematics and science, but even this protection left institutions responsible for finding areas where they could cut costs, such as the £150 million reduction demanded in 2015 (Morgan 2015).

A consistent outcome of austerity policies is the exacerbation of income and wealth inequality, which often manifests in housing policy. Britain faced both rising prices and reductions in housing subsidies. The former is a cumulative effect of long-term market liberalization. As in Spain, market growth resulting from increased financial capital investment by wealthy buyers enjoying expanded lending opportunities, particularly in urban and high-end markets, drove substantial increases in housing costs. These increases imposed hardships on lower-income renters and first-time homebuyers (Smith 2002).

Austerity added to the impact of market forces by decreasing available resources to help fund housing in the inflated market. After 2010, British policymakers cut publicly funded affordable housing initiatives while increasing taxation based on unused rooms in public housing units. The so-called "Bedroom Tax" was designed to increase revenue through a direct cut in a "subsidy," but ended up increasing the rental costs for those living in public housing (Gibb 2015; Moffatt et al. 2015).

Austerity imposition from 2010 to the present has imposed distinct hardships on the majority of Britons, while simultaneously facilitating the upward distribution of wealth. Neither deficit nor debt reduction goals ever achieved their promised ends despite dramatic reductions in service delivery and public spending (Reeves et al. 2013). Perversely, the decline of public sector employment, sustained wage stagnation, and rising cost burdens made subsidization and state assistance *more* necessary, while at the same time eviscerating state capacities to meet constituent material demands. Indeed, austerity policies have not achieved growth levels that differ from non-austerity periods (Armingeon & Baccaro 2012; Blyth 2013; Lehndorf 2013; Rosenow & Eyre 2016), and in the case of the United Kingdom they have actually depressed growth (Hay 2013).

Anti-austerity campaigns responded to these policies throughout the country. Beginning in 2010, massive protests in London (estimated at half a million in March 2011) directly responded to spending cuts and tuition increases at British universities. Successive strike actions occurred on a national scale. Several formal organizations emerged out of the actions, such as the People's Assembly Against Austerity, mobilizing many popular actions and garnering support from opposition politicians including the Labour Party's Ed Miliband and Jeremy Corbyn. Despite broad popular disapproval, minority governments sustained austerity policies, maintaining the central message that austerity continued to be a necessity. Eventually, the British government began to run budget surpluses and see some debt reductions. However, its adherence to austerity has not resulted in increased economic growth, wage increases, or cost stabilization.

Devolution, a central strategy of neoliberalization, posed significant challenges to universal austerity imposition in Britain. As operational authority and budgetary responsibilities shifted, pressures on local governments increased (Gordon & Whitty 1997; Murtaugh & Shirlow 2012). Devolution also created distinct opportunities for local policy adaptation and change that at times ran counter to dominant federal neoliberal or austerity proscriptions (Scott & Mooney 2009).

For example, devolution created opportunities to deviate from central (primarily English) policies and develop alternative systems of care and delivery, even while remaining tied directly to central government funding and formulaic distribution (Connolly et al. 2010). Devolving authority to Northern Ireland, Scotland, and Wales provided opportunities for their respective parliamentary bodies to determine the manner and form of central government grants in areas such as social services, healthcare, and education. In the case of Scotland, for instance, successive rounds of austerity on the part of the central UK government resulted in direct funding reductions (approximately 12.5%), which then translated into reduced service delivery on the part of Scottish authorities (UNISON Scotland 2016: 12).

These budgetary restrictions impacted Scotland the same way as everywhere else austerity has been implemented: the more economically vulnerable the population, the more drastic the adverse effect. Since 2010, increases in both poverty and overall economic inequality in Scotland have increased demand for public services simultaneous with recurring budget cuts, as the current Conservative government seeks to deepen austerity measures already in place. As one Scottish government official noted in response to the recent rise in local poverty, "We know that in the face of UK Government cuts and continuing austerity, which are having a damaging impact on thousands of Scottish households, our actions mean we are fighting poverty with one hand tied behind our back" (Macnab 2018).

Similarly, Wales's ability to meet social service demands, fund education and healthcare, as well as finance initiatives to address other needs such as affordable housing, are all negatively impacted by austerity cuts, as funding sources are reduced (Drakeford 2012). As material conditions in Wales continued to mirror those elsewhere in the United Kingdom, the downward pressures led the Welsh Finance Minister to demand the end of central austerity in 2017. In response, UK government ministers suggested that devolved tax authority could be a way forward for local governments unhappy with austerity cuts (BBC 2017). In effect, the devolution of operational authority also becomes an attempt to defer political responsibility through the encouragement of additional taxation on already struggling constituencies in Scotland and Wales.

In contrast, the role of devolution in Northern Ireland allowed the local government to resist cuts in social service provision. The Northern Ireland government elected to refuse funding cuts to social service provision, citing the explicit need to maintain such spending in one of the United Kingdom's most unequal and impoverished regions (Horgan 2006; McEwen & Parry 2008; Murtaugh & Shirlow 2012). In response, the central government introduced a series of fines to both create long-term political pressure on the devolved government and recoup short-term financial gains expected as a result of spending cuts (Mac Flynn 2015).

The political response emerging from an era of austerity has taken a decidedly reactionary turn. The Scottish National Party (SNP) began to push a strong anti-austerity platform and quickly saw its electoral support rise considerably (Glencross 2015). The broad unpopularity of sustained austerity gave the SNP enough confidence to hold a referendum on Scottish independence in 2014, which it lost by just 11 percentage points. The imposition of austerity on Scotland provided the SNP with a means to argue that independence was an avenue to end the imposed policy restrictions – in fact, the broad acceptance of austerity by other major British political parties (including Labour) left the SNP as the sole anti-austerity proponent in Scotland (BBC 2014). Sovereignty, it was argued, was the only way to escape the external imposition of austerity and conditions detrimental to the economic and social health of Scotland.

The irony of the Scottish independence referendum was that while it was broadly opposed outside of Scotland, the same logic permeated the drive to remove Britain from the EU. The successful Brexit vote in 2016 was driven by several nationalist initiatives, including anti-immigration rhetoric voiced by the far-right British National Party, but the impact of austerity policies on vulnerable Britons also played a decisive role (Gietel-Basten 2016; Jessop 2017). It is important to note the link between the reaction to austerity effects and the desire to escape the political conditions/constraints that reduce local capacities to resist austerity imposition. While the general downward pressures of neoliberalization have encouraged constituencies to seek culturalist/nationalist alternatives to global market capitalism (Blad 2015; Habermas 2001; Yúdice 2003), austerity has exacerbated those tendencies and opened up political opportunities for formerly marginal political actors. This violent reaction against conventional political practices amid the broad acceptance of austerity by traditional political parties has led to the rise of more than just individual political parties such as the UK Independence Party (UKIP), it has pushed hardship-ridden communities to seek ideological alternatives to the poverty of the status quo.

Austerity among the (Relatively) Wealthy

Our European cases help trace the continuities and differences in global austerity. As we have throughout, we focus in this chapter on issues of national power and the sources by which austerity came to be imposed, tracing the way it became hegemonic, the hardships populations endured, and the resistance those hardships generated.

The cases in this chapter differ from others in this book, with the exception of the United States, in that they are relatively wealthy nations. Although not matching the wealthiest of nations such as Australia, Iceland, and Ireland, all of these nations enjoyed dramatically greater wealth than the Latin American, Asian, and African nations we've examined. Each of them also entered austerity with a history of political democracy, although Spain's and Greece's democratic tradition was much shorter than that of the United Kingdom. In short, it is clear, as it is in the United States, that neither wealth nor democratic governance provides a bulwark against austerity. All of the countries in question were ushered into austerity via crisis, although those crises differed from other cases we examine.

As we mentioned in the introductory chapter, the European critique of Great Recession-driven austerity neglected the recognition of the long history of those policies within the Global South. This neglect may be in part due to the different origins of European and Global South experiences; austerity in the latter cases was driven by existing public debt while austerity in the former cases – with the partial exception of the United Kingdom – was driven by the Great Recession and how states were forced to take on the responsibility for private debt. But the analytic neglect is also a symptom of power: the unwillingness to address European austerity within a global trajectory may reflect the different rankings of state economic and political capacities. How can we think through the similarity of experiences in nations of such widely varying economic and political power?

All of our European cases are instructive in this way. The global power of the United Kingdom did not shield it from becoming an early adopter of austerity policies similar to those across the developing world nor later in response to the Great Recession. Greece's and Spain's respective backgrounds are in some ways more similar to the Global South cases we've addressed, because despite their long histories and relative power, they are considered peripheral nations in comparison to the EU's core nations. Greece's similarity to Latin American indebted nations is even more striking. Global creditors were left blameless despite their problematic loan decisions during Greece's entry into the EU, not unlike the way risky loans were honored across Latin America. As peripheral nations, they were forced to accommodate the demands of the EU, its core powers, and less directly the credit rating agencies, just as Mexico and other nations were forced to yield to similar demands of the IMF and the United States. Again we see how austerity has touched nations across the globe despite their relative positions of power.

But just as the crises by which austerity was introduced differed across the Global North and South, so too were the powers enforcing it. The credit agencies were much more important as signaling institutions in the North, as the waves of financialization and globalization have made these institutions increasingly important to global investors. In addition, despite their consistent participation as members of the Troika, the role of the IMF in the European cases differed from its previous roles, at times seeming to be a reluctant partner. The IMF's unwillingness to endorse some of the policy of the Troika (Varoufakis 2017) in what would become the third Greek bailout, and its diverging positions from the German government, demonstrate that although austerity was hegemonic in influence, the participation of more and different actors may have opened cracks in the policymakers' unity.

Cracks in that unity, however, provide even more evidence to our argument that austerity has become hegemonic policy. Even with the occasional unease of the IMF, formerly one of the greatest champions of austerity, these nations and the EU failed to genuinely entertain any other alternative for anything but a limited time. National governments that took office as explicit critics of austerity soon reversed their stances. Indeed, austerity was imposed even against the rules of imposing organizations. Varoufakis (2017) reminds us that EU rules against financing of public debt were broken during Greece's second bailout. Finally, the very participation by new actors in the imposition of austerity, even taking over the lead among the Troika, demonstrates the hegemonic place of austerity policies as the answer to all crises. The ideologues so necessary in Latin America and the United States became less important as austerity gained hegemonic status and the credit raters grew more powerful. Certainly, Europe has a long history of intellectuals driving neoliberalism, such as those in the Mont Pelerin Society. But the intellectual energy of this group had moved to the United States, and the very point of the EU was to lift up nations and citizens across Europe to diminish the chances of conflict. Given this context, how was austerity so readily adopted in all three cases, and so quickly in Greece and Spain?

The answer lies in the root of the "debt crisis" often cited as the primary reason for austerity implementation. As neoliberal states gradually (or quickly) withdrew from tax (i.e., public) revenue generation, their increased dependency on private capital (i.e., debt) allowed politicians to claim tax reduction victories while maintaining the relative fiscal health of the state. This rhetorical victory came at the cost of significant shifts in funding priorities. This structural reality means that debt reduction and debt management became increasingly dictated by creditor institutions, and, in Greece and Spain, by more powerful nations. Indeed, credit rating agencies such as Moody's have played an increasingly influential role in governmental economic policy decisions. Austerity, of course, is desirable to financial institutions because it facilitates investment opportunities through privatization and investible wealth accumulation. The increased power of financial sectors drives austerity owing to its ability to generate short-term capital growth, while ignoring the long-term costs that are leveled on non-investors. These costs drove political opposition in the streets and governing bodies across Europe.

The similarity of protest responses, common across the South and North alike, reminds us of the global character of the political impacts generated by austerity. Even national governments whose ideological character and expressed opposition caved in to austerity demands, as was the case in nations like Mexico, Ecuador, and others in Latin America. Anti-austerity movements in Greece and Spain, not to mention Italy, spurred the creation of new partisan options, which demonstrated significant electoral power within very short periods. Austerity came to define not only the economics of Europe, but its politics as well.

7

Why Austerity Persists

Why has austerity persisted across the globe over the past 45 years? In the preceding chapters, we've explored how austerity has been imposed in rich nations and poor, in democratic nations and authoritarian ones, and by external powers and a combination of external and internal elites. We've examined cases where repressive force was important, and where austerity emerged more slowly, linked to changing political economies. We've seen how austerity both facilitates and is facilitated by other neoliberal policies and trends. We presented cases in which ideologues have been crucial, and demonstrated how austerity has become a hegemonic policy with policymakers exploring few alternatives, especially in response to economic crisis. The hegemony of austerity has been contested by both social movements and governments, but it has persisted despite its limited beneficiaries in contrast to previous moments of capitalism. Below we highlight some of our findings, first more broadly and then by region. We then further unpack the persistence of austerity. We conclude with some suggestions that may dislodge austerity's hegemonic position.

There is a clear trajectory between the components and results of austerity across time and place. Greece and Spain were confronted with the inevitability of neoliberalism and austerity in large part because Chile, and later other nations, first suffered through austerity. The results of austerity, from growing inequality to shrinking social services and diminished labor rights, were broadly similar. But the political conditions under which earlier and later austerity have been imposed differ significantly. Chile suffered austerity at the point of a bayonet, and many people died in order for the experiment of neoliberalism to proceed. The social movement history across cases also differed: the Chilean junta violently squelched opposition and demobilized the citizens as much as they could, while in other cases austerity generated social movement and partisan opposition. Over the intervening years, despite its failure to generate equitable economic growth, the imposition of austerity has been decreasingly accompanied by the overt use of violence. Instead, austerity became characterized by the structural violence of steady economic pain for majorities of each nation's citizens. The more overt violence suffered at times in the Global South paved the way for its imposition in seemingly more democratic ways.

Our case studies demonstrate the consistency of the kinds of policies that have comprised austerity. These include wage cuts and freezes, especially for public sector workers; imposition of new taxes, usually regressive; slashing of social welfare spending; and privatization of national assets. The consistent result is the growing immiseration of most of the public, accompanied by the growth of inequality with the top incomes rising while middle and lower incomes stagnate or fall.

Another consistent outcome has been the political changes that austerity has generated. Sovereignty over economic decision-making was transferred to different externally powerful actors: the IMF and the United States played a key role in much of the Global South, while the EU as an institution, and singularly powerful nations within that body, became more important for European nations. Over time, credit rating agencies also became increasingly important as signals of the preferences of global capital. The predominance of external power in many cases was supplemented by true-believing neoliberal policymakers and others in positions that could influence policy. The dependence on external power for economic guidance coincides with an increased reliance on private global financial capital for state revenues in an era of tax reductions for the wealthy amid sustained spending demands from the poor and middle class. This contradiction of austerity is increasingly evident as claims of a need to reduce debt through spending cuts conflict with vested financial interests eager to increase profits on the back of increased government lending. Debt reduction claims of austerity proponents ring hollow in this environment and will continue to do so as managing debt remains such a profitable enterprise.

Cracks in the unity around austerity occasionally appeared, as the IMF seemed more reluctant to bring harsh austerity to bear than other Troika actors in the European experiences. Indeed, the

IMF even suggested stimulus packages in the early years of the Great Recession, matching the initial response of the G20 nations in their summits of 2008 and 2009. But austerity once again trumped stimulus when the core nations of the EU insisted that bailouts were to be contingent on debt payback, which offered little room for stimulus or debt relief. Earlier efforts at debt relief came with the Highly Indebted Poor Countries Program, which largely targeted Africa, but only after long periods of austerity and debt payback.

In most cases, the political response included protest, and in many, new partisan alternatives. Sometimes protest worked to roll back austerity measures, at least for a time. In other cases, however, it was relatively absent, as in the slow roll-out of austerity in the United States. The short-lived activity of the Occupy movement in the US should be considered as an anti-austerity protest, but its impact was limited. Elsewhere, newly elected governments came to power on the wings of their anti-austerity rhetoric. In some places, that opposition was maintained and generated alternative policy; in others, the opponents of austerity quickly capitulated to its powerful advocates.

We've shown that differential political power did not matter to the advocates of austerity. States as powerful as the United Kingdom and the United States underwent austerity just as weaker economic and political actors did. Differential power did, however, influence how austerity policies were rolled out – it took time for the creeping and cumulative scarcity to affect the United States to the extent that neoliberals could argue for austerity. In weaker nations, the legacy of dependency allowed the powerful IFIs and the US government to move much more quickly and impose austerity as the cure to debt.

We've also demonstrated that one of the changes in austerity is the increasingly overt attack on labor. In nations like Mexico, labor's role was mostly to support the government's freezing and cutting of wages and jobs. Mexican labor was complicit in this way largely because the unions, long tied to the single-party government, hoped to forestall more harm and maintain their relatively privileged relationship. By the time austerity reached South Africa, and later Greece and Spain, the attack on labor standards and right to collective bargaining had increased substantially. The reduction of labor protection is an increasingly characteristic component of austerity packages.

We've also seen austerity become the singular, hegemonic policy, applied as a magic antidote to many different economic ills: whether public debt taken on for development needs, but then magnified owing to inflated interest, as in Latin America; inherited debt and political change, as in African nations; "hot money" speculation, as in Asia; deindustrialization, tax policy changes, and devoting state incomes to corporate desires in order to avoid job flight, as in the United States; or private debt, as in the EU.

In many ways, Latin America provided the laboratory for austerity policies. Closely tied to the United States, Latin American nations were influenced to pursue austerity policies by both internal and external elites. The fierce repression of Chile's authoritarian government paved the way for the normalization of austerity as the socialist alternative was destroyed amid the economic innovations of the "Chicago Boys." Coercive military violence gave way to institutional coercion, with the history of Chile facilitating IFI pressure on democratizing governments in Mexico and Ecuador. In each nation, we recognize the disciplinary nature of austerity policies, as governments were criticized for intervening in the economy – the greatest error a state could make, according to the emerging neoliberal orthodoxy. Those interventions included moving to a socialist welfare state and taking on too much debt. In all cases, the hard-won protections on labor were stripped with austerity.

The Latin American cases reveal the power dimensions behind austerity, first as Chile's government was immediately supported by the US government and the IFIs, and later when those same actors held creditors blameless even for irresponsible loans to Mexico and Ecuador. The IFIs and the United States remained the dominant policymaking actors throughout these impositions of austerity, prioritizing debt repayment over social needs, and thus further demonstrating the overwhelming balance of power. Throughout Latin America, neoliberal ideologues took on increasing importance over time as internal elites were convinced of the propriety of austerity and neoliberalism. Political opposition to austerity arose on the streets and in the halls of government, but few of these opponents were able to maintain their opposition. Across the continent, middle-income and poorer nations have been subjected to austerity.

In Africa, we find that neither a democratic nor an authoritarian state could withstand the global powers demanding austerity. Zimbabwe's emergent freedom was constrained by property agreements that left racial economic privilege intact, and crisis soon limited the government's social welfare efforts as it became an increasingly rigid one-party state. Even the new South African government, emerging triumphantly and with substantial political support from its successful battle against apartheid, was unable to resist austerity. As we've seen, both nations' political elites came to power committed to policies generating economic prosperity in newly democratic governments. Each nation was relatively wealthy, despite the deeply polarized ownership of that wealth. In South Africa, external elites had already made inroads into the thinking of the new policymakers, who turned fairly quickly to austerity policies. In Zimbabwe, the negotiated restrictions on rectifying the racially divided possession of wealth meant that reversing economic inequality translated into relying on debt, and in the neoliberal era, debt often transitions into austerity.

In both cases, the hegemony of austerity overcame even the commitment to resolving longstanding racial inequalities. Austerity was indeed demonstrably hegemonic because it helped local elites – our restricted beneficiaries – consolidate economic power, just as the external elites also benefited. Extending control over labor was a crucial component; even though those sectors were closely linked to the liberation movements, they did not escape the cuts. In Africa, race was central to how austerity was implemented, as racial colonialism left a legacy of inequality that could not be disrupted when austerity policies were prioritized.

In Asia and Oceania, neoliberal policies preceded the imposition of austerity, as deregulation and growing financialization helped pave the way for crises in Thailand, Indonesia, and, to a lesser extent, New Zealand. In Indonesia and Thailand, external powers played a significant role as the IFIs forced certain responses to crises upon willing internal elites; in New Zealand, internal elites mirrored the policies of other Commonwealth members. The influence of credit rating agencies increased, especially in Thailand. These cases also again demonstrate the legacy of racial colonialism, as austerity was more fiercely imposed on Thailand and Indonesia than on New Zealand, reflecting different histories of racial domination. New Zealand is an atypical case within the context of Asia and Oceania, but perhaps more typical in comparison with other nations more commonly thought of as developed. This case serves as a transition for us as we begin to examine austerity in other developed states. More than that, though, New Zealand highlights both the differential experiences of developed and developing countries and the role of colonial investment or extraction and the legacies left as a result of capitalist integration during the colonial period. The ability to retain capital and invest locally facilitated New Zealand's development in ways that were restricted in other countries, not just in Asia and Oceania, but elsewhere throughout the Global South. Therefore, New Zealand's relationship with austerity is much more aligned with those of European and North American cases.

The nations we examine in the Global South demonstrate how global and local elites challenged state-centered development. External powers in the IFIs and the US government, reinforced by US academic departments, pushed austerity in ways that limited the economic policymaking prerogatives of national governments. Those external powers soon found willing collaborators among internal elites, who found reasons to enjoy the shifting fortunes resulting from austerity. The early innovations experienced in Latin America blossomed throughout the 1980s across less-developed nations, as the communist alternative failed. As communism revealed its weaknesses, both ideological and concrete resources for development became less available. Over time, the successful disciplining of governments in their welfare state and labor protection roles provided clear trajectories for policymaking in post-2008 crisis Global North.

As we turned to the Global North, we focused first on the United States, and its unique transition to austerity. In the US, the most economically powerful nation we examined, political economic changes created an environment that made austerity seem inevitable. Despite the United States' history as a rich and democratic nation, neither its welfare state nor its labor protections were as extensive as those of its European counterparts. For the United States, the diagnosis of crisis to which austerity had to respond moved more slowly than elsewhere. A variety of policy choices, influenced by the US experience of globalization, diminished even the comparatively weaker welfare state and facilitated the transition to austerity. As other nations updated much of their industrial production infrastructure, and as technological innovations in both communication and transportation challenged US primacy in production, US elites looked for other ways to increase declining profits. Those who stayed in bricks-and-mortar production sought to increase their profits by threatening to leave. Such threats allowed firms to demand increasing incentives from local governments, or to diminish wages, benefits, and security for workers, or both. Other corporate powers moved away from their traditional activities in favor of financial speculation and investment, ceding production to commodity chains that increased industrialization elsewhere. Regardless of the path, power shifted dramatically to corporations, as locales and labor were forced into concessions.

Changes in policies intended to help the poor further disciplined labor. Poverty alleviation efforts, never generous in the United

States, became more draconian and even more associated with stigma during the Reagan and Clinton presidencies. Tax policy further shifted the power dynamic: the resources available to governments to address social needs diminished as expectations that the rich and corporations would pay high taxes yielded to neoliberal cuts. The slow transition to the inevitability of austerity was driven by ideologues in think tanks and US universities, with Keynesian thought steadily displaced by neoliberalism. The strategy of neoliberal thinkers proved sophisticated, as they devised a division of labor of critique, policymaking, and even writing legislation for a new crop of conservative lawmakers. The combination of policymaking and the ideological drive to neoliberalism slowed the path to austerity in the United States compared to other nations, owing to its tradition of democratic governance and predominant political power. But those changes, shielded by this ideological bulwark, made austerity the seemingly inevitable choice.

Our European cases again focused on comparatively wealthy nations with democratic governments, but reveal the stratification within the EU. The European experience after 2008 highlighted the role of external powers in the imposition of austerity, but these differed from those molding the Global South. The importance of the United States and even the IMF shrank, although the latter still served the Troika agenda of austerity. Germany, the EU, the ECB, and the credit rating institutions elevated their importance over the IMF in policing and maintaining austerity. By the time of the Eurozone crisis, policymakers were deeply entrenched in meeting neoliberal demands; in effect, the work of the ideologues so important elsewhere was completed. This demonstrates the ongoing policy hegemony of austerity, as different actors adopt it as accepted wisdom without any real examination of alternatives.

In Greece and Spain, austerity was again crisis-driven, with sovereign governments forced to take over private debt while mirroring the Global South's protection of investors and creditors above citizens. Like others, we agree with the argument that the rhetoric of government overspending as a cause of the crisis was dramatically overstated, and that austerity policies have yielded counterproductive results. Yet the comparison of Greece and Spain to the early cases in the developing world also shows accelerated contention against austerity, as street protests and electoral transition intersected to provide resistance and, potentially, the beginning of an alternative. The case of the United Kingdom was certainly impacted by the 2008 recession, but the permanent austerity conditions accompanying

British neoliberalization exacerbated household financial hardships as post-crisis austerity was imposed. In a sense, the imposition of crisis-driven austerity on the back of permanent austerity conditions pushed many – particularly those already struggling in the face of postindustrial neoliberalization – to embrace alternatives to traditional political party loyalties and political projects, and support withdrawal from the EU. The Brexit vote occurred because of a confluence of factors, but it is impossible to ignore the impact of persisting economic hardship and the shift of many former Labour voters to isolationist parties such as UKIP. The sustained conditions of broad economic adversity created an opportunity for Brexit proponents to marshal support as an alternative to the status quo, which was defined by austerity conditions.

The Hegemony of Austerity

In recent years, the discussion of austerity has centered only on the 2008 crisis. As we have noted throughout this book, this perspective is incomplete. Austerity is a truly global set of policies that have been brought to bear in response to different economic ills across the past 45 years. The actors most important to the imposition of austerity have varied over time, most notably across more and less powerful nations, but the policies themselves have proven similar. Austerity has been used as a tool to make the poor and the working and middle classes pay for those changes in the global political economy that might otherwise have forced economic elites to diminish profits; investors and creditors are consistently protected even while slashing welfare states endanger the economic health of nations and citizens. Austerity policies have been proven ineffective in promoting promised growth, but have exacted substantial material hardships on many countries utilizing this policy framework. The paradox of how the state weakens itself and its citizens is central to this book, as is who forces the imposition of austerity, how that has changed across time and place, and what are the purposes of that action. Its origins also have differed, as it has been generated by crises of different kinds, often pulled back in response to protest only to be imposed again. This flexibility shows its hegemony: its very ability to remain broadly the same at different times when imposed by different powers in response to varied causes.

Throughout the period we've examined, austerity has taken on the status of a hegemonic policy, the go-to cure despite its record of economic harm. Unlike Gramsci's focus on hegemony as requiring some popular support, we find the hegemony of austerity benefiting only a few. The lack of efficacy amid the broad unpopularity of such programs raises the question: Why have austerity policies persisted as the solutions to economic crises?

Clearly, elites have benefited from their control of economic policy and the diminishing of alternatives. The upward redistribution of gains from austerity policies to both affluent individuals and corporate entities helps us understand the persistence of austerity, but we argue that this provides only a partial explanation. The policy choices of the powerful help us understand austerity, but structural changes prove important too.

Advanced capitalist states have shifted funding strategies and revenue generation from tax-based strategies to debt-based strategies since the early 1980s through the present (Streeck 2014). This shift has made an increase in debt inevitable and, indeed, a central feature of contemporary state organization. While austerity might focus on controlling debt as a means of managing budgets and conditioning national economies, states increasingly need that debt to finance their operations. The seeming paradoxes inherent in this trend are less contradictory if we take into account where austerity has proven effective. Austerity has provided further rationale for restricting the expansion of state-funded public programs and policy initiatives through the tool of debt ceiling restrictions. In an environment dependent on debt financing, the dual pursuit of both debt restrictions and austerity policies can only serve to limit state-funded initiatives. Thus, austerity policies also serve a political purpose in limiting the size and scope of state welfare and regulatory capacities.

But debt also serves as a profit generator, particularly in the context of expanding financialization (Krippner 2005; van der Zwan 2014). The pivot from taxation to debt with regard to public financing has certainly contributed to this trend; however, the context of austerity goes far beyond increasing public debt. Accompanying deregulation (e.g., of mortgage sectors) and privatization create investment opportunities for transnational financial entities and are essentially products of austerity imposition. The deregulation of mortgage sectors opened substantial opportunities for speculative capital investment that contributed directly to the 2008 financial crisis (Aalbers 2008). Similarly, the shedding of public spending responsibilities that often accompanies austerity imposition shifts public goods and services to the financial sector at extremely low costs. In fact, privatization initiatives such as charter schools in the United States remain essentially publicly funded (through debt and tax revenues) but consolidate capital in the private sector. The privatization of formerly public utilities, as another example, represents profit potential on the back of publicly funded infrastructure development.

At the same time that austerity creates market opportunities for private capital, the mechanism of debt serves as a persistent danger for both national populations and the financial entities profiting from debt dependency. While financialization through austerity-driven deregulation and privatization creates substantial investment opportunities, the expansion of debt also increases financial market instability. As we have seen from the inevitable financial crises that arise from overspeculation and financial excess (commonly characterized as risk), markets can fail. Subsequently, financial market beneficiaries turn to austerity policies as a way to manage debt and lessen risk while simultaneously using the same policies to promote financial market expansion and integration. This schizophrenic relationship with austerity certainly carries systemic risk, but also allows significant profit potential. Austerity, for those not directly benefiting from investment capital, will exacerbate economic hardship conditions, hence the broad popular dissatisfaction referenced throughout this book. Sustained and expanded financialization accompanies austerity as financial markets seek to condition labor markets and mitigate the risks of debt dependency to enhance profitability. As we have seen time and again, however, these policies cannot mitigate risk and in fact worsen social costs and increase local precarity.

We've also emphasized the role of ideologues in the hegemony of austerity. Despite the early and ongoing neoliberal ideology generated by the Europe-based Mont Pelerin Society, the United States provided especially fertile ground in which to grow support for and disseminate neoliberalism and austerity policies. The impact of neoliberal intellectual entrepreneurs expanded from their European origins, coalescing to espouse a widely shared set of neoliberal ideas, including the need for austerity policies to rein in overly powerful states. Think tank staff researchers, writers, and others "helped apply the abstract contributions ... [and] ... when the economic crisis of the 1970s forced politicians and public servants to look around for new ideas, the transatlantic neoliberal network was well established to provide them" (Jones 2012: 135). One important exemplar of think tank innovators, Charles Koch, used his family's vast resources to nurture and generate anti-state thinkers. These efforts culminated in the formation of the Koch-controlled ALEC, as well as the Koch takeover of the Heritage Foundation, another organization that has proven to be "crucial in the American context in bringing together neoliberal thinkers and their ideas with Republican politicians" (Jones 2012: 165). As a result of the well-funded and articulated ideology project, austerity choked out alternative policymaking, especially once the fall of the Soviet Union was taken to mean that state-centered development was terminally discredited.

Yet as important as the power of ideas has proven to be, arguments focusing only on the ideological roots and spread of neoliberalism are not enough to explain the hegemony of austerity. Although Gramsci focused on how hegemony required some level of consent, he also recognized the importance of coercion. How could he fail to do so while writing in a jail cell? Later cases of austerity could not have happened without the laboratory of Chile providing a model, and Chile's economic transition could not have occurred without the repression that the junta enthusiastically brought to bear. Neither can the ongoing pressure of debt and the actions of the IFIs and the United States be understood as anything but coercive. Although austerity has indeed become hegemonic policy, coercion paved the way.

The hegemony of austerity always relied on the threat of example for the economically vulnerable. Chile loomed in the background for the Global South, while allegiance to the benefits of a monetary union kept Europe in check. For the United States, a long process of attacking an economic base that had widened wealth, and slow eating away at the function of government made austerity inevitable – and so again hegemonic.

The experiences of the first terms of Prime Minister Michael Manley in Jamaica (1972–6) and President Alan García in Peru (1985–90) are also instructive Both stood up to the IMF and continued to push social democratic policies rather than allow global policymakers to intrude on sovereign policy. The IFIs and the United States responded by ostracizing those nations, denying them access to aid and markets, leading to crushing inflation and violence. The early example of nations that dared to stand up to the austerity policymakers warned others not to follow their lead.

Austerity policies became and remain hegemonic also because the real-world implementation of the policy diverts from a crucial component of neoliberal ideology. Despite rhetoric to the contrary, the scope and power of the state does not shrink under austerity and neoliberalism. Instead, those who benefit from austerity find state power to be a useful tool. As Harvey (2005) demonstrated, neoliberalism gained its ideological power when other forms of elite power faltered. We've shown that austerity has been used to diminish those forms of state-centered development that addressed popular needs, as in Latin America, or could have aided in the transition to majority rule in Africa. The use of austerity in Greece and Spain helped maintain German and other European bankers' profits, forcing nations to bear the brunt of private debt rather than the creditors themselves. It is less important that states shrink with austerity, although it is clear that their social welfare and protection capacity does. It is more to the point that the importance of certain constituencies shifts; austerity serves the political interests of the powerful as well as their economic desires.

Removal of states from their central role in providing welfare reveals new strategies of how state elites become economic elites. This transition is clear in our African cases, but Latin America and Asia and Oceania also reveal how state elites enjoyed increasing enrichment, especially using privatization to reward themselves and their cronies. Austerity proves useful not only for investors and speculators requiring protection for their profitmaking capacity, but also for corruptible state elites who paved the way for such policymaking.

The very character of globalization has reinforced the hegemony of austerity by maintaining the vulnerability of weaker economies. The economic makeup of many nations has changed over the past five decades, with fewer relying only on the extraction of agricultural and natural resource wealth characteristic of slavery, empire, and then dependency. Yet globalization has maintained the hierarchy of nations, even when the membership in the hierarchy has shifted. With the end of the Soviet era, ideological alternatives appeared to shrink. But importantly, so too did resource alternatives. With Soviet aid a thing of the past, neoliberals effectively had the globe largely under their power with regard to resources they could extract and use to entice recalcitrant nations to their side.

With the removal of the communist threat, development strategies evolved that were meant to nurture poorer nations. Grant making became a less common tool than loan making. Here too, the augmented link of debt to profitmaking benefited elites, as they found fewer avenues in the wake of declining profitmaking through bricks-and-mortar economies in the West. As financialization became increasingly central to profitmaking, not only did debt loads grow, but debt cancellation also became less of an option. Loans to nations became an increasingly important part of the financial architecture as capital relied on that source of profit.

Hegemony, however, does not equate with inevitability. We've been careful in this book in using the phrase "seemingly inevitable" at various times. Although admittedly clunky and inelegant, it does allow us to think beyond hegemony. One of the ways to do so is to understand how austerity conflicts with legitimacy.

Austerity and Political Legitimacy

Austerity, as a tactic in support of broader neoliberalization, always carries political risk. Everyone, from proponents to critics to casual observers, is well aware that austerity policies are deeply unpopular. The fact that austerity creates material hardships for national majorities has been made abundantly clear through both economic statistics and worldwide protests. Benefits gained from austerity imposition are heavily skewed toward elite capital beneficiaries, which invariably created difficulties in attempting to legitimate both policies and the political actors putting them in place.

Political actors acquiescing to the broader structural demands of neoliberalization or the temporal demands of austerity are politically unable to address material adversities in any but temporary ways. When they've carried the austerity agenda, support for social democratic and labor parties has declined significantly, including among traditional constituents. The willingness of labor and social democratic parties to embrace neoliberalism and their political inability (see Greece and Spain) or unwillingness to resist austerity (see the United States and the United Kingdom) have contributed greatly to the discrediting of those parties. Left-leaning parties' embrace of market reforms and austerity policies not only directly contributed to material hardships, but also signaled a willingness to abdicate traditional roles as advocates of labor and protectors of national economies.

As a result of "Third Way" or "new economic" politics, national populations experiencing the hardships of austerity continue to search out political allies that will assume the protectionist mantle formerly held by social democratic and labor parties. These have ranged from non-traditional politic actors (e.g., in the United States and Italy), tertiary parties (e.g., in France and Germany), to once-shunned nationalist parties (e.g., in Sweden and India), resulting in unprecedented electoral success (Della Porta et al. 2017; Norris & Inglehart 2019). Indeed, the persistent search for someone, anyone, to resolve deep economic despair and create jobs, lower costs, and provide material dignity is at the root of the turn to both the new populism and new left alternatives. As a result, neoliberal and austerity advocates will have to choose between losing control over the neoliberal project as unsympathetic populist or critical opposition politicians gain power, or reverting to authoritarian strategies to maintain what is a deeply unpopular political economic ideology. Austerity is hegemonic, as we've noted, among elite economic policymakers, but the popular response on both right and left demonstrates it is deeply contested on the streets and in the halls of government. The illegitimacy of austerity, and how it has been contested by movements and governments, leads us to think about how its hegemony might be disrupted. The final sections of this chapter suggest what paths away from austerity may look like.

Paths Away from Austerity

Just like it did in African, Asian, and Latin American nations, the post-recession Eurozone push for austerity-based solutions to the so-called "sovereign debt crisis" generated substantial political opposition to this externally imposed but state-led process. Following Polanyi (2001; see also Block & Somers 2014), we should expect a protectionist counter-movement to focus its attention on those same culpable actors and institutions that have brought austerity to bear. This is, of course, what we find; however, there are particular characteristics that complicate a strict Polanyian interpretation of events.

Austerity elicited a variety of responses in societies in which such economic policies were enacted. Among cases we've examined, significant and rapid social spending decreases in the United Kingdom generated protest action throughout 2011, not to mention significant student mobilization in response to tuition increases the year before. Additionally, the M-15 or *indignados* movement was rooted in similar opposition to Spanish government attempts to weaken labor. As we've shown, another notable example of anti-austerity protest took place in Greece beginning in 2010. Despite differences across cases, social movement activity responding to austerity is consistent.

From 2008 to 2015, Portugal's experience was much like Greece and Spain. The government followed the Troika's direction toward austerity, amid some social movement protest. With the 2015 victory of the Socialist Party leading a leftist alliance, the new government bucked the austerity orthodoxy, instead choosing to "reverse cuts to wages, pensions and social security, and offered incentives to businesses" (Alderman 2018). Despite creditors' disquiet, production, exports, and employment all grew, as did foreign investment in productive industries. As Prime Minister António Costa declared: "What happened in Portugal shows that too much austerity deepens a recession, and creates a vicious circle." Instead, his government "devised an alternative to austerity, focusing on higher growth, and more and better jobs" (Alderman 2018). A leftist government elected under promises to beat back austerity did just that, reversing wage cuts to public workers, as well as other wage and pension cuts. Portugal is still seen as vulnerable, especially owing to its debt, the largest in the Eurozone. But the challenge to austerity may provide the government with the legitimacy required for further social progress that may require more time, especially as the government's efforts continue to direct investment into expanding jobs.

Mobilization in Italy, Ireland, France, Turkey, and elsewhere confirms that opposition to austerity has been transnational. There is certainly strong evidence of inter-movement collaboration and strategic cooperation among anti-austerity movements, including the use of social media from organization to promotion to branding and beyond (Costanza-Chock 2012; Flesher Fominaya & Cox 2013). In all these cases, we see evidence of the "double movement," with popular action challenging state imposition of austerity.

Despite transnational cooperation, national responses have varied significantly. Here too, this is consistent with Polanyi, who recognized that the response to increased market fundamentalism was neither singular nor inevitably social democratic. Social movement mobilization has occurred in a distinctly national context focusing on state institutions/actors. Transnational institutions (e.g., international investment firms, the IMF, the EU) and external states (e.g., Germany in the case of Greece and others) are certainly secondary targets and sources of movement motivation, but the clear impetus to action remains deteriorating local economic conditions and state implementation of austerity. As we've seen, and others have argued (e.g., Della Porta et al. 2017), national protest and subsequent partisan political action provide some potential for a more significant attack on austerity.

Importantly, both European and Global South anti-austerity mobilization regularly crosses class lines. In all of the cases we've examined, protest participants have included members of trade unions, state workers, students, the unemployed, the impoverished, the urban poor, and others with specific interests but a singular target (Hughes 2011; Rüdig & Karyotis 2014). This trend confirms the Polanyian assumption that unrestrained market liberalism would not simply affect the impoverished. A key constituency of these movements has been middle-class actors who are reacting to the attack on public sector workers as well as the attack on labor security (Ruggie 1982; Holman & van der Pijl 1996). Clearly, each individual case is motivated by particular conditions: severe austerity cuts and declining quality of life in Greece; evictions and youth unemployment in Spain; spending cuts and subsequent cost increases in the United Kingdom. But the scope of austerity and subsequent hardships motivates counter-movement responses that transcend traditional class boundaries and specific occupational/socio-economic interests (Flesher Fominaya & Cox 2013; Della Porta & Mattoni 2014). These trends also promote coalitions in opposition to austerity that may prove effective and long-lasting.

Policy Imperatives

What kind of policies might address the problems with austerity? The power of capital mobility to spur crises is one issue to be addressed. A tax on cross-border financial transactions, long ago advocated by James Tobin, with a variant supported by Eurozone powers in 2009, would diminish the volume and speed of capital flight while building a reserve that could be used to attack debt. Additionally, shrinking the size of giant banks reduces the power of certain economic actors and diminishes the risk of their failure for the global economy – addressing the foundations of some crises.

In addition to regulating financial transactions, international debt laws require attention. In 2014, the United Nations General Assembly voted to create a new debt restructuring mechanism. The history of crisis and austerity demonstrates that debt managers, such as the IMF, are dominated by creditors and investors, and enact policy in their favor. The United Nations may be in a position to address debt crises by providing regulation on responsible borrowing and lending, declaring some debt as unsustainable if it interferes with the development and wellbeing of a nation, legitimizing halts on debt payments, and generally encouraging more transparency and accountability. Such a call has recently been made by the European Network on Debt and Development (Stichelmans 2015).

Any effort to forge a path away from austerity must include debt cancellation. Many precedents exist for such a policy: one comes from the 1953 London Debt Agreement, when many of the former European countries allied against Nazi-era Germany were convinced to write off much of Germany's prewar debt (Varoufakis 2016). Even while championing austerity, the World Bank and the IMF have recognized debt cancellation is necessary. In 1988, Paris Club creditors embarked on a new approach for heavily indebted, impoverished countries by proposing a one-third elimination of debt to encourage both foreign investment and national GDP growth. In 1994, the allowable debt forgiveness rose to 67%, and in 1996, the IMF and World Bank institutionalized the policy by creating the Heavily Indebted Poor Countries (HIPC) Initiative. But debt relief remained linked to neoliberal conditions, as eligibility for debt relief through the HIPC Initiative still required adherence to IMF guidelines.

The HIPC Initiative was enhanced several times, first in 1999 by adding a requirement that poor countries and the IFIs "focus on poverty reduction as a fundamental goal of their operations in these countries" (Andrews et al. 1999). The Multilateral Debt Relief Initiative (MDRI) in 2005 provided up to 100% relief for multi-lateral loans administered through IMF- and/or World Bank-affiliated organizations. But conditions continued to mark both programs, as access was determined first and foremost by the demonstration of "good performance" with respect to IMF-defined structural reforms (Santiso 2001).

By 2018, these programs "relieved 36 participating countries of $99 billion in debt" (World Bank 2018), but simple eligibility for debt relief continues to be based on established adherence to neoliberal and austerity policies. The maintenance of conditions, including austerity, highlights the unequal power over national economic policy. It also once again demonstrates the utility of Polanyian analysis, as the pressures of the market are somewhat relieved even while other market conditions are added. The addition of poverty relief require-ments partially addressed one of the main problems of the HIPC Initiative: the fact that it deepened existing material hardships among national populations. This approach to debt relief, however, remains ineffective. First, the policy re-creates unequal power: the creation of Poverty Reduction Strategy Papers (PRSPs)[1] is the responsibility of the indebted nation but must be approved by authorized MDRI personnel. PRSPs must exist in order to meet eligibility criteria and cannot interfere with neoliberal conditions, including adherence to austerity policies. Second, although MDRI conditionality provides increased space for social service funding, countries still must adhere to externally defined spending limitations and restrictions.

The contradiction between poverty alleviation and social services, on one side, and austerity and neoliberal conditionality, on the other side, is likely to be resolved in favor of the latter in the absence of wider structural changes. The link between debt alleviation and the mitigation of hardship conditions is tenuous without attending to the numerous historical and structural conditions that have led to the deep poverty that pervades the Global South, and the inequality that increasingly characterizes the Global North.

The conditions attached to debt forgiveness schemes have sustained the hegemony of austerity and the final authority of global powers over the less powerful. To disrupt this path, debt forgiveness must be freed from conditionality, unencumbered, and able to address the very real material hardships that have been exacerbated by austerity. Debt relief can be a good thing, especially when monies spent on debt can instead be spent on programs by which nations can become less unequal, more fair, and healthier. But when imposed by institutions that reinforce global inequality, debt relief alone does nothing to change the hierarchy that brought austerity to hegemonic policy status. Debt relief does not diminish the power of creditor over debtor, of multinational agency over national domestic policy prerogative, of rich nation over poor, of a global financial power over global members of middle and working classes. Debt relief without a wider base of reforms retains austerity as the go-to policy when nations suffer from economic crises that are not fully of their own making. Even if debts are diminished, the threat of austerity remains a political tool to maintain power, and an economic tool to maintain extraction. Debts must be negotiated downward, but this will not be sufficient to put brakes on the expansion of neoliberal authority. The hegemony of austerity must be disrupted by social movements and progressive governments whose citizens have suffered for so long under these policies.

Paths away from austerity will have to include the pressures of national social movements on states, as pain is felt nationally and states provide the closest targets. Movements will, however, have to forge and maintain transnational links in order to keep pressure on those for whom austerity is the medicine to cure all ills. The goals of the movements must include both the casting off of external powers advocating the imposition of austerity, and the return to greater national sovereignty for economic policymaking, as well as debt cancellation. Jubilee 2000 appeared for a time to be such a movement. A coalition of religious organizations, various social movements, and NGOs, Jubilee 2000 advocated "cancellation of the foreign debts of the poorest nations, reached its zenith in the late 1990s and 2000 – and then, by design, shut down. In the space of a few years, it became one of the most successful international, non-governmental movements in history" (Roodman 2010).

As a movement, Jubilee 2000 was able to build on its religiously based legitimacy first to publicize the harmful impact of debt, and then to push the IMF and World Bank for real debt relief programs. The movement framed austerity policies among the most highly indebted nations as both an ethical/religious affront and an obstacle to development. Its successes included not just debt cancellation, but rechanneling aid to development purposes, notably to fighting AIDS in Africa. According to its estimate, Jubilee 2000's efforts pushed the World Bank to clear $100 billion of debt owed by 35 nations, which paved the way to use those savings for development needs and poverty reduction. The movement's strategies included substantive research, and action inside and outside of the hallways of power. The latter culminated in a demonstration of over 70,000 people at the 1998 G7 meeting.

Jubilee 2000 disbanded, as planned, in 2000, leaving a leadership vacuum for debt relief campaigners that its successor, Drop the Debt, has been unable to fill. Despite Jubilee 2000's success, however, part of its scope of analysis was insufficient. Debt and austerity are, of course, obstacles to development. But they are also part of a wider program that seeks to maintain economic and political power by shrinking the welfare and labor protection capacity of states. In so doing, debt is not just used to repay creditors at all costs, certainly a problematic priority in itself. It is also a tool of discipline and a method of extraction from either poor nations, or the poor and working class within poor nations and others.

Paths away from austerity remain open but they must be first paved by national social movements with articulate and unyielding opposition to austerity. A return to the social movement opposition to debt remains possible, especially based on the cross-national model established by Jubilee 2000. A multi-class, multinational movement would have to rely not only on reversing debt, but also on revising bankruptcy standards, which in neoliberal days far favor creditors over debtors, despite the lack of due diligence on the part of the former. These movements can embolden and invigorate national parties to stand up against debt. Both movements and parties must supplement their national work with transnational links to provide the solidarity needed to launch alternatives. One possibility might be the formation of debtor cartels; the current international financial institutions certainly constitute a cartel for creditors.

But forging an alternative to the hegemony of austerity must be an ideological project in addition to an organizational and political project. Some years ago, Arrighi and Zhang (2011) hoped for a "new Bandung" emerging from China which would articulate a genuinely alternative economic model. That source for such a model now seems unlikely, as it is difficult to describe China's expansion as progressive. But the hope remains for a counter-hegemonic ideology, and we argue it is fed by the consistent failure of austerity. The counter-hegemonic imagination may be nourished by a number of currents, including environmentalism, indigenous rights and philosophies, the emergence of new parties with less allegiance to stagnant ideological foundations, and changing values around work lives. As important to the creation of an ideological alternative to austerity, to which our work contributes, is the realization by people worldwide that austerity has been tested by time and it does not work.

Notes

Chapter 1 Many Paths to Austerity

1 The IMF reaction was notable in its inflexibility, despite IMF President Michel Camdessus's letter to the President where he expressed that he was "'profoundly moved' by the many deaths that occurred during the rioting. Nevertheless, he 'confirmed that the economic policies were well-conceived; we back them and will continue to back them'" (Ellner 1989: 8).

2 The fact that Greece had lied about its economic health to enter the EU helped this analysis spread (Panageotou & Shefner 2015).

3 O'Cinneide (2014: 186) is one of the few recent authors who recognizes the historical trajectory of austerity, writing "austerity is perhaps better understood as involving the intensification of already existing policy trends." Rakopoulos (2018) and his contributors also recently address the global scope of austerity.

4 We align with Harvey's position that neoliberalism is a theory that prioritizes the functioning of the market over control by states, and individual freedom over that of a collective.

5 Less critical analysts of austerity define it differently: "Austerity, or a commitment to budgetary discipline and sound monetary principles, has become a key credential of economic governance in a globalized world" (Kaplan 2013: 26).

6 We recognize that states are consistently considered enemies by some citizens within their own nations, often for good reason. Austerity drives even relatively privileged citizens to attribute new hardships to states.

Chapter 2 From Development to the Lost Decade in Latin America

1 For classic work on dependency, see Cardoso & Faletto (1979).

2 Comisíon Económica para América Latina y el Caribe, or ECLAC, the Economic Commission for Latin America and the Caribbean, a regional commission of the United Nations, formed in 1948.

3 Some estimates have reached as high as 80,000 dead and disappeared.

4 Important work, especially by Peter Kornbluh (2013), documents the involvement in Chilean affairs and the attempts to keep the US role hidden.

5 See Valdés (1995) and Collins & Lear (1995) for the history of how the "Chicago Boys" were integrated into the junta's economic team.

6 Even during Mexico's most substantial period of economic planning, however, the seeds of neoliberalism were being sown. Ludwig von Mises served as a visiting professor at Mexico City's UNAM (Universidad Nacional Autonoma de Mexico, or Autonomous National University of Mexico) with the sponsorship of Luis Montes de Oca, a former director of Mexico's Central Bank. While there, Mises anticipated later neoliberal policymaking in his "book on the economic problems of Mexico, including a proposal to privatize Mexico's railroad system" (Plehwe 2009: 243).

7 The tight reins on the Mexican economy were somewhat loosened in the wake of the Mexico City earthquake of 1985, which devastated the city and required some greater economic flexibility from government.

8 At the time, Mexico was the world sixth largest producer of crude oil and the fourth largest oil exporter; oil accounted for 40% of the nation's revenue.

9 Like many struggles in Mexico from the late 1980s into the 2000s, some of what were clear responses to austerity were integrated into partisan electoral struggles. The leftist PRD used the threats to PEMEX to its advantage, with party leaders taking the lead in protests.

10 By 1995, "more than 15,000 companies closed their doors, more than 2 million Mexicans lost their jobs, inflation raged, the annual wage of the typical worker shrank from $3,981 to $2,550, and interest rates soared to as much as 140 percent. Virtually overnight, there were hundreds of thousands of people whose outstanding loans doubled, but whose salaries and savings were cut in half" (Anderson 1996).

11 In 2018, Andrés Manuel López Obrador defied the PRI and traditional opposition parties to win the Mexican presidency and Congress. López Obrador, a populist and critic of Mexico's economic policy, may reverse some of the nation's unbroken history of austerity, but only time will tell.

12 As Sawyer (2004) notes, the size of Ecuador's indigenous population is a moving target, with estimations ranging from 7% to 45%. National censuses find the lowest figures, indigenous activist groups the highest, and the World Bank found indigenous peoples make up 39% of Ecuador's total population. The different numbers have less to do with concrete numbers and more to do with a non-static cultural identity. See also Vázquez & Saltos (2008).

13 The hegemony of neoliberalism also required a political organizing project to overcome Keynesian dominance, led by intellectuals integrated into the Mont Pelerin Society, a process documented in Mirowski & Plehwe (2009).

Chapter 3 African Austerity

1 An alternative view finds ANC political elites willing to work with global capital and its representatives, while maintaining suspicion of South African white economic elites (Seekings & Nattrass 2011).

2 The IFIs' earlier influence during the apartheid era increased owing to a loan from the IMF accompanied by common conditions such as deficit reduction through government expenditure cuts (including civil service wages), tight monetary policies, and private wage restraint (Kahn 2000). But the fact that the loan was paid by 1998 without IMF imposition of structural adjustment made it clear that similar policies were pursued by the newly democratic government itself.

3 As BEE developed, it widened to additionally focus on "management representation, employment equity, skills development, preferential procurement, enterprise development and corporate social investment" (Ponte et al. 2007: 934).

4 The ANC has been criticized for patronage in its party operations, and this was seen as increasingly penetrating state hiring and budgets. But observers find the Zuma administration's patronage efforts surpassed those of all other ANC party and government traditions (Southall 2016).

Chapter 4 Austerity in Asia and Oceania

1 Net FDI in Indonesia increased 511% from 2009 to 2015 in current US dollars (World Bank Databank).

2 The shift in platform ideology on the part of the National Party illustrates the near ubiquity of neoliberal ideological integration among formerly Keynesian or welfare capitalist parties. The novelty here is that a right-leaning party embraces neoliberalism whereas many examples are of social democratic or labor-oriented parties shifting to an embrace of neoliberal reforms (such as the Democratic Party in the United States under Bill Clinton).

Chapter 5 The United States and the Inevitability of Austerity

1 Cowie and Heathcott note that those following Bluestone and Harrison's lead on deindustrialization are myriad. For a comprehensive list up until 2003, see Cowie and Heathcott (2003: 306 n. 3).

2 It is important to note that these funds are on top of the federal bailout money dispersed in response to the Great Recession of 2008.

3 All of these examples draw on Story (2012).

4 The Chattanooga VW plant also provides a fascinating case of not only state funding, but also government intervention against the efforts to unionize the plant, despite VW's willingness to do so. See McKenney (2018).

5 Just months after the Trump tax cuts, Republican officials began planning to offset the revenue loss by cutting imposing limits on Medicare and Social Security.

6 In 2015, the poverty line was $20,090.

7 Freedom House, which publishes a yearly Freedom Index, notes a startling decline in its measure of freedom in the United States in the last 10 years (Freedom House 2019).

Chapter 6 Austerity Lands in the European Union

1 This case study draws heavily on Panageotou & Shefner (2015).

2 See Della Porta et al. (2017) for an important analysis of how austerity drove the creation and flourishing of new political parties in Europe.

3 Real government spending actually increased by an average of 1% per year from 1979 to 1990. There were significant cuts in spending, particularly in 1985 and 1989, but those cuts were offset by earlier increases in the 1980s (Eaton 2013).

4 The "Third Way" was a term popularized by British sociologist Anthony Giddens (1998) as a means to describe a compromise political philosophy that blends neoliberal and social democratic ideas. Tony Blair and other center-left politicians embraced the terminology as a platform foundation in the late 1990s. The practical outcome of Third Way politics was a shift toward fiscal conservatism combined with so-called "social justice" values (Freeden 2004: 197–8).

Chapter 7 Why Austerity Persists

1 PRSPs are required analytical statements that are a part of more-recent IMF and World Bank development agreements. In short, the respective country in question must develop and monitor broad efforts to reduce poverty as a part of receiving IMF and World Bank loans. PRSPs are also a requisite component of debt relief initiatives enacted by the IMF and World Bank.

References

Aalbers, M. B. (2008) "The financialization of home and the mortgage market crisis," *Competition & Change* 12: 148–66.

Abramovitz, M. (2016) "Welfare reform in the United States: gender, race and class matter," *Critical Social Policy* 26: 336–64.

Acemoglu, D., Johnson, S., & Robinson, J. A. (2001) "The colonial origins of comparative development: an empirical investigation," *American Economic Review* 91: 1369–401.

Agkyridou, N. (2013) "Greece's doctors to get dose of austerity medicine," *CNBC Markets*, December 4. Available at: http://www.cnbc.com/id/101245803

Alavi, H. (1972) "The state in post-colonial societies: Pakistan and Bangladesh," *New Left Review* 74: 59–81.

Alderman, L. (2018) "Portugal dared to cast aside austerity. It's having a major revival," *The New York Times*, July 22. Available at: https://www.nytimes.com/2018/07/22/business/portugal-economy-austerity.html

Alderman, L., & Thomas, L. J., Jr. (2014) "Taking a risk, investors snap up once-shunned Greek debt," *The New York Times*, April 10. Available at: https://www.nytimes.com/2014/04/11/business/international/greece-trumpets-its-return-to-international-bond-market.html

Anand, G. (2016) "Narendra Modi struggles to fulfill his plan to rejuvenate India," *The New York Times*, February 29. Available at: https://www.nytimes.com/2016/03/01/world/asia/narendra-modi-india.html

Anderson, J. (1996) "Debtors disrobe in banking protest," *The Washington Post*, June 15, p. A17.

Andrews, D., Boote, A. R., Rizavi, S. S., & Singh, S. (1999) "Debt relief for low-income countries: the enhanced HIPC Initiative," *IMF Pamphlet Series* 51. Available at: https://www.imf.org/external/pubs/ft/pam/pam51/contents.htm

Anwar, S., & Gupta, D. (2006) "Financial restructuring and economic growth in Thailand," *Global Economic Review* 35: 113–27.

Armingeon, K., & Baccaro, L. (2012) "Political economy of the sovereign debt crisis: the limits of internal devaluation," *Industrial Law Journal* 41: 254–75.

Aron-Dine, A. (2007) *New Study Finds "Dramatic" Reduction since 1960 in the Progressivity of the Federal Tax System: Largest Reductions in Progressivity Occurred in 1980s and since 2000.* Washington, DC: Center on Budget and Policy Priorities.

Aron-Dine, A. (2017) "Senate tax bill would add 13 million to uninsured to pay for tax cuts of nearly $100,000 per year for the top 0.1 percent." Center on Budget and Policy Priorities, November 15. Available at: https://www.cbpp.org/blog/senate-tax-bill-would-add-13-million-to-uninsured-to-pay-for-tax-cuts-of-nearly-100000-per-year

Arrighi, G. (2010) *The Long Twentieth Century: Money, Power, and the Origins of our Times.* New York: Verso.

Arrighi, G., & Zhang, A. L. (2011) "Beyond the Washington Consensus: a new Bandung?" In: Shefner, J., & Fernández-Kelly, P. (eds.) *Globalization and Beyond: New Examinations of Global Power and Its Alternatives.* University Park: Pennsylvania State University Press.

Auty, R. M. (2007) "Natural resources, capital accumulation and the resource curse," *Ecological Economics* 61: 627–34.

Babb, S. (2001) *Managing Mexico: Economists from Nationalism to Neoliberalism.* Princeton: Princeton University Press.

Bair, J. (2009) "Taking aim at the new international economic order." In: Mirowski, P., & Plehwe, D. (eds.) *The Road from Mont Pelerin : The Making of The Neoliberal Thought Collective.* Cambridge, MA: Harvard University Press.

Baker, C., & Phongpaichit, P. (2014) *A History of Thailand,* 3rd edn. Cambridge: Cambridge University Press.

Barbero, I. (2015) "When rights need to be (re)claimed: austerity measures, neoliberal housing policies and anti-eviction activism in Spain," *Critical Social Policy* 35: 270–80.

Barr, B., & Taylor-Robinson, D. (2016) "Recessions are harmful to health," *British Medical Journal* 354: i4631.

Barr, B., Kinderman, P., & Whitehead, M. (2015) "Trends in mental health inequalities in England during a period of recession, austerity and welfare reform 2004 to 2013," *Social Science and Medicine* 147: 324–31.

BBC (2011) "Greek government austerity measures," October 19. Available at: https://www.bbc.com/news/business-13940431

BBC (2014) "Scottish independence: post-yes Scotland 'to end austerity,'" June 16. Available at: https://www.bbc.com/news/uk-scotland-scotland-politics-27868468

BBC (2017) "Budget 2017: 'end austerity' plea from Welsh and Scottish governments," October 26. Available at: https://www.bbc.com/news/uk-wales-politics-41763468

Becatoros, E. (2013) "Greek strike: thousands protest austerity cuts as services shut down," *Huffington Post*, November 6. Available at: http://george-islandnews.blogspot.com/2013/11/greek-strike-thousands-protest.html

Becker, M. (2007) "State building and ethnic discourse in Ecuador's 1944–1945 *asemblea constituyente*." In: Clark, A. K., & Becker, M. (eds.) *Highland Indians and the State in Modern Ecuador*. Pittsburgh: University of Pittsburgh Press.

Beja, E., Jr., Junvith, P., & Ragusett, J. (2005) "Capital flight from Thailand, 1980–2000." In: Epstein, G. A. (ed.) *Capital Flight and Capital Controls in Developing Countries*. Cheltenham: Edward Elgar.

Berglund, O. (2018) "Contesting actually existing austerity," *New Political Economy* 23: 804–18.

Black, W. K. (2014) "Spain rains on the austerity victory parade," *Challenge* 57: 42–53.

Block, F. (2008) "Swimming against the current: the rise of a hidden developmental state in the United States," *Politics and Society* 36: 169–206.

Block, F., & Keller, M. (2011) *State of Innovation: The US Government's Role in Technology Development*. Abingdon: Routledge.

Block, F., & Somers, M. R. (2014) *The Power of Market Fundamentalism*. Cambridge, MA: Harvard University Press.

Bluestone, B. (2003) "Foreword." In: Cowie, J., & Heathcott, J. (eds.) *Beyond the Ruins: The Meanings of Deindustrialization*. New York: ILR Press.

Bluestone, B., & Harrison, B. (1982) *The Deindustrialization of America: Plant Closings, Community Abandonment, and the Dismantling of Basic Industry*. New York: ILR Press.

Blyth, M. (2013) *Austerity: The History of a Dangerous Idea*. Oxford: Oxford University Press.

Bond, P. (2006) "Resource Extraction and African Underdevelopment," *Capitalism Nature Socialism* 17: 5–25.

Bond, P., & McInnes, P. (2007) "Decommodifying electricity in postapartheid Johannesburg ." In: Leitner, H., Peck, J., & Sheppard, A. E. (eds.) *Contesting Neoliberalism: Urban Frontiers*. London: Guilford Press.

Brett, E. A. (2005) "From corporatism to liberalization in Zimbabwe: economic policy regimes and political crisis, 1980–97," *International Political Science Review* 26: 91–106.

Bullard, N., Bello, W., & Mallhotra, K. (1998) "Taming the tigers: the IMF and the Asian crisis," *Third World Quarterly* 19: 505–56.

Bungarten, P. (1999) "The crisis of Thailand and the International Monetary Fund," *Internationale Politik und Gesellschaft* 3: 253–62.

Cardoso, E., & Helwege, A. (1992) "Below the line: poverty in Latin America," *World Development* 20: 19–37.

Cardoso, F. H., & Falatto, E. (1979) *Dependency and Development in Latin America*. Los Angeles: University of California Press.

Carmody, P. (2001) *Tearing the Social Fabric: Neoliberalism, Deindustrialization, and the Crisis of Governance in Zimbabwe*. Portsmouth, NH: Heinemann.

Cassano, G., & Dello Buono, R. A. (2010) *Crisis, Politics, and Critical Sociology*. Boston: Brill.

Centeno, M. A. (1997) *Democracy within Reason: Technocratic Revolution in Mexico*, 2nd edn. University Park: Pennsylvania State University Press.

Cervero-Liceras, F., McKee, M., & Legido-Quigley, H. (2015) "The effects of the financial crisis and austerity measures on the Spanish health care system: a qualitative analysis of health professionals' perceptions in the region of Valencia," *Health Policy* 119: 100–6.

Chari, A., and Henry, P. B. (2015) "Two tales of adjustment: East Asian lessons for European growth," *IMF Economic Review* 63: 164–96.

Chiengkal, W. (1983) "The transformation of the agrarian structure of central Thailand, 1960–1980," *Journal of Contemporary Asia* 13: 340–60.

Chomthongdi, J.-c. (2000) "The IMF's Asian legacy," Global Policy Forum, September. Available at: https://www.globalpolicy.org/component/content/article/209/42924.html

Chorafas, D. N. (2013) *Public Debt Dynamics of Europe and the US*. New York: Elsevier.

Chua, I., & Papachristou, H. (2014) "Fitch upgrades Greece by a notch to 'B'; outlook stable," Reuters, May 23. Available at: https://www.reuters.com/article/greece-ratings-fitch/update-1-fitch-upgrades-greece-by-a-notch-to-b-outlook-stable-idUSL6N0O919920140523

Clawson, D., & Clawson, M. A. (1999) "What has happened to the US labor movement? Union decline and renewal," *Annual Review of Sociology* 25: 95–119.

Colitt, R. (1995) "Ecuador energy strike launched," *Financial Times*, July 14, p. 3.

Collins, C., & Hoxie, J. (2017) "Billionaire bonanza 2017: the Forbes 400 and the rest of us," Inequality, November 8. Available at: https://inequality.org/great-divide/billionaire-bonanza-2017/

Collins, J., & Lear, J. (1995) *Chile's Free-Market Miracle: A Second Look*. Oakland, CA: Institute for Food and Development Policy.

Conde-Ruiz, J. I., & Marín, C. (2013) "The fiscal crisis in Spain." In: *Austerity Measures in Crisis Countries: Results and Impact on Mid-Term Development*. Heidelberg: ZBW – Leibniz Information Centre for Economics. Available at: https://www.ceps.eu/system/files/article/2013/02/Forum.pdf

Connolly, S., Bevan, G., & Mays, N. (2010) *Funding and Performance of Healthcare Systems in the Four Countries of the UK before and after Devolution: A Longitudinal Analysis of the Four Countries*. London: Nuffield Trust.

Costanza-Chock, S. (2012) "Mic check! Media cultures and the Occupy movement," *Social Movement Studies* 11: 375–85.

Cowie, J., & Heathcott, J. (eds.) (2003) *Beyond the Ruins: The Meanings of Deindustrialization*. Ithaca, NY: ILR Press.

Crouch, C. (2011) *The Strange Non-Death of Neoliberalism*. Cambridge: Polity.

Cypher, J. M. (2004) "Pinochet meets Polanyi? The curious case of the Chilean embrace of 'free' market economics," *Journal of Economic Issues* 38: 527–35.

Cypher, J. M., & Delgado Wise, R. (2010) *Mexico's Economic Dilemma: The Developmental Failure of Neoliberalism.* Lanham, MD: Rowman & Littlefield.

Damián, A., & Julio Botvinik, A. D. (2006) "A table to eat on: the meaning and measurement of poverty." In: Hershberg, E., & Rosen, F. (eds.) *Latin America after Neoliberalism: Turning the Tide in the 21st Century?* New York: The New Press.

Darline, J. (1997) "Factions reach agreement in Ecuador crisis," *Los Angeles Times*, February 9, p. A1.

Dashwood, H. (2000) *Zimbabwe: The Political Economy of Transformation.* Toronto: University of Toronto Press.

Davison, P. (1995) "Middle classes bear the brunt of Mexico's pain: austerity measures are causing unrest but failing to revive the economy," *The Independent*, March 22 p. 15.

Debrun, X., Moulin, L., Turrini, A., Ayuso-i-Casals, J., & Kumar, M. S. (2008) "Tied to the mast? National fiscal rules in the European Union," *Economic Policy* 23: 297–362.

Della Porta, D., & Mattoni, A. (eds.) (2014) *Spreading Protest: Social Movements in Times of Crisis.* Pretoria: ECPR Press.

Della Porta, D., Fernández, J., Kouki, H., & Mosca, L. (2017) *Movement Parties against Austerity.* Cambridge: Polity.

Dello Buono, R. A., & Lara, J. B. (2007) "Neoliberalism and resistance in Latin America." In: Dello Buono, A., & Lara, B. (eds.) *Imperialism, Neoliberalism and Social Struggles in Latin America.* Boston: Brill.

Denemark, D. (2001) "Choosing MMP in New Zealand: explaining the 1993 electoral reform." In: Shugart, M. S., & Wattenberg, M. P. (eds.) *Mixed Member Electoral Systems: The Best of Both Worlds?* Oxford: Oxford University Press.

Díaz-Parra, I., Roca, B., & Martín-Díaz, E. (2018) "Indignados, municipalism and Podemos: mobilisation and political cycle in Spain after the Great Recession." In: Díaz-Parra, I., Roca, B., & Martín-Díaz, E. (eds.) *Challenging Austerity: Radical Left and Social Movements in the South of Europe.* London: Routledge

Directorate-General for Economic and Financial Affairs (2011) *The Economic Adjustment Programme for Greece.* Brussels: European Commission.

Drake, P. W. (2006) "Latin America and the United States." In: Hershberg, E., & Rosen, F. (eds.) *Latin America after Neoliberalism: Turning the Tide in the 21st Century?* New York: The New Press.

Drakeford, M. (2012) "Wales in the age of austerity," *Critical Social Policy* 32: 454–66.

Dresser, D. (1991) *Neopopulist Solutions to Neoliberal Problems: Mexico's National Solidarity Program.* La Jolla, CA: UCSD Center for US–Mexican Studies.

Dussel Peters, E. (2000) *Polarizing Mexico: The Impact of Liberalization Strategy*. Boulder, CO: Lynne Rienner.

Eaton, G. (2013) "How public spending rose under Thatcher," *New Statesman*, April 8. Available at: https://www.newstatesman.com/politics/2013/04/how-public-spending-rose-under-thatcher

The Economist (2012) "Labour reform in Spain: Spanish practices," February 18. Available at: https://www.economist.com/europe/2012/02/18/spanish-practices

Ekathemerini (2014, 1 April) "Eurogroup clears tranches, Greece eyes bond issue," April 1. Available at: http://www.ekathimerini.com/4dcgi/_w_articles_wsite1 _1_01/04/2014_538659

Elliott, L. (2015) "Greece: the election is over, the economic crisis is not," *The Guardian*, September 20. Available at: https://www.theguardian.com/world/2015/sep/20/greece-the-election-is-over-the-economic-crisis-is-not

Ellner, S. (1989) "Organized labor's political influence and party ties in Venezuela: Acción Democrática and its labor leadership," *Latin American Politics and Society* 31: 91–130

Escobar Latapí, A., & Roberts, B. (1991) "Urban stratification, the middle classes, and economic change in Mexico." In: González de la Rocha, M., & Escobar Latapí, A. (eds.) *Social Responses to Mexico's Economic Crisis of the 1980s*. San Diego, CA: Center for US–Mexican Studies.

Eurostat (n.d.-a) "Government consolidated gross debt by components, annual data." Available at: https://ec.europa.eu/eurostat/tgm/table.do?tab=table&init=1&language=en&pcode=tipsgo11&plugin=1

Eurostat (n.d.-b) "People at risk of poverty or social exclusion." Available at: https://ec.europa.eu/eurostat/tgm/refreshTableAction.do?tab=table&plugin=1&pcode=t2020_50&language=en

Eurostat (n.d.-c) "Severely materially deprived people." Available at: https://ec.europa.eu/eurostat/tgm/table.do?tab=table&init=1&language=en&pcode=tipslc30&plugin=1

Eurostat (n.d.-d) "Youth Unemployment Rate – % of Active Population Aged 15–24." Available at: https://ec.europa.eu/eurostat/tgm/refreshTable-Action.do?tab=table&plugin=1&pcode=tipslm80&language=en

Evans, L., Grimes, A., Wilkinson, B., & Teece, D. (1996) "Economic reform in New Zealand, 1984–95: the pursuit of efficiency," *Journal of Economic Literature* 34: 1856–902.

Faiola, A. (1999a) "Economic crisis triggers general strike in Ecuador," *The Washington Post*, March 11, p. A27.

Faiola, A. (1999b) "Ecuador not ready to go to market: economic reforms are slowed by strikes," *The Washington Post*, March 24, p. A17.

Faiola, A. (1999c) "Ecuadoran economy near collapse; bank closures, proposed austerity measures trigger widespread protests," *The Washington Post*, March 16, p. A22.

Falkus, M. (1991) "The economic history of Thailand," *Australian Economic History Review* 31: 53–71.

Farah, D. (1995) "Mexico plan wins praise, helps peso: loss of 1 million jobs seen possible this year," *The Washington Post*, March 11, p. A19.

Farmer, B. (2015) "VW commits to Chattanooga plant as Tennessee lawmakers heap praise on troubled automaker," WPLN Radio, October 29. Available at: https://tnfinance.wordpress.com/2015/10/

Fernández Rodríguez, F. C., Rojo, R. I., & Lucio, M. M. (2016) "Austerity and collective bargaining in Spain: the political and dysfunctional nature of neoliberal deregulation," *European Journal of Industrial Relations* 22: 267–80.

Ffrench-Davis, R. (2010) *Economic Reforms in Chile: From Dictatorship to Democracy*, 2nd edn. Houndmills: Palgrave Macmillan.

FIER (Foundation for Economic and Industrial Research) (2012) *The Greek Economy* (Report No. 67). Athens: Foundation for Economic and Industrial Research.

Flesher Fominaya, C., & Cox, L. (eds.) (2013) *Understanding European Movements: New Social Movements, Global Justice Struggles, Anti-Austerity Protest*. London: Routledge.

Formisano, R. P. (2015) *Plutocracy in America: How Increasing Inequality Destroys the Middle Class and Exploits the Poor*. Baltimore, MD: Johns Hopkins University Press.

Foster, J. B., & Magdoff, F. (2009) *The Great Financial Crisis: Causes and Consequences*. New York: Monthly Review Press.

Foweraker,, J., & Craig, A. (eds.) (1990) *Popular Movements and Political Change in Mexico*. San Diego, CA: Center for US–Mexican Studies.

Francis, S. (2003) "Indonesia's battle of will with the IMF," Global Policy Forum, February 25. Available at: https://www.globalpolicy.org/component/content/article/209/43040.html

Frank, T. (2016) *Listen, Liberal: or Whatever Happened to the Party of the People?* New York: Metropolitan Books.

Freeden, M. (2004) *Liberal Languages: Ideological Imaginations and Twentieth-Century Progressive Thought*. Princeton: Princeton University Press.

Freedom House (2019) *Democracy in Retreat: Freedom in the World 2019*. Available at: https://freedomhouse.org/report/freedom-world/freedom-world-2019/democracy-in-retreat

Freeman, L. (2014) "A parallel universe – competing interpretations of Zimbabwe's crisis," *Journal of Contemporary African Studies* 32: 349–66.

Freund, B. (2007) "South Africa: the end of apartheid & the emergence of the 'BEE elite,'" *Review of African Political Economy* 34: 661–78.

Frieden, J. A. (2006) *Global Capitalism: Its Fall and Rise in the Twentieth Century*. New York: W. W. Norton.

Friedmann, S., Lustig, N., & Legovini, A. (1995) "Mexico: social spending and food subsidies during adjustment in the 1980s." In: Lustig, N. (ed.) *Coping with Austerity*. Washington, DC: Brookings Institution.

Galbraith, J. K. (2015) *The End of Normal: The Great Crisis and the Future of Growth*. New York: Simon & Schuster.

García Rada, A. (2013) "Child poverty and malnutrition rise in Spain as austerity measures bite," *British Medical Journal* 347: f5261.

Gatopoulos, D., & Paphitis, N. (2013) "Greek parliament approves austerity measures," *Greek News*, July 17. Available at: http://www.greeknewsonline. com/greek-parliament-approves-new-austerity-measures/

Gellert, P. K. (2010) "Extractive regimes: toward a better understanding of Indonesian development," *Rural Sociology* 75: 28–57.

George, S. (1992) *The Debt Boomerang: How Third World Debt Harms Us All.* Boulder, CO: Westview Press.

Gerlach, A. (2003) *Indians, Oil and Politics: A Recent History of Ecuador.* Wilmington, DE: Scholarly Resources.

Gibb, K. (2015) "The multiple policy failures of the UK Bedroom Tax," *International Journal of Housing Policy* 15: 148–66.

Giddens, A. (1998) *The Third Way: The Renewal of Social Democracy.* Cambridge: Polity.

Giddens, A. (2013) *Turbulent and Mighty Continent: What Future for Europe?* Cambridge: Polity.

Gietel-Basten, S. (2016) "Why Brexit? The toxic mix of immigration and austerity," *Population and Development Review* 42: 673–680.

Giles, C., & Harding, R. (2013) "Austerity hurts … but is it working?," *Financial Times,* April 26. Available at: https://www.ft.com/content/ e1532c9a-aceb-11e2-b27f-00144feabdc0

Giles, C., & Parker, G. (2008) "Tax hit to fund £20bn fiscal stimulus," *Financial Times,* November 24 Available at: https://www.ft.com/ content/4a9f5776-ba36-11dd-92c9-0000779fd18c

Glencross, A. (2015) "Going it alone? The choice of political union in British politics," *The Political Quarterly* 86: 555–62.

Glyn, N., & Drenkard, S. (2013) "Prop 13 in California, 35 years later," Tax Foundation, June 6. Available at: https://taxfoundation.org/ prop-13-california-35-years-later

Gogoll, T. (1997) "Ecuador unions call for general strike; US exporters worried over new restrictions," *Journal of Commerce,* February 3, p. 5A.

Golden, T. (1995) "Defiant workers in Mexico protest government policies," *The New York Times,* May 2, Available at: https://www.nytimes. com/1995/05/02/world/defiant-workers-in-mexico-protest-government-policies.html

González de la Rocha, M. (2001) "From the resources of poverty to the poverty of resources? The erosion of a survival model," *Latin American Perspectives* 28(4): 72–100.

González de la Rocha, M., & Escobar Latapí, A. (eds.) (1991) *Social Responses to Mexico's Economic Crisis of the 1980s.* San Diego, CA: Center for US–Mexican Studies.

Good, K. (1976) "Settler colonialism: economic development and class formation," *Journal of Modern African Studies* 14: 597–620.

Gordon, L. I. Z., & Whitty, G. (2010) "Giving the 'hidden hand' a helping hand? The rhetoric and reality of neoliberal education reform in England and New Zealand," *Comparative Education* 33: 453–67.

Green, D. (2003) *Silent Revolution: The Rise and Crisis of Market Economics in Latin America*, 2nd edn. New York: Monthly Review Press.

Gregson, J. (2019) "The richest countries in the world," Global Finance, April 15. Available at: https://www.gfmag.com/global-data/economic-data/richest-countries-in-the-world

Grindle, M. S. (2004) "Good enough governance: poverty reduction and reform in developing countries," *Governance* 17: 525–48.

The Guardian (2018) "The Guardian view on schools and austerity: more than a funding crisis," March 16. Available at: https://www.theguardian.com/commentisfree/2018/mar/16/the-guardian-view-on-schools-and-austerity-more-than-a-funding-crisis

Gunson, P. (1996) "Final bus strike gesture proves a cross too far," *The Guardian*, April 6, p. 12.

Habib, A., & Padayachee, V. (2000) "Economic policy and power relations in South Africa's transition to democracy," *World Development* 28: 245–263.

Hall, A. (2006) "From Fome Zero to Bolsa Família: social policies and poverty alleviation under Lula." *Journal of Latin American Studies* 38: 689–709.

Hallerberg, M., Strauch, R., & von Hagen, J. (2007) "The design of fiscal rules and forms of governance in European Union countries," *European Journal of Political Economy* 23: 338–59.

Harrison, B., & Bluestone, B. (1988) *The Great U-Turn: Corporate Restructuring and the Polarizing of America*. New York: Basic Books.

Harrison, G. (2005) "Economic faith, social project and a misreading of African society: the travails of neoliberalism in Africa," *Third World Quarterly* 26: 1303–20.

Harrison, R. V., & Jackson, P. A. (eds.) (2010) *The Ambiguous Allure of the West: Traces of the Colonial in Thailand*. Hong Kong: Hong Kong University Press.

Harsch, E. (2001) "South Africa tackles social inequities," *Africa Recovery* 14: 12–19.

Harvey, D. (2005) *A Brief History of Neoliberalism*. Oxford: Oxford University Press.

Hawke, G. R. (1985) *The Making of New Zealand: An Economic History*. Cambridge: Cambridge University Press.

Hay, C. (2010) "'Things can only get worse …': the political and economic significance of 2010," *British Politics* 5: 391–401.

Hay, C. (2013) "Treating the symptom not the condition: crisis definition, deficit reduction and the search for a new British growth model," *British Journal of Politics and International Relations* 15: 23–37.

Hershberg, E., & Rosen, F. (2006) *Latin America after Neoliberalism: Turning the Tide in the 21st Century?* New York: The New Press.

Hiam, L., Dorling, D., Harrison, D., & McKee, M. (2017) "Why has mortality in England and Wales been increasing? An iterative demographic analysis," *Journal of the Royal Society of Medicine* 110: 153–62.

Hobson, J., Russel, D., & Raphelson, S. (2017) "As Trump proposes tax cuts, Kansas deals with aftermath of experiment," NPR, October 25. Available at: https://www.npr.org/2017/10/25/560040131/as-trump-proposes-tax-cuts-kansas-deals-with-aftermath-of-experiment

Holman, O., & van der Pijl, K. (1996) "The capitalist class in the European Union." In: Kourvetaris, G., & Moschonas, A. (eds.) *The Impact of European Integration: Political, Sociological, and Economic Changes.* London: Praeger.

Horgan, G. (2006) "Devolution, direct rule and neo-liberal reconstruction in Northern Ireland," *Critical Social Policy* 26: 656–68.

Houston Chronicle (1992) "Workers launch strike," September 24, p. 19.

Huang, Y. (1999) *Inflation and Investment Controls in China: The Political Economy of Central–Local Relations during the Reform Era.* Cambridge: Cambridge University Press.

Hughes, N. (2011) "'Young people took to the streets and all of a sudden all of the political parties got old': the 15M movement in Spain," *Social Movement Studies* 10: 407–13.

Husy, D. (2000) "Growth, poverty and inequality: South Africa Reports," *Social Watch.* Available at: http://www.socialwatch.org/node/10709

Ifanti, A. A., Argyriou, A. A., Kalofonou, F. H., & Kalofonos, H. P. (2013) "Financial crisis and austerity measures in Greece: their impact on health promotion policies and public health care," *Health Policy* 113: 8–12.

IMF (International Monetary Fund) (1997) "Press release: IMF approves stand-by credit for Thailand." International Monetary Fund Press Release No. 97/37, Available at: https://www.imf.org/en/News/Articles/2015/09/14/01/49/pr9737

IMF (International Monetary Fund) (2014) "World economic outlook database." Available at: http://www.imf.org/external/pubs/ft/weo/2014/02/weodata/index.aspx

ITEP (Institute on Taxation and Economic Policy) (2013) *Tax Incentives: Costly for States, Drag on the Nation.* Washington, DC: ITEP.

James, W. E., & Fujita, N. (1989) "Import substitution and export promotion in the growth of the Indonesian industrial sector," *ASEAN Economic Bulletin* 6: 59–70.

Jessop, B. (1996) "Post-fordism and the state." In: Greve, B. (ed.) *Comparative Welfare Systems.* London: Palgrave Macmillan UK.

Jessop, B. (2017) "The organic crisis of the British state: putting Brexit in its place," *Globalizations* 14: 133–41.

Jitsuchon, S., & Siamwalla, A. (2009) "Economic shocks and vulnerable Thailand: a case study of rising food and fuel prices." Paper submitted to United Nations, Thailand Development Research Institute, February. Available at: https://www.childimpact.unicef-irc.org/documents/view/id/102/lang/en

Johnson, C. (1982) *MITI and the Japanese Miracle*. Stanford: Stanford University Press.

Jones, D. S. (2012) *Masters of the Universe: Hayek, Friedman, and the Birth of Neoliberal Politics*. Princeton: Princeton University Press.

Kahn, B. (2000) *Debates over IMF Reform in South Africa* (IMF Special No. 6). Bonn: Friedrich Ebert Stiftung.

Kaplan, S. (2013) *Globalization and Austerity Politics in Latin America*: Cambridge: Cambridge University Press.

Kar, S. (2017) "Austerity welfare: social security in the era of finance," *Anthropology Today* 33: 12–15.

Karagiannis, N., & Kondeas, A. G. (2012) "The Greek financial crisis and a developmental path to recovery: lessons and options," *Real-World Economics Review* 60: 54–73.

Karanikolos, M., & Kentikelenis, A. (2016) "Health inequalities after austerity in Greece," *International Journal for Equity in Health* 15: 83.

Karanikolos, M., Mladovsky, P., Cylus, J., Thomson, S., Basu, S., Stuckler, D., ... & McKee, M. (2013) "Financial crisis, austerity, and health in Europe," *The Lancet* 381: 1323–31.

Karger, H. (2014) "The bitter pill: austerity, debt, and the attack on Europe's welfare states," *Journal of Society & Social Welfare* 41: 33–53.

Karseno, A. R. (1997) *Structural Adjustment in Indonesian Economy* (Working Paper No. 48). Jakarta: Center for Policies and Information Studies. Available at: http://www.esri.go.jp/jp/archive/wor/wor048/wor048a.pdf

Kelsey, J. (2015) *The New Zealand Experiment: A World Model for Structural Adjustment?* Wellington: Bridget Williams Books.

Kentikelenis, A. E., Stubbs, T. H., & King, L. P. (2016) "IMF conditionality and development policy space, 1985–2014," *Review of International Political Economy* 23: 543–82.

Kickert, W., & Ysa, T. (2014) "New development: how the Spanish government responded to the global economic, banking and fiscal crisis," *Public Money and Management* 34: 453-57.

Kitsantonis, N. (2018) "Macedonia agrees to change its name to resolve dispute with Greece," *The New York Times*, June 12. Available at: https://www.nytimes.com/2019/01/11/world/europe/macedonia-greece-name-change.html

Kohli, A. (2006) "Politics of economic growth in India, 1980–2005: Part I: The 1980s," *Economic and Political Weekly*, April 8, pp. 1251–9.

Kornbluh, P. (2013) *The Pinochet File: A Declassified Dossier on Atrocity and Accountability*. New York: The New Press.

Kotios, A., & Roukanas, S. (2013) "The Greek crisis and the crisis in Eurozone's governance." In: Sklias, P., & Tzifakis, N. (eds.) *Greece's Horizons*. Berlin: Springer.

Krippner, G. R. (2005) "The financialization of the American economy," *Socio-Economic Review* 3: 173–208.

Krippner, G. R. (2011) *Capitalizing on Crisis: The Political Origins of the Rise of Finance*: Cambridge, MA: Harvard University Press.

The Lancet (2018) "Progress in the USA for autistic spectrum disorder," *The Lancet* 391: 1750.

Lane, T. (1999) "Program design." In: Lane, T., Ghosh, A., Hamann, J., Phillips, S., Schulze-Ghattas, M., & Tsikata, T. (eds.) *IMF-Supported Programs in Indonesia, Korea and Thailand: A Preliminary Assessment*. Washington: IMF.

Lane, T., & Schulze-Ghattas, M. (1999) "Overview." In: Lane, T., Ghosh, A., Hamann, J., Phillips, S., Schulze-Ghattas, M., & Tsikata, T. (eds.) *IMF-Supported Programs in Indonesia, Korea and Thailand: A Preliminary Assessment*. Washington, DC: IMF.

Lane, T., Schulze-Gattas, M., Tsikata, T. M., Phillips, S., Ghosh, A. R., and Hamann, A. J. (1999) *IMF-Supported Programs in Indonesia, Korea and Thailand*. No. 178. Washington, DC: IMF.

Lapavitsas, C., Kaltenbrunner, A., Labrinidis, G., Lindo, D., Meadway, J., Michell, J., ... & Vatikiotis, L. (2012) *Crisis in the Eurozone*. New York: Verso.

Larmer, B. (1989) "Austerity plan hits poor hardest," *Christian Science Monitor*, June 21, p. 3.

Larráin, F., & Vergara, R. (2000) "Un cuarto de siglo de reformas fiscales." In: Larráin, F., & Vergara, R. (eds.) *La Transformación Económica de Chile*. Santiago: Centro de Estudios Politicos.

Lauridsen, L. S. (1998) "The financial crisis in Thailand: causes, conduct and consequences?," *World Development* 26: 1575–191.

LAWR (*Latin American Weekly Report*) (1992) "No *caracazo*, at least not yet: unions and Indians measure up strength for general strike," September 24, p. 11.

LAWR (*Latin American Weekly Report*) (1993a) "Ecuador: IMF verdict," March 11, p. 115.

LAWR (*Latin American Weekly Report*) (1993b) "Government defies 'indefinite' strike," June 10, p. 256.

LAWR (*Latin American Weekly Report*) (1993c) "Teachers begin hunger strike," December 2, p. ???.

LAWR (*Latin American Weekly Report*) (1994a) "Choruses of protests continue to swell," February 24, p. 77.

LAWR (*Latin American Weekly Report*) (1994b) "Ecuador: resuming payments," April 28, p. 175.

LAWR (*Latin American Weekly Report*) (1997a) "Ecuador: IMF help sought," April 22, p. 187.

LAWR (*Latin American Weekly Report*) (1997b) "Opposition forces gather momentum," January 21, p. 45.

Lawrence, T., & Andrews, J. (2018) *School Funding Pressures in England*. London: Education Policy Institute.

Leachman, M., & Mai, C. (2014b) *Most States Funding Schools Less than before the Recession*. New York: Center on Budget and Policy Priorities.

Lehndorff, S. (ed.) (2012) *A Triumph of Failed Ideas: European Models of Capitalism in the Crisis*. Brussels: ETUI.

Leibbrandt, M., Finn, A., & Woolard, I. (2012) "Describing and decomposing post-apartheid income inequality in South Africa," *Development Southern Africa* 29: 19–34.

Lessig, L. (2011) *Republic, Lost: How Money Corrupts Congress, and a Plan to Stop It*. New York: Hachette Book Group.

Lesufi, I. (2002) "Six years of neoliberal socioeconomic policies in South Africa," *Journal of Asian and African Studies* 37: 286–98.

Loopstra, R., McKee, M., Katikireddi, S. V., Taylor-Robinson, D., Barr, B., & Stuckler, D. (2016) "Austerity and old-age mortality in England: a longitudinal cross-local area analysis, 2007–2013," *Journal of the Royal Society of Medicine* 109: 109–16.

Lowndes, V., & Gardner, A. (2016) "Local governance under the conservatives: super-austerity, devolution and the 'smarter state,'" *Local Government Studies* 42: 357–75.

Lucero, J. A. (2007) "Barricades and articulations: comparing Ecuadorian and Bolivian indigenous politics ." In: Clark, A. K., & Becker, M. (eds.) *Highland Indians and the State in Modern Ecuador*. Pittsburgh: University of Pittsburgh Press.

Lustig, N. (1998) *Mexico: The Remaking of an Economy*, 2nd edn. Washington, DC: Brookings Institution.

Lynn, M. (2011) *Bust: Greece, the Euro, and the Sovereign Debt Crisis*. Hoboken, NJ: John Wiley & Sons.

Mac Flynn, P. (2015) "Austerity in Northern Ireland: where are we and where are we going?" NERI, May 6. Available at: https://www.nerinstitute.net/blog/2015/05/06/austerity-in-northern-ireland-where-are-we-and-whe/

Macnab, S. (2018) "One million Scots now living in poverty as austerity bites," *The Scotsman*, March 22. Available at: https://www.scotsman.com/news/politics/one-million-scots-now-living-in-poverty-as-austerity-bites-1-4710590

Major, A. (2014) *Architects of Austerity: International Finance and the Politics of Growth*: Stanford: Stanford University Press.

Mamdani, M. (2009) "Lessons of Zimbabwe: Mugabe in context," *Concerned African Scholars Bulletin* 82: 1–13.

Manolopoulos, J. (2011) *Greece's "Odious" Debt*. London: Anthem Press.

Marais, H. (1998) *South Africa: Limits to Change*. London: Zed Books.

Marconi, S. (ed.) (2001) *Macroeconomica y Economia Politica en Dolarización*. Quito: Abya-Yala.

Marmot, M., Bloomer, E., & Goldblatt, P. (2013) "The role of social determinants in tackling health objectives in a context of economic crisis," *Public Health Reviews* 35: 1–24.

Martin, P. (2014) "On eve of Merkel visit, massive anti-austerity strike in Greece," Global Research, April 10. Available at: http://www.globalresearch.ca/on-eve-of-merkel-visit-massive-anti-austerity-strike-in-greece/5377395

Matsaganis, M., & Leventi, C. (2014) "The distributional impact of austerity and the recession in Southern Europe," *South European Society and Politics* 19: 393–412.

Matthews-King, A. (2017) "Landmark study links Tory austerity to 120,000 deaths," *Independent*, November 16. Available at: https://www.independent. co.uk/news/health/tory-austerity-deaths-study-report-people-die-social-care-government-policy-a8057306.html

Mayer, J. (2016) *Dark Money: The Hidden History of the Billionaires behind the Rise of the Radical Right*. New York: Doubleday.

Mazzucatto, M. (2013) *The Entrepreneurial State: Debunking Public vs. Private Sector Myths*. London: Anthem Press.

McClure, M. (2013) *A Civilised Community: A History of Social Security in New Zealand 1898–1998*. Auckland: Auckland University Press.

McDonald, D. (2008) *World City Syndrome: Neoliberalism and Inequality in Cape Town*. London: Routledge.

McEwen, N., & Parry, R. (2008) "Devolution and the preservation of the United Kingdom welfare state." In: McEwen, N., & Moreno, L. (eds.) *The Territorial Politics of Welfare*. London: Routledge.

McGlone, M. S., & Wilmshurst, J. M. (1999) "Dating initial Maori environmental impact in New Zealand," *Quaternary International* 59: 5–16.

McKenney, Z. (2018) *The State of the Union? Transnational Manufacturing and the US Labor Movement* (PhD dissertation). University of Tennessee, Knoxville.

McKinley, D. (2016) "Lessons in community-based resistance? South Africa's anti-privatisation forum," *Journal of Contemporary African Studies* 34: 268–81.

Mercado, D. (2018) "New year, new tax brackets. Here's where you stand," CNBC, January 1. Available at: https://www.cnbc.com/2017/12/29/heres-where-you-stand-in-the-new-2018-tax-brackets.html

Meredith, M. (2002) *Our Votes, Our Guns: Robert Mugabe and the Tragedy of Zimbabwe*. New York, Public Affairs.

Merrick, R. (2017) "Chancellor Philip Hammond accused of more 'failed austerity' after demanding extra spending cuts before the election," *The Independent*, February 28. Available at: https://www.independent.co.uk/news/uk/politics/chancellor-philip-hammond-latest-budget-spending-cuts-austerity-social-care-john-mcdonnell-a7603096.html

Miami Herald (1991a) "Americas," February 1, p. 4.

Miami Herald (1991b) "Biggest union group plans general strike," July 21, p. 15.

Middlebrook, K. (1991) *Unions, Workers, and the State in Mexico*. San Diego, CA: Center for US–Mexican Studies.

Miley, T. J. (2017) "Austerity politics and constitutional crisis in Spain," *European Politics and Society* 18: 263–83.

Mirowski, P. (2013) *Never Let a Serious Crisis Go to Waste*. London: Verso.

Mirowski, P., & Plehwe, D. (2009) *The Road from Mont Pelerin: The Making of the Neoliberal Thought Collective.* Cambridge, MA: Harvard University Press.

Mishel, L., Biens, J., Gould, E., & Shierholz, H. (2012) *The State of Working America,* 12th edn. Ithaca, NY: ILR Press.

Mngxitama, A. (2002) "The taming of land resistance: lessons from the National Land Committee," *Journal of Asian and African Studies* 41: 39–69.

Moffatt, S., Lawson, S., Patterson, R., Holding, E., Dennison, A., Sowden, S., & Brown, J. (2015) "A qualitative study of the impact of the UK 'Bedroom Tax,'" *Journal of Public Health* 38: 197–205.

Moore, D. (2001) "Neoliberal globalisation and the triple crisis of 'modernisation' in Africa: Zimbabwe, the Democratic Republic of the Congo and South Africa," *Third World Quarterly* 22: 909–29.

Morgan, J. (2015) "HEFCE reveals 150 million cut," *Times Higher Education,* July 22. Available at: https://www.timeshighereducation.com/news/hefce-reveals-ps150m-cut

Moyo, S., & Yeros, P. (2007) "The radicalised state: Zimbabwe's interrupted revolution," *Review of African Political Economy* 34: 103–21.

Moyo, S., & Yeros, P. (2011) *Reclaiming the Nation: The Return of the National Question in Africa, Asia, and Latin America.* London: Pluto Press.

Murray, M. (1994) *Revolution Deferred: The Painful Birth of Post-Apartheid South Africa.* London: Verso.

Murtagh, B., & Shirlow, P. (2012) "Devolution and the politics of development in Northern Ireland," *Environment and Planning C: Government and Policy* 30: 46–61.

Narsiah, S. (2002) "Neoliberalism and privatisation in South Africa," *GeoJournal* 57: 29–38.

Navarro, V. (2013) "The social crisis of the Eurozone: the case of Spain," *International Journal of Health Services* 43: 189–192.

New York Times Editorial Board (2014) "Kansas' ruinous tax cuts," *The New York Times,* July 13. Available at: http://www.nytimes.com/2014/07/14/opinion/kansas-ruinous-tax-cuts.html

Newsome, J. (1998) "Ecudaor subsidy cuts spark protests," *Financial Times,* October 2, p. 3.

Newsome, J. (1999) "Ecuador President struggles to fulfil his promise: Jamil Mahuad's efforts to restore stability have failed and economic difficulties are looming large," *Financial Times,* February 26, p. 3.

Newsome, J., & Lapper, R. (1999) "Ecuador crisis grows as banks stay closed," *Financial Times,* March 10, p. 37.

Norris, P., & Inglehart, R. (2019) *Cultural Backlash: Trump, Brexit, and Authoritarian Populism.* Cambridge: Cambridge University Press.

Nyabereka, M. C. (2017) "An exploration of the effects of structural adjustment and BRICS engagement on development in Zimbabwe over the periods 1991–1995 and 2009–2013," *Politikon* 44: 111–31.

O'Cinneide, C. (2014) "Austerity and the faded dream of a 'social Europe.'"

In: Nolan, A. (ed.) *Economic and Social Rights after the Global Financial Crisis*. Cambridge: Cambridge University Press.

O'Connor, J. (1973) *The Fiscal Crisis of the State*. New Brunswick, NJ: Transaction.

O'Hara, M. (2015) *Austerity Bites: A Journey to the Sharp End of Cuts in the UK*. London: Policy Press.

Oldfield, S., & Stokke, K. (2007) "Polemical politics, the local politics of community organizing, and neoliberalism in South Africa." In: Leitner, H., Peck, J., & Sheppard, E. (eds.) *Contesting Neoliberalism: Urban Frontiers*. London: Guilford Press.

Ollstein, A. (2015) "Scott Walker's corporate tax breaks come back to haunt him," Think Progress, May 7. Available at: http://thinkprogress. org/politics/2015/05/07/3655893/scott-walkers-corporate-tax-breaks-come-back-haunt/

Orange, C. (2015) *The Treaty of Waitangi*. Wellington: Bridget Williams Books.

Ornellas, A., Martínez-Román, M. A., Tortosa-Martínez, J., Casanova, J. L., das Dores Guerreiro, M., & Engelbrecht, L. K. (2017) "Neoliberalism and austerity in Spain, Portugal and South Africa: the revolution of older persons," *Journal of Gerontological Social Work* 60: 535–552.

Panageotou, S., & Shefner, J. (2015) "Crisis management and the institutions of austerity: a comparison of Latin American and Greek experiences," *Comparative Sociology* 14: 301–27.

Papachristou, H. (2014) "Greek recession slightly deeper than expected in 2013," Ekathemerini, March 11. Available at: http://www.ekathimerini.com/158500/article/ekathimerini/business/greek-recession-slightly-deeper-than-expected-in-2013

Papadopoulos, T., & Roumpakis, A. (2012) "The Greek welfare state in the age of austerity: anti-social policy and the politico-economic crisis." In: Kilkey, M., Ramia, G., & Farnsworth, K. (eds.) *Social Policy Review 24: Analysis and Debate in Social Policy*. Bristol: Policy Press.

Park, M. (2013) "Lessons from the Asian Financial Crisis for the Eurozone: a comparative analysis of the perilous politics of austerity in Asia and Europe," *Asia Europe Journal* 11: 189–99.

Pasiouras, F. (2012) *Greek Banking: From the Pre-Euro Reforms to the Financial Crisis and Beyond*. London: Palgrave Macmillan.

Pastor, M. (1987) *The International Monetary Fund and Latin America: Economic Stabilization and Class Conflict*. Boulder, CO: Westview Press.

Peck, J. (2014) "Pushing austerity: state failure, municipal bankruptcy and the crises of fiscal federalism in the USA," *Cambridge Journal of Regions, Economy and Society* 7: 17–44.

Peet, R. (2002) "Ideology, discourse, and the geography of hegemony: from socialist to neoliberal development in postapartheid South Africa," *Antipode* 34: 54–84.

Penders, C. L. M. (2002) *The West New Guinea Debacle: Dutch Decolonisation and Indonesia, 1945-1962*. Adelaide: University of Hawaii Press.

Perez, S. A., & Matsaganis, M. (2018) "The political economy of austerity in Southern Europe," *New Political Economy* 23: 192–207.

Perez-Caldentey, E., & Vernengo, M. (2012) *The Euro Imbalances and Financial Deregulation: A Post-Keynesian Interpretation of the European Debt Crisis* (Working Paper 702). New York: Levy Economics Institute of Brad College.

Petrakis, M. (2014) "Olympic park tests Greek recovery talk after privatization flops," Bloomberg, February 10. Available at: https://www.bloomberg.com/news/articles/2014-02-10/olympic-park-tests-greek-recovery-talk-after-privatization-flops

Pew Research Center (2015) *More Mexicans Leaving than Coming to the US*. Washington: Pew Research Center.

Phillips-Fein, K. (2009) "Business conservatives and the Mont Pelerin Society." In: Mirowski, P., & Plehwe, D. (eds.) *The Road from Mont Pelerin: The Making of the Neoliberal Thought Collective*. Cambridge, MA: Harvard University Press.

Picot, G., & Tassinari, A. (2017) "All of one kind? Labour market reforms under austerity in Italy and Spain," *Socio-Economic Review* 15: 461–82.

Pierson, P. (1998) "Irresistible forces, immovable objects: post-industrial welfare states confront permanent austerity," *Journal of European Public Policy* 5: 539–60.

Pierson, P. (2002) "Coping with permanent austerity: welfare state restructuring in affluent democracies," *Revue Française de Sociologie* 43: 369–406.

Pincus, J., & Ramli, R. (1998) "Indonesia: from showcase to basket case," *Cambridge Journal of Economics* 22: 723–34.

Pitcher, A. (2012) "Was privatisation necessary and did it work? The case of South Africa," *Review of African Political Economy* 39: 243–60.

Piven, F. F., & Cloward, R. A. (1993) *Regulating the Poor: The Functions of Public Welfare*, 2nd edn. New York: Vintage Books.

Plehwe, D. (2009) "The Origins of the Neoliberal Economic Development Discourse." In: Mirowski, P., & Plehwe, D. (eds.) *The Road from Mont Pelerin: The Making of the Neoliberal Thought Collective*. Cambridge, MA: Harvard University Press

Plehwe, D., Walpen, B. J. A., & Neunhöffer, G. (eds.) (2007) *Neoliberal Hegemony: A Global Critique*. Abingdon: Routledge.

Polanyi, K. (2001) *The Great Transformation: The Political and Economic Origins of Our Times*. Boston: Beacon Press.

Ponte, S., Roberts, S., & van Sittert, L. (2007) "'Black economic empowerment': business and the state in South Africa," *Development and Change* 38: 933–55.

Porras Velasco, A. (2005) *Tiempo de Indios: La Construcción de la Identidad Política Colectivea del Movimento Indio Ecuatoriano*. Quito: Abya-Yala.

Portes, A. (1997) "Neoliberalism and the sociology of development: emerging trends and unanticipated facts," *Population and Development Review* 23: 229–59.

Poverty USA (2016) "Poverty facts." Available at: https://www.povertyusa. org/facts

Presidency (2009) *Development Indicators 2009*. Pretoria: Republic of South Africa

Preston, J. (1999) "Student strike in capital jarring all of Mexico," *The New York Times*, June 24. Available at: https://www.nytimes.com/1999/06/25/world/student-strike-in-capital-jarring-all-of-mexico.html

Quade, E. A. (2007) "The logic of anticorruption enforcement campaigns in contemporary China," *Journal of Contemporary China* 16: 65–77.

Quigley, J. M. (2001) "Real estate and the Asian crisis," *Journal of Housing Economics* 10: 129–61.

Raftopoulos, B. (2000) "The labour movement and the emergence of opposition politics in Zimbabwe," *Labour, Capital and Society* 33: 256–86.

Rakopoulos, T. (ed.) (2018) *The Global Life of Austerity: Comparing Beyond Europe*. New York: Berghahn Books.

Ramiro, L., & Gomez, R. (2017) "Radical-left populism during the great recession: Podemos and its competition with the established radical left," *Political Studies* 65: 108–26.

Ranger, T. (1985) *Peasant Consciousness and Guerrilla War in Zimbabwe: A Comparative Study*. Berkeley: University of California Press.

Reeves, A., Basu, S., McKee, M., Meissner, C., & Stuckler, D. (2013) "Does investment in the health sector promote or inhibit economic growth?," *Globalization and Health* 9: 43.

Reeves, A., McKee, M., Basu, S., & Stuckler, D. (2014) "The political economy of austerity and healthcare: cross-national analysis of expenditure changes in 27 European nations 1995–2011," *Health Policy* 115: 1–8.

Renaud, B., Zhang, M., & Koeberle, S. (1998) "How the Thai real estate boom undid financial institutions: what can be done now." In: NESDB Seminar on Thailand's Economic Recovery and Competitiveness, Bangkok.

Reygadas, L. (2006) "Latin America: persistent inequality and recent transformations." In: Hershberg, E., & Rosen, F. (eds.) *Latin America after Neoliberalism: Turning the Tide in the 21st Century?* New York: The New Press.

Rich, B. (1994) *Mortgaging the Earth: The World Bank, Environmental Impoverishment, and the Crisis of Development*. Boston: Beacon Press.

Ricklefs, M. C. (2008) *A History of Modern Indonesia since c. 1200*, 4th edn. New York: Palgrave Macmillan.

Roach, S. S. (2012) "Lessons from Asia: austerity can work," Al Jazeera, March 9. Available at: https://www.aljazeera.com/indepth/opinion/2012/0 3/20123781637209922.html

Robberson, T. (1995a) "Mexico faces banking and credit crisis; rising interest rates cause loan defaults," *Washington Post*, March 15, p. A1.

Robberson, T. (1995b) "Zedillo's plan for austerity faces trouble; markets fail to revive Peso; public backlash intensifies," *Washington Post*, March 17, p. A19.

Rodney, W. (1972) *How Europe Underdeveloped Africa*. Washington, DC: Howard University Press.

Rohter, L. (1990) "Stop the world, Mexico is getting on," *The New York Times*, June 3, p. 1.

Roll, R. (2018) "The international crash of October 1987," *Financial Analysts Journal* 44: 19–35.

Roman, R., & Velasco, E. (2001) "Neoliberalism, labor market transformation, and working-class responses: social and historical roots of accommodation and protest," *Latin American Perspectives* 28: 52–71.

Roman, R., & Velasco, E. (2014) "Mexico: the state against the working class," *NACLA Report on the Americas* 47: 23–6.

Roodman, D. (2010) "The arc of the Jubilee," Center for Global Development, October 26. Available at: http://www.cgdev.org/content/publications/detail/1424539

Rosenow, J., & Eyre, N. (2016) "A post mortem of the green deal: austerity, energy efficiency, and failure in British energy policy," *Energy Research and Social Science* 21: 141–4.

Ross, M. (2003) "The natural resource curse: how wealth can make you poor." In: Collier, P., & Bannon, M. (eds.) *Natural Resources and Violent Conflict: Options and Actions*. London: World Bank.

Roubini, N., & Mihm, S. (2010) *Crisis Economics: A Crash Course in the Future of Finance*. New York: The Penguin Press.

Rüdig, W., & Karyotis, G. (2014) "Who protests in Greece? Mass opposition to austerity," *British Journal of Political Science* 44: 487–513.

Ruggie, J. G. (1982) "International regimes, transactions, and change: embedded liberalism in the postwar economic order," *International Organization* 36: 379–415.

Sachs, J. D., & Williamson, J. (1985) "External debt and macroeconomic performance in Latin America and East Asia," *Brookings Papers on Economic Activity* 2: 523–73

Salmon, K. (2017) "A decade of lost growth: economic policy in Spain through the Great Recession," *South European Society and Politics* 22: 239–60.

Sanger, D. E. (1998) " IMF now admits tactics in Indonesia deepened crisis," *New York Times*, January 14. Available at: https://www.nytimes.com/1998/01/14/business/international-business-imf-now-admits-tactics-in-indonesia-deepened-the-crisis.html

Santiso, C. (2001) "Good governance and aid effectiveness: the World Bank and conditionality," *The Georgetown Public Policy Review* 7: 1–22.

SAPRIN (Structural Adjustment Participatory Review International Network) (2004) *The Policy Roots of Economic Crisis, Poverty and Inequality*. London: Zed Books.

Sawyer, S. (2004) *Crude Chronicles: Indigenous Politics, Multinational Oil, and Neoliberalism in Ecuador*. Durham, NC: Duke University Press.

Schelzig, E. (2016) "Haslam's $30M secret project draws criticism,"

Knoxblogs, March 29. Available at: http://knoxblogs.com/humphreyhill /2016/03/29/gov-adds-30m-to-budget-for-secret-ecd-project/

Schemo, D. (1997) "Ecuadoreans rally in drive to oust President," *The New York Times,* February 6. Available at: https://www.nytimes.com/1997/02/06/ world/ecuadoreans-rally-in-drive-to-oust-president.html

Schoenbaum, T. J. (2012) *The Age of Austerity: The Global Financial Crisis and the Return to Economic Growth.* Northampton: Edward Elgar.

Schott, L., Pavetti, L., & Floyd, I. (2015) "How states use federal and state funds under the TANF block grant," Center on Budget and Policy Priorities, October 15. Available at: https://www.cbpp.org/research/family-income-support/ how-states-use-federal-and-state-funds-under-the-tanf-block-grant

Schoultz, L. (2006) "Latin America and the United States." In: Hershberg, E., & Rosen, F. (eds.) *Latin America after Neoliberalism: Turning the Tide in the 20th Century?* New York: The New Press.

Schui, F. (2014) *Austerity: The Great Failure.* New Haven: Yale University Press.

Schwarz, A. (1994) *A Nation in Waiting: Indonesia in the 1990s.* Boulder, CO: Westview Press.

Scott, G., & Mooney, G. (2009) "Poverty and social justice in the devolved Scotland: neoliberalism meets social democracy?," *Social Policy and Society* 8: 379–89.

Seekings, J., & Nattrass, N. (2011) "State–business relations and pro-poor growth in South Africa," *Journal of International Development* 23: 338–57.

Segatti, A., & Pons-Vignon, N. (2013) "Stuck in stabilisation? South Africa's post-apartheid macro-economic policy between ideological conversion and technocratic capture," *Review of African Political Economy* 40: 537–55.

Sen, S., & Dasgupta, Z. (2014) *Economic Policy in India: For Economic Stimulus, or for Austerity and Volatility?* (Working Paper No. 813). New York: Levy Economics Institute of Bard College.

Shefner, J. (2001) "Coalitions and clientelism in Mexico," *Theory & Society* 30: 593–628.

Shefner, J. (2008) *The Illusion of Civil Society: Democratization and Community Mobilization in Low-Income Mexico.* University Park: Pennsylvania State University Press.

Sheridan, M. B. (1996) "Mexico plans to repay much of US bailout 2 years early," *Los Angeles Times,* June 19, p. D1.

Sherlock, M. F., & Marples, D. J. (2014) *Overview of the Federal Tax System.* Washington, DC: Congressional Research Service.

Sigmund, P. E. (1977) *The Overthrow of Allende and the Politics of Chile, 1964–1976.* Pittsburgh: University of Pittsburgh Press.

Smith, J. (1999) "Mexico clamps down on tortilla prices," *Los Angeles Times,* January 7, p. C1.

Smith, N. (2002) "New globalism, new urbanism: gentrification as global urban strategy," *Antipode* 34: 427–50.

Southall, R. (2016) "The coming crisis of Zuma's ANC: the party state confronts fiscal crisis," *Review of African Political Economy* 43: 73–88.

Statistics New Zealand (2013) "Rental affordability 1998–2012: regional distributions." Available at: *http:*//www.stats.govt.nz

Statistics South Africa (2009) *Quarterly Labour Force Survey: Quarter 4.* Available at: http://www.statssa.gov.za/publications/P0211/P02114th Quarter2009.pdf

Steiner, Y. (2009) "The neoliberals confront the trade unions." In: Mirowski, P., & Plehwe, D. (eds.) *The Road from Mont Pelerin: The Making of the Neoliberal Thought Collective.* Cambridge, MA: Harvard University Press.

Stevens, R. (2014) "Greek parliament approves new attacks on workers," International Committee of the Fourth International, April 1. Available at: http://www.wsws.org/en/articles/2014/04/01/gree-a01.html

Stichelmans, T. (2015) *Why a United Nations Sovereign Debt Restructuring Framework is Key to Implementing the Post-2015 Sustainable Development Agenda.* London: Eurodad.

Stiglitz, J. E. (2000) "What I learned at the world economic crisis." In: Driscoll, W. J., & Clark, J. (eds.) *Globalization and the Poor: Exploitation or Equalizer?* New York: IDEA.

Stiglitz, J. E. (2002) *Globalization and Its Discontents.* New York: W. W. Norton.

Stiglitz, J. E. (2006) *Making Globalization Work.* London: Allen Lane.

Story, L. (2012) "As companies seek tax deals, governments pay high price," *The New York Times,* December 1. Available at: http://www.nytimes. com/2012/12/02/us/how-local-taxpayers-bankroll-corporations.html

Story, L., Fehr, T., & Watkins, D. (2012) "Government incentives," *The New York Times,* December 1. Available at: http://www.nytimes.com/ interactive/2012/12/01/us/government-incentives.html

Streeck, W. (2014) *Buying Time: The Delayed Crisis of Democratic Capitalism.* London: Verso.

Tax Foundation (2013) *Federal Individual Income Tax Rates History: Inflation Adjusted (Real 2012 Dollars) Using Average Annual CPI during Tax Year Income Years 1913–2013.* New York: Tax Foundation.

Tax Foundation (2014) *State Individual Income Tax Rates, as of January 1, 2014.* New York: Tax Foundation.

Taylor, M. (2006) *From Pinochet to the Third Way: Neoliberalism and Social Transformatoin in Chile.* London: Pluto Press.

Tomba, L. (2004) "Creating an urban middle class: social engineering in Beijing," *The China Journal* 51: 1–26.

Tshitereke, C. (2006) *The Experience of Economic Redistribution: The Growth, Employment and Redistribution Strategy in South Africa.* London: Routledge.

Tzanetaki, T. (2013) "Greek economy and employment," Institute of Labor of the Greek General Confederation of Labor. Available at: https://www. etui.org/content/download/11649/97847/file/Greek+Economy+and+Em ployment+2013.pdf

Unger, D. (1998) *Building Social Capital in Thailand: Fibers, Finance and Infrastructure.* Cambridge: Cambridge University Press.

UNISON Scotland (2016) *The Impact of Austerity on Scotland: Damage Done and Routes to Recovery*. London: UNISON Scotland.

US Census Bureau (2012) *Statistical Abstract of the United States 2012*. New York: US Census Bureau.

Utting, P., Razavi, S., & Buchholz, R. V. (2012) "Overview: social and political dimensions of the global crisis: possible futures." In: Buchholz, R. V., & Utting, P. (eds.) *The Global Crisis and Transformative Social Change*. London: Palgrave Macmillan.

Uxó, J., & Álvarez, I. (2017) "Is the end of fiscal austerity feasible in Spain? An alternative plan to the current stability programme (2015–2018)," *Cambridge Journal of Economics* 41: 999–1020.

Valdés, J. G. (1995) *Pinochet's Economists: The Chicago School in Chile*. Cambridge: Cambridge University Press.

van der Zwan, N. (2014) "Making sense of financialization," *Socio-Economic Review* 12: 99–129.

Varoufakis, Y. (2016) *And the Weak Suffer What They Must? Europe's Crisis and America's Economic Future*. New York: Nation Books.

Varoufakis, Y. (2017) *Adults in the Room*. New York: Farrar, Straus and Giroux.

Varoufakis, Y., Holland, S., & Galbraith, J. K. (2013) "A modest proposal for resolving the Eurozone crisis, Version 4.0." Available at: https://varoufakis.files.wordpress.com/2013/07/a-modest-proposal-for-resolving-the-eurozonecrisis-version-4-0-final1.pdf

Vázquez, L., & Saltos, N. (2007) *Ecuador: Su Realidad*. Quito: Fundación José Peralta.

Vickers, A. (2005) *A History of Modern Indonesia*. Cambridge: Cambridge University Press.

Walton, J., & Seddon, D. (1994) *Free Markets and Food Riots: The Politics of Global Adjustment*. Oxford: Blackwell

Walton, J., & Shefner, J. (1994) "Latin America: popular protest and the state." In: Walton, J., & Seddon, D. (eds.) *Free Markets and Food Riots: The Politics of Global Adjustment*. Cambridge, MA: Blackwell.

Ward, P. (1986) *Welfare Politics in Mexico: Papering Over the Cracks*. London: Allen & Unwin.

Weisbrot, M. (2014) "Greece: signs of growth come as austerity eases," *The Guardian*, January 22. Available at: https://www.theguardian.com/commentisfree/2014/jan/22/greece-growth-austerity-eases-europe-imf

Williamson, J. (1990) *Latin American Adjustment How Much Has Happened?* Washington, DC: Peterson Institute for International Economics

Winn, P. (2004) *Victims of the Chilean Miracle*. Durham, NC: Duke University Press.

Woods, N. (2006) *The Globalizers: The IMF, the World Bank, and Their Borrowers*. Ithaca, NY: Cornell University Press.

World Bank (1985) *World Development Report 1985*. Washington, DC: Oxford University Press.

World Bank. (1990) *World Development Report 1990: Poverty*. Washington, DC: Oxford University Press.

World Bank (2018) "Heavily Indebted Poor Country (HIPC) Initiative," January 9. Available at: http://www.worldbank.org/en/topic/debt/brief/hipc

Young, M. (2006) *From Pinochet to the "Third Way": Neoliberalism and Social Transformation in Chile*. London: Pluto Press.

Yúdice, G. (2003) *The Expediency of Culture: Uses of Culture in the Global Era*. Durham, NC: Duke University Press.

Zamosc, L. (1994) "Agrarian protest and the Indian movement in the Ecuadorian highlands," *Latin American Research Review* 29: 37–68.

Zieger, R., & Gilbert Gall, T. M. (2014) *American Workers, American Unions: The Twentieth and Early Twenty-First Centuries*. Baltimore, MD: Johns Hopkins University Press.

Index